The Backpack Diaries

Two Friends.
Two Paths.
One Remarkable Journey.

By Traci Bogan & Amy Oberstadt

Today is the
perfect day
To dream a
new dream!
Live it!

SATORI PUBLISHING
Publication Date: 2015
©2015 by Traci R. Bogan. All Rights Reserved.
Printed in USA
10 9 8 7 6 5 4 3 2

ISBN #978-0-9795069-3-2
Library of Congress Control Number 2011912780

Edited by: Valerie Hennen: valhennen@yahoo.com
            Amy Oberstadt: aloberstadt@yahoo.com
Design, Layout, and Graphics Design: Valerie Moody: val.moody@gmail.com
Cover Design: Kimb Manson

This book is based on the real life perspectives, personal experiences, and opinions of the two authors based on their two year backpacking adventure around the world. Please note some names, places, and events may have been changed to protect the identity of those involved. Some of the segments after the chapter "Parting Ways" have been embellished for effect and entertainment. None of the second or third hand information or facts told to them on their adventure has been verified. Neither the author nor the publisher will be held liable or responsible to any person or entity with respect to any misinformation or damages caused, or alleged to be caused, directly or indirectly, by any information contained within this book.

Contact the Authors:
Traci Bogan: Traci@TraciBogan.com
Amy Oberstadt: aloberstadt@yahoo.com

Other Books by Traci Bogan:

Romance - 411:

Your Little Black Book of Romantic Ideas

Romance - 911:

Your Emergency Guide to Romance

Cracking the Dream Code:

6 Keys to Achieving Your Goals & Dreams

Speaking / Workshops / Keynotes by Traci Bogan:
Dare to Dream: Live the Life You've Always Imagined
Dare to Achieve Coaching: Turn Your Passion into Profit
Dare to Thrive: Weekend Retreat
Dare to Manifest: Mastermind
Dare to Adventure: Adventure Mastermind Around the World

Connect with Traci:
traci@TraciBogan.com
www.TraciBogan.com
fb.com/dreamplanlive
LinkedIn/tracibogan
Twitter/tracibogan

Try our #1 Client Retention Tool FREE
www.amcards.com/traci OR www.sendoutcards.com/planb

Dedication

This book is dedicated to all the people who said we could and all the people who said we couldn't. Each of you in your own unique way was the fuel that kept us going. May you reach your own seeming impossible dreams, whatever they may be.

Acknowledgements

Thank you for supporting our journey with care packages, notes of encouragement, and donations to our adopted schools and villages: Rick & Nanci Bogan, Jennifer Bogan Bassett, John & Dolores Oberstadt, Wendy Oberstadt, Vicki Oberstadt, Pat Deprey, Bob & Leslie Mudge, Lou & Sue Lesperance, Sally Kuhlman, Jacque Schaeffer, Dulaney Collins, Dave & Lolly Bohn, Jackie Oney, Judy Gower & Family, Dan Suprak, and Dr. Gene Kremer.

Thank you to friends and strangers alike who came together and contributed to making this book better: The Adventure Center, Nicola Allen, Mische Hamilton, Mike Cieslewicz, David Henry Saaski, Charlie Petrach, Michael LaPoint, Mike Zielonka, Valerie Hennen, Valerie Moody, Kimb Manson, A.S. Raju, Brian Barnes, Skye Tan, Parker Fillmore, Deb Tasnadi, Keith Frost, Hansong Zhang, JM Suarez for use of Ganges River photo, and to all of my Facebook friends who threw in their two-cents and offered opinions, advice, and support. You guys are the best!

Contents

About the Authors

Traci Bogan, Dreampreneur

Dreampreneur [dreem pruh-noor]
*noun, one who has the unrelenting will
to achieve their boldest goals, most daring
dreams, and live their authentic empowered
life - despite all fear, obstacles, and opposition.*
–Traci Bogan

Traci Bogan is the world's first Dreampreneur and leading expert on goal mastery and self-empowerment. She has backpacked 75,000 miles, in six continents, through 54 countries. Traci has made a career of putting herself front and center to show others how to break through their fears and achieve their boldest goals and most daring dreams through her books, workshops, and coaching programs. She has been featured on FOX, ABC, NBC, CBS, as well as many radio shows and has published four books. She has lived in China, teaching English at the World Exchange College of Language, as well as Alaska, Hawaii, Arizona, and Wisconsin. The breadth of Traci's life experiences is beyond ordinary. As a survivor of childhood sexual abuse, she spearheaded a campaign to increase the Criminal Statute of Limitations for sex crimes on children. Her grassroot efforts helped change Wisconsin's law on child sexual abuse. It is dubbed "The Bogan Bill." Traci is dedicated to working with entrepreneurs who are committed to higher achievement, increasing wealth, and living an authentic empowered life.

Book your FREE 30 Minute Goal Strategy Session with Traci: tracibogan.com/booknow

Amy Oberstadt

Amy's thirst for travel began shortly after graduating from the University of WI-Madison in 1989 when she signed up for a tour through what was then the Soviet Union. She returned to UW-Madison in 1995 and supplemented her college studies with medical mission trips to El Salvador and Belize. She has lived in Hawaii, Colorado, Texas, Alaska, and China and has traveled through 30 countries. She graduated from the University of Wisconsin-Madison with degrees in Physical Therapy and Physician Assistant studies. She is currently working as a Physician Assistant and has earned a graduate degree in Public Health. After leaving her world tour with her best friend and co-author, Traci Bogan, she returned to her Wisconsin roots and now resides in Appleton. She continues to travel throughout the world.

How to Use This Book

The Backpack Diaries is composed of actual diary entries from Amy and Traci's two year world tour. Elements were added to make your experience more enjoyable.

Icons: At the beginning of each journal entry, a visual icon has been placed to help you identify the writer.

 Traci: Backpack icon   Amy: Footprint icon

Videos and QR Codes: More than 200 photos and QR code video links have been included amongst the journal entries to give you a better sense of what it was like to be there. Some are relevant to what is written, others were just some of their favorites.

Follow the instructions below to use QR codes on either a smartphone or an iPad. To view the video on a computer, simply type the URL into the web browser on your computer.

QR Code Instructions:
1. Install a free QR code reader app onto your smartphone or iPad.
2. Open the QR code app and scan the code with your device. You will be directed to the video.

FAQs: People often ask questions about the trip such as cost, favorite memory, lessons learned, favorite country, etc. At the end of the book the authors answer the top FAQs on video using QR code links at the end of the book.

"We hope you vicariously enjoy our adventure." - Traci and Amy

Prologue

Now or Never

"A journey of a thousand miles must begin with a single step."
- Lao Tzu

Traci

It's now or never, I thought, as we sipped Captain Morgan and cokes at our regular weekend watering hole, watching the white, fluffy, wintery weather fall past the window beside our table. We day-dreamed of all the sand and sun filled places that we could run away to. Amy began with Mexico, Australia, or the Bahamas, and I threw out Florida, Arizona, and Hawaii. We both jokingly agreed that Hawaii would be the ultimate escape from the harsh Wisconsin winters and an exciting new alternative to our mundane routine of meeting every weekend to scope for boys. As cocktails flowed and hours passed our dreams became more inflated, and by the end of the night we had a sure plan to move to "paradise" for a year-long adventure. The next day, after the fog cleared from my head, I gathered the courage to ask Amy if she was serious about wanting to move to Hawaii for a year. Ideally, such a trip is made when you're in your twenties and you are unjaded and unidentified by a career and the trappings that it buys. She had just bought a house a few months earlier and had a great job as a Director of a Physical Therapy Department, so I didn't think the dream of paradise would actually materialize. To my surprise, she said if I was serious about it, she would seriously consider it. I was in! I excitedly shouted, "Let's chuck life as we know it and do it!" She chuckled at my quick response and said, "Okay, we'll do that!" We talked almost daily for the next several weeks, set a departure date, and began devising a to-do list and a plan. We kept our plan a secret from coworkers, friends, and family members. Finally when our plans were concrete we sent out resumes, searched for Hawaiian housing in our local library newspapers, sold our possessions, and said goodbye to family and friends.

Amy

It's now or never I thought, and there will never be a better time. I met Traci when she had just graduated from high school and I was just out of college and new to Racine, starting my career as a Physical Therapist. She took me under her wing and her family welcomed me as one of their own. We became close quickly, best friends. I was flab-bergasted when Traci shared secrets from her childhood. She and her family seemed so normal. The idea of chucking everything and moving to Hawaii had a certain cachet. Although I had a great job and had just bought a new house I was ready for an adventure.

We arrived in Hawaii on April Fool's Day with each of our worldly belongings condensed into two suitcases. We moved into the first fully furnished apartment we looked at and each opened a Hawaiian bank account. Several months later when our money was running lower than what we were comfortable with and the novelty of laying on Waikiki beach for 4-5 hours/day was wearing off, we both found jobs at Straub Medical Center in Honolulu. I worked as a Physical Therapist and Traci did drug screenings and physicals on the seafarers.

🎒 Traci

I had never felt surer, clearer, or happier in my life with the decision that we had made. From our small, one bedroom apartment in Waikiki we devised a plot to further our adventure together and loosely outlined a plan to go backpacking around the world. The year

was 1991, and the plan was to spend a year touring the beautiful Hawaiian Islands as we worked and saved enough funds to continue our sojourn for our second year through the South Pacific and heading west

into Asia and Africa. But life, circumstances, and relationships led us on separate paths and journeys. After six months of Hawaiian living, Amy was homesick and returned to Wisconsin. I stayed in Hawaii for ten fruitful years.

👣 Amy

Fast forwarding to April of 2001, I flew to Hawaii for a week to celebrate my birthday with Traci. We began reminiscing that it was exactly ten years to the day that we had made the brave move to Hawaii. We talked about our abandoned plans to see the world together. I told her that I regretted not pursuing that dream of backpacking around the world and had thought about it several times throughout the years, and she admitted her own regrets. Two months later I called and asked her if she remembered our "regret" conversation. Was she willing to go now because I was fresh out of a relationship and ready for a change? To my surprise she said yes immediately. I would give up my Physician Assistant job at National Jewish Medical Center and apartment in Denver and move into her three bedroom home in Hawaii Kai so we could share expenses, fine tune a plan, and leave from Hawaii. We took several months to research our itinerary and as it was being finalized, a major kink was thrown into our plans when on the morning of September 11, 2001, terrorists flew two planes into the World Trade Center. Thirteen days later Traci lost her job working at a prominent plastic surgery center as people were no longer so quick to open their pocketbooks for expensive, elective plastic surgery.

Traci

I'll never forget the day when my roommate Kristin, publicist of the popular TV show Baywatch Hawaii, banged on my bedroom door in the early morning hours of September 11th and informed me of the

terrorist attacks on the World Trade Center. Thirteen days later I lost my job working for a prominent plastic surgeon. Elective surgery was replaced by a spending freeze.

Traci & The Baywatch Girls Out On The Town

After losing my lucrative and glamorous position I tried to make myself feel better by going out every night and pickling my liver in alcohol and other indulgences and spending the money I had been saving for our world tour. For a couple of months I was not only off track, but on a bad track, living out of focus and out of integrity with who I know I am. I was lost and didn't know what I wanted. I had been dodging Amy's calls until a breaking point was reached. After another night hitting the town in limousines and helicopters with my rich and famous friends, thinking I was hot shit, I woke up with one of the worst hangovers I've ever had and I thought I was having a heart-attack. I looked into the mirror as I splashed cold water on my face and said "I AM MORE THAN THIS!"

It was a pivotal moment in my life that forced me to ask myself some tough questions: Who am I? What am I doing? Where am I going? What is my purpose? What is my life's plan? What do I want? What do I really, really, really, really want? After a wasted day on the couch, moving back and forth between couch and toilet, getting sick, I woke

Beaching The Boat At The Kahala Hotel & Resort, A Sunday Morning Bloody Mary Ritual

up the next morning with a soulful "knowingness" that it was time to leave my beautiful Hawaii and abandon my reckless and high maintenance lifestyle. In one instant, I made the decision to wholeheartedly change my life, pursue my dreams, and find the answers to my life's questions and meaning. Amy happened to call within minutes of this life-changing decision. I picked up the phone and said "We are leaving

NOW"! She replied "Well hello to you too Traci! Now how are you going to do this NOW?" And in typical Traci fashion, I told her I would figure it out on the way. In the next 72 hours, I gave up my lease, putting an imposition on Kristin, gave away all of my earthly possessions, found a home for my cat, and sold my cute little sports car within hours of my departing flight. I left Hawaii with the same two suitcases I had arrived with ten years earlier. I was Wisconsin bound and Amy was meeting me there. We would spend the Thanksgiving and Christmas holiday with our families, finalize plans, and leave for our world tour from there.

🥾 Amy

I had always wanted to sign up with a traveling healthcare organization and see different parts of the United States and this became the new plan to earn money for our travels. It eliminated housing costs as the healthcare organization paid for all travel and housing expenses. Six weeks later Traci and I were driving cross-country to Monahans, Texas, where we would spend the next 5 months working and taking in the sites of this beautiful Lone Star state on long weekend excursions. When that gig was finished we flew to Alaska, a place we had both wanted to see and where supposedly the generous wages made up for the isolation and cold temperatures.

Car Full Of Aluminum Cans Worth $50

I worked as many hours as possible as a Physician Assistant while Traci bartered services and found various cash paying jobs: cleaning wealthy people's homes, delivering newspapers, selling plasma, dog walking, and house sitting. Our free time was spent collecting aluminum cans, researching at the library, reading travel books, and exploring Alaska on the weekends. We loosely outlined an itinerary that began in China and crawled westward through Europe. Our Tour De World finally seemed real.

Traci

We were growing more excited every day about exploring the underbelly of new cultures, mindsets, and lifestyles of our international counterparts, especially since we had been working so hard and saving every cent.

Consequences of 9-11 persisted. The war in Afghanistan had already been launched and the sympathy that 9-11 had garnered for Americans was wearing thin as President Bush talked increasingly of invading Iraq as well. Travel warnings for Americans were still in effect, and it seemed that we would not be welcomed anywhere we went. Our families became increasingly concerned for our safety as the time was approaching to leave the relatively safe confines of the United States. We were determined not to let this atmosphere of fear disturb our travel plans, so we became Canadians! We sewed Canadian patches on our backpacks and purchased two Canadian hats. If anyone were to ask us where we were from, we would tell them Toronto. We couldn't say we were from Montreal because neither of us could speak French, and we knew nothing about the province of Quebec, but we thought we could fake our way as Toronto residents. Our plan was preserved.

Amy

After six months of living in Alaska and finalizing the daunting task of planning our route, chasing visas, updating passports, getting travel shots, pawning our belongings, arranging transportation, purchasing travelers checks, and overcoming all the hurdles and roadblocks that modern nations put in the way of would-be-travelers, we cemented our departure date: November 2nd, 2002. We would leave just before the perpetual winter darkness of the Last Frontier arrived. I'm looking forward to the adventure.

Traci

I just had a pleasant telephone conversation with my parents. They are concerned about our safety, but are supportive of the adventure and happy that we are pursuing our dream. I told them that Amy and I would like to adopt a school or a village in each country we visit, by sending a package of Western goodies to the first local person who takes an interest in learning about us or who invites us into their home. Mom has agreed to do the shopping and shipping for us and is excited to have a supporting role in our journey. I joked that she will make a wonderful "God Mother." We will keep our friends and family updated through emails and our geocities website: www.atworldtour.com (short for Amy & Traci's World Tour). Everyone seems pretty excited to vicariously share our adventure and follow us around the globe. Hopefully internet connections will be plentiful so we can regularly post our photos, journal entries, and whereabouts. I just broke the news to Amy that I am interested in visiting an ashram for 1-2 weeks when we get to India. She asked why. I told her that I am ready to "find myself" and discover my life's purpose. I'm pretty sure I saw her eyes roll as she made it clear that she has no interest in joining me but had no problem finding something else to do while I am there. I further confessed that I am hoping to get closure from my broken engagement and released from the shackles of being sexually abused as a child. She expressed concern that my concentrated soul-seeking quest is going to get in the way of our adventure and I expressed concern that she is going to get sick of traveling halfway through our ensuing adventure and return home, as she has done in the past. And so it is cemented; Amy is on a journey to see the world, and I'm on a journey to discover my role in it.

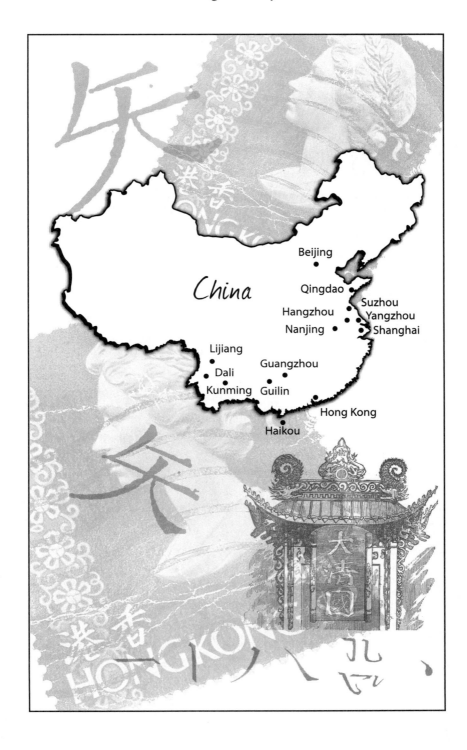

China

"Leave nothing but your footprints. Take nothing but photographs. Kill only with kindness. Die with peace not war. Remember, you are only passing through." - Unknown

 Departure Day
Amy's Diary Entry
November 2nd, Anchorage, Alaska

Well we were on the airplane safely seated in our designated seats, but it was a close call. Our last day in Alaska was quite stressful, and I was irritated at Traci almost all day. She wasn't feeling well, so I was left to do all the last minute errands by myself, yet she felt well enough to sip cocktails with the people she cleans houses for. So typical! I packed and repacked and then made new lists out of old lists to make sure that I had everything. My backpack was so heavy that I couldn't believe I was going to haul it around for a year. By the time the final packing was done, it was midnight and the alarm went off at 2 AM. Good thing we had a long plane ride ahead of us because I needed to get some sleep. At least Traci's new friend John, who manages some pawn shops, showed up to pick us up and drop us off. I had visions of him not

showing up as he never seemed like a particularly energetic guy and
I envisioned us scrambling for a last minute taxi but Traci swore he
would show up, and she was right. He was even early. Traci's backpack
was over the 40# weight limit, so there we were at the check-in gate
while she rummaged through her pack, trying to decide what to get rid
of and what to try to stuff in the little backpacks that we were carrying
onto the airplane with us. I'm sure the passengers behind us were
rolling their eyes and grumbling about those 2 idiots with the backpacks and rightfully so. I had told her repeatedly about the weight
limit. She finally had to make some last minute donations to the
airport garbage. I hope she doesn't end up needing those shoes that
she had to get rid of. We sat at the wrong gate for 2 hours, and I was
wondering why there were so few people at the gate since this was an
international flight going to Seoul, South Korea and I was sure more
than 10 people would be hopping on the airplane with us. At first we
just thought that the plane was late until I heard the faint overhead call
for the final boarding for Inchon, South Korea, and it dawned on me
they were calling our flight!!! I couldn't believe we had been sitting and
dozing at the wrong gate. We hadn't bothered to get up and find out
why our plane wasn't boarding. It's a good thing the Anchorage airport
is small as we had to run through it as fast as we could. We wouldn't
have stood a chance if we had been at O'Hare airport in Chicago.
My thrift shop travel pants started to fall down as the side cinch plastic
fastener wouldn't hold, so one of my hands had to hold them up so that
I could keep running. The zipper had already broken when I put them
on this morning, but I didn't have time to sort through my backpack
to find other ones, so I just used safety pins to hold them together.
I guess there was a good reason why they were at the second hand
store. At least we made it and learned a valuable lesson… international

cities are not always called the same name in America as in other parts of the world. My irritation with Traci dissolved, and now I was just excited and nervous to be sitting on the plane. I'm glad Traci is here with me as I know I wouldn't do this by myself. I hate flying. I am always convinced that my plane is going to crash, and my last minutes on earth are going to be spent in a terrifying downward spiral into the ocean. Any little turbulence sent me into prayer mode while others comfortably read or slept. Every time I met a pilot (which wasn't often) I asked them about the danger of turbulence, and every time they reassured me that it was nothing to be concerned about but I still didn't believe them. I already missed my family. It's only been 6 months since we left Wisconsin for Alaska and that has been about the longest that I've gone in my life without seeing them. Now I'm leaving for another year. Alaska was an incredible experience in and of itself, and I'm so glad I was able to spend time there. I'd move to Alaska before I moved to Hawaii again. Visiting Denali Park and seeing the grizzly bears, going salmon fishing, going to Seward for our little cruise, walking on a glacier, driving past moose as they grazed in the ditches alongside roads… they were all very cool experiences. Plus I made some decent cash working in the walk-in clinic as a Physician Assistant. Good-bye Alaska… China here we come.

*Amy & Traci
at Glacier Bay
National Park*

A Baby Moose Zooms By Our Boat
As We Are Salmon Fishing
http://j.mp/k3iiUz

Good Bye Alaska

Traci's Diary Entry
November 2nd, Anchorage, Alaska

It's a few hours past dawn and for the last time I sit quietly alone in a beautiful place that lies freshly awoken. The early morning sun reveals not just a new day, but a new journey to a whole new place. The water sparkles like diamonds and I feel lost in its reflection. I reminisce about the last six months and what is yet to come. My love affair with the timeless wilderness of Alaska will soon be only a distant memory. I will miss the song of the loons echoing across the water, the smell of crisp arctic air, and the impressions of Caribou tracks around our new homeland. I'll miss skidding to avoid a grizzly running in front of our vehicle, walking on glaciers, floating down the Kenai Peninsula while sipping cold beer and eating salmon hours after catching them. I recall water plane rides for picnics and sunsets with new friends. The silence and the roar of this vast state has opened my eyes to a new appreciation of the greatest and the smallest of things. I am grateful for every tiny moment that my time in Alaska has brought. But today is "D" Day, as in "Departure" day or "Dream" day. I can't believe this day is finally here! I'm going around the world…

a dream come true, even if it is ten years later. I'm nervous, excited, and plagued with doubt and fear about our decision to do the unthinkable, inconceivable, and unconventional. I've had butterflies and knots in my stomach for days, wondering if we will have enough money, if we will be safe, if it will be all that we dreamed it to be, if we will still be friends after this is over, if Amy will back out of her commitment as she usually does…

Amy is anxiously looking at her watch and staring out the window waiting for our ride from my new friend John, who I befriended at the pawn shop after hocking our bicycles and a few miscellaneous items we inherited after six months of exploring these majestic lands. Every few minutes I can sense her sending disapproving vibes or glares in my direction but I'm pretending not to notice. It's been a little quiet and

Dinner On The Kenai Peninsula
With Cousin Dan

tense around here this morning. We haven't even left yet, and it seems as if we are on each other's nerves. I know she's been irritated that I have not read one iota about any of the places we are going, and Ms. Bookworm has spent more than 200 hours reading and researching this trip. I've done all I needed to do; I've circled every place I want to go, and listed everything I want to see and do when I get there. I have gotten my shots and purchased our Round-the-World travel passes. To me, half the fun and the adventure is in just showing up and figuring it out and reading about where I am when I get there, but she needs to have a written plan, a daily breakdown, reservations set up days in advance for hostels and hotels, and all the transportation lined up for not only the current destination, but the next one as well! After a couple decades of being best friends she should know me by now. I am spontaneous and not a planner. She is so analytical about everything that it drives me crazy! She is a bookish person with a true greed for knowledge and culture, who is inclined to live within the limits of "normal," obeying common sense and tradition. She trusts no one. I, on the other hand, am experiential and social in nature, always pushing past the boundaries of "normal" and coloring outside of the lines of tradition and ideology. I love everyone. My god, she is already convinced that John is going to leave us stranded after only meeting him once. I have faith in my new friend, and I know he will be here. I know this is going to be a wonderful journey ahead, and I welcome and embrace every unscripted moment to come throughout the next year. Headlights are creeping up the driveway now! I knew he'd show up! Ready, fire, aim…We're off! Goodbye styling mousse, blow dryers, curling irons, hairspray, make-up, and razors! – And Mom, Dad, and Jen.

Beijing Arrival

Amy's Diary Entry
November 3rd, Beijing, China

Here we were… in Beijing, China, the other side of the world, and what a new, strange world we had walked into. I had read the Lonely Planet China book over and over before leaving Alaska and read it once again on the plane ride over here. I thought I was all prepared and would be able to get us to our hostel without a hitch. Boy was I wrong.

When we first got off the airplane, we followed the signs through immigration and customs and thought this whole China experience was going to be a walk in the park since there were signs everywhere in English. So far everyone we encountered in the airport could speak passable English. We picked up our 40# backpacks from the baggage claim and hoisted them on our backs while our smaller backpacks rode on our fronts. We were backpack sandwiches. My pants were still a hindrance to walking comfortably, and I couldn't wait to take them off and throw them away. We finished all of the airport obligations and were soon standing on the wide sidewalk outside one of the Beijing airport's main entrances. We were looking for the free shuttle bus to our hostel, the one that the Lonely Planet guidebook assured us was easy to find, but out here on the sidewalk all of the English signs were gone as were the nice, polite Chinese that generously attempted to speak passable English. Instead there were only Chinese signs and Chinese people who had no interest in trying to communicate with us. We walked up and down the sidewalk in front of the airport for 15 minutes, not wanting to believe the airport attendant when she told us that the shuttle bus to the hostel didn't exist. What?! Lonely Planet, my bible of travel, said it did!! It had to… we did not have a backup plan. Maybe the shuttle bus did exist, but if we took the shuttle bus the airport attendant wouldn't get her commission for getting us on another bus. I had read about these people. Instead we were directed onto a city bus that would supposedly take us to a local "drop-off" place and from there we could catch a taxi to our hostel. Now how were we supposed to figure out what stop to get off of when no one spoke English anymore and all the signs were in Chinese? We had no other choice, so we climbed aboard the bus. The bus driver would not let us put our bulging backpacks in the storage area under the bus for whatever reason, so we had to haul our packs onto a bus that was almost fully loaded with Chinese riders, hitting most of them with our packs as we lumbered past them to the few open seats available. Of course, the open seats were in the back of the bus. We tried to apologize and smile to each person we hit, but when we turned slightly to offer our apology, our backpack would then hit the person on the other side of the aisle. Some accepted our apologies with return smiles, and some were not so accepting, returning our smiles with glares of indignation. We took our seats, jamming our big backpacks between our legs and started trying to figure out how we were ever going to know where and when to get off. We contemplated getting off and just taking a taxi directly to the hostel but we were already in cheap travel mode and didn't want to pay the taxi fare. We were afraid we were going to end up even farther away from the hostel than where we were now or where this bus was going to puke us out. Our voices were rising and we were starting to get mad at each other for this farce when Lily, a beautiful, young woman sitting in the seat in front of us, heard our dilemma and fluently in English asked us where we were trying to go. She not only confirmed with the bus driver that we were on the right bus, but she got off with us at the appropriate stop, hailed us a taxi, and rode with us to the hostel to make sure we were not cheated by the taxi driver. Thank you God for Lily! Lily had learned English from her father who she said was "very old," more than 75 years old. He had learned English before the Cultural Revolution. She patiently answered all of our questions about herself, her family, and her job as the taxi driver veered in and out of traffic. When we were dropped off at the hostel we tried to pay her taxi fare to her next destination, but she refused to accept it. I did not want to see her drive off. I wanted her to hold our hands for a couple of days. I hoped that getting to the hostel would be our last bad experience in China and if not, that there would be more Lilys along the way.

The hostel staff welcomed us with lukewarm acknowledgement, but we were expecting much greater fan fare. Didn't they realize that we had just traveled half way around the world to be here? Didn't they realize that we had worked and scrimped for the last year and a half, selling almost every material possession that we had in order to get here? Weren't they appreciative that we had chosen Beijing, China, as the start of this expedition? Nope. To them we were just another pair of travelers on another day that had arrived tired, disheveled, and a bit disoriented. We abandoned our big backpacks in our room and ventured out for a walk. This city is funny. Crossing a street in Beijing is not like crossing a street in Milwaukee, WI, or any other city in the United States I'm sure. People congregated in bunches and crossed the street as a group as there was safety in numbers. The pedestrian walk signs on the intersection traffic lights meant virtually nothing to the cars and their crazy drivers. Cars made right turns in front of us as we stepped off the sidewalk with the walk sign flashing, and then when we were half way across the street, other cars would make left turns in front of us as if we were not there. If they did see us, they certainly did not seem to care nor made any attempt to avoid hitting us. At first we thought maybe it was because we were foreigners, but then saw they would do the same thing with regular Chinese people. Out of real fear we held onto each other's arms every time we crossed a street, but we always tried to be in the middle of a group and moved with them. The outside people would then absorb any impact of the car, and hopefully we would remain safe and unharmed. There were not only thousands of cars on the roads but bicycles everywhere. There were bicycles carrying passengers, cages of chickens, cases of water, plants, lumber, and tires. The cars did not seem to care much about the bikes either. Cars always had the right of way, simply because of their size and speed. Within a few minutes we saw a bike pedaled by an elderly Chinese man, hit the side of a car because the car turned in front of him. The elderly man fell over on his bike and was lying on the road when the driver of the car got out of his car and started yelling at the elderly biker as he was on the ground. He did not seem to care at all that this old man was lying on the ground with his bike on top of him. They started arguing until they either came to an agreement or at least had their say, and they both moved on. So much for the respect

supposedly given to the elderly in China. We were both so tired by this point that we gave in to our fatigue and returned to our hostel. Our big adventure had begun in earnest.

First Hostel Beijing

 3rd World Culture Shock
Traci's Diary Entry
November 3rd, Beijing, China

It's 11 AM. We are descending into Beijing… in ten short minutes we will be in a new world and on a new journey into the unknown. I am filled with an indescribable source of excitement. Even though I've been away from home and criss-crossing America for nearly a year (as if this didn't count), this is the moment my "Dream" finally feels realized. I can hardly wait for the next year to get here!

My feet have just touched their first Asian soil…walking out of the safe confines and English signs of that airport and onto the street we are assaulted by mobs of yellow people robotically rushing and unconsciously spitting, hawking out snot rockets, burping, and farting without embarrassment. Seas of blaring cars, busses, scooters, taxis, and bicyclists are weaving in and out of our paths and zooming all around us. I am in compete CULTURE SHOCK! There are a billion people in China and I think they are all right here! The flashing, lighted, wacky character signs are like Las Vegas on steroids, only illegible. I feel like I am on the verge of having an anxiety attack, but maybe it is just an out of world experience! Okay, Amy is right; I should have read about this place before arriving rather than after. It would have been much easier to know where we are going or at least where we can find some English speaking people or know what bus to get on to take us to our hostel. All I can say is OMG! Where in the world are we?!

We finally arrive at the Hostel International hours after landing. What a nightmare! Our first currency exchange is interesting; it is like monopoly money. It just doesn't seem real or valuable. The currency here is called YUAN or RMB and it is 8 RMB to 1 USD. This hostel offers different pricing options: a spacious private room with heat, heated blankets, and a western toilet for 170 RMB or $21.25 per night, a double room with private bath and heat for 70 RMB or $8.75, or a simple dorm room for 10 RMB per night or $1.50. We take the middle option.

We walk into our meager room and realize there is no bathroom or shower. After depositing our bags, we snoop around the facility and find a co-ed bathroom and shower area. Our heads simultaneously turn toward each other with a smirk of disbelief when we lay eyes on our first squatter toilet. We both need to use it, but notice that there is no toilet paper, hand soap, or drying towels, so I go back to the front

desk and ask. I am informed that almost everywhere you go in China, it is BYOTP (bring your own toilet paper) and BYOS (bring your own soap)… so I chime in and say "Let me guess, BYDT stands for bring your own drying towels" and in a belittling tone she informs me that they don't use "drying towels." Good-bye western toilets and hello buying our own toilet paper for 4 RMB or 50 cents a 10 pack.

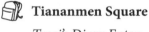

Hostel Squatter Toilet

🎒 Tiananmen Square

Traci's Diary Entry
November 4th

Our first excursion into Beijing is Tiananmen Square. On our way out the door of our hostel, we ask the front staff for directions and refuse to believe them when they tell us it is a 3 hour walk. They keep insisting that we take a taxi, but we assume that it is a ploy to squeeze some more money out of us; they laugh at us when we tell them we were going to walk there. But what do they know? We have a map from our Lonely Planet Book, and it certainly doesn't look like it is that far of a walk, so off we go...walking and walking and walking and stopping to ask for direction a few times along the way. Three hours later we acknowledge their "knowledge," but we don't mind too much as it is a sunny, fall day, and the streets are filled with sights that are all new to us. The streets are very clean with minimal litter and no graffiti anywhere, including the subways and underground walkways. People seem very orderly, and neatly line up in rows to catch a train, bus, or a taxi or enter an attraction in contrast to the usual chaotic globs of people pushing and shoving their way in, like in the U.S.

At Tiananmen Square we find that WE are the main attraction for many of the Chinese people. A few Chinese couples nearby pose for each other as they pretend to take each other's picture, but we notice that the camera lens always lands on us before they snap their pictures. We signal them to actually come and sit next to us for a picture, which they each do a number of times. This seems to tickle them greatly. Once we are seen by others as agreeable photo opportunities we have dozens and dozens of other groups that want their pictures taken with us, first as a group and then with each person separately. They even shove their babies or young children into our arms for poses. Communication is without words, but the emotions are easy to read. We may feel like movie stars, but they are probably mocking us as we look like aliens to them with our yellow hair, colored eyes, and tanned skin.

We look out at the expanse of Tiananmen Square, the largest city square (880 meters by 500 meters) in the center of Beijing, China, and largest city square in the world, and feel dwarfed. The square is named after the Tiananmen Gate (Gate of Heaven's Pacification) located to its

North, separating it from the Forbidden City. We don't notice any memorial plaques commemorating the victims of the Tiananmen Square uprising in 1988 but we each collectively remember where we had been when we heard the news on that day and all the news footage we had seen during that historic time. None of the locals we meet are willing to elaborate on their thoughts or feelings about what happened there.

To our surprise, we find McDonalds, KFC, and Pizza Hut, the most common franchises, having lines of people outside the door, waiting to get in. On the walk back to our hostel, we decide to grab an early dinner at Pizza Hut as we are hesitant to venture into an authentic Chinese restaurant so soon. It turns out to be a disappointment. The

Delivery Boy

menu selections are slim, the portions sizes much smaller, and it just doesn't taste like the flavor of "home." We actually leave still hungry, so we walk next door and top our day off with hot fudge sundaes from McDonalds, using the excuse that we need the sugar boost to sustain us on the 3 hour trek back to our hostel. Alas, a flavor from "home" in China! And it fit right into our budget. We no longer view McDonalds as a greedy, corporate, money factory, churning out cheap, fatty food with no nutritional value. Now the golden arches represent a relatively clean Western toilet, toilet paper, and a sink to wash your hands in. But more importantly it means an ice cream cone for about 20 cents. Any McDonald's value meal costs 16 RMB or $2.00.

It was great seeing everyday life in Beijing and hitting some of the top attractions like: Retan Park, Jingshan Park, Chaoyang Theater, Dashanzi Art District, Beijing Silk Market, Xiang Shan Park and the Azure Clouds Temple, Buddhist Monastery Temple, Donghuamen Night Market, Peking Opera, Beijing Zoo, and the Imperial Place.

Washing Windows 18 Stories High With No Safety Straps

Playing A Board Game In The Middle Of The Sidewalk

🐾 The Great Wall of China

Amy's Diary Entry
November 8th, Beijing, China

We took our first organized tour today instead of just wandering around the city streets thinking that we know where we're going. This tour cost us each $12.00 and so far we've managed to skimp by on only $8.00 a day even though I'm always hungry. My pants were already looser. The bus trip to the Great Wall took 3 hours and could have been a tourist attraction by itself. The first hour was spent getting out of the city of Beijing. Thank God we were in a bigger, taller bus that offered us a little protection from all the other vehicles that didn't seem to realize our bus was a lot bigger than their cars. Lanes of traffic merged without signaling their intent to do so and merged with only inches to spare between vehicles. Add to that motorbikes, dodging in and out of lanes at will, and the pedal bikes trying to maintain safety closer to the sides of the highways. We reached a 2 lane highway once outside the city walls and the horn became like elevator music, constantly in the background. It was used to let a bike, or pedestrian, or another car know that they will soon be passed and missed by mere inches. Pedestrians were walking their pigs and sheep along the side of the road with only a stick to keep them from venturing into the traffic and being hit. Our driver passed whenever he wanted to simply because he had the bigger vehicle, and the biggest vehicle always seemed to have the right of way. They passed on curves, seemingly blind curves to us, and sometimes on hills as well. They passed while going through villages, and they passed when there were oncoming cars. The 2 lane highway would be forced into a 3 lane highway in order to make room for all the vehicles. I had to stop paying too much attention, but I wondered what the daily mortality count was on the roads of China.

The Great Wall of China was incredible. We started at Simatai and ended up several hours later at Jinshanling. There weren't many tourists at all, maybe 3 groups of 20-30 people, and we were spread out along several miles. Parts of the wall were newly renovated or in the process of renovation to prepare for the onslaught of tourists that will accompany the 2008 Olympics. The renovated parts of the Great Wall had smooth, safe steps that were free of debris with intact walls but a fair amount of the walkway was crumbling and hazardous, with gravelly debris littering the walkway. We never walked on a flat surface. Either we were walking uphill or downhill, or we were climbing up or down stairs. I don't remember the Chinese ever being known in history for their height but most of the stairs were of a height, appropriate for a 6 or 7 foot warrior, not 5 foot something women. Periodically there were towers or brick enclosures that one always had to climb up to and through, and from there I could span the horizon and see the Great Wall stretch to the highest peaks until it disappeared. Considering that it was built between 2,000 and 2,500 years ago, with primitive instruments, animals, and back-breaking labor it was truly a stunning testament to the wonder of the man-made world.

Local villagers plied us with postcards and trinkets before we even set foot on the wall itself but they were eventually convinced that we weren't interested in their treasures after the 200th "No thank-you." Several villagers continued walking with us anyway. They seemed very nice, offering to help us climb up and down the stairs, offering to take our pictures, and sharing what they knew about the Great Wall. When they didn't try to sell us anything, we assumed they were part of our tour and were being paid by our tour company to accompany us, so we were much nicer to them. We tried to keep our distance because they had very bad breath. Thirty minutes later they also pulled out their goods and tried to convince us to buy from them. One of them tried to sell us a large hard covered picture book. It may have been a bargain at $3.50, but since we were already struggling just to carry ourselves forward, we repeatedly refused to add another 2 pound picture book to our backpacks. They finally gave up on us as well and went in search of new tourists. These villagers, easily in their 40's or 50's, never shed a stitch of clothing as they walked along in long pants, heavy overcoats, and boots while we had rolled our pants legs as high as they would go and wore only our t-shirts, having shed our sweatshirts within 15 minutes of starting out. They never drank an ounce of water while we drank our limited water like it would last forever. Good thing it was

November and not July. I was hoping that we were close to done at the 90 minute point, but it took us 3 hours to get to the end of our climb. It felt so good just to sit on the bus on the way back to Beijing and stare

Great Wall

out the windows in peaceful repose. I had to tell Traci that I needed some quiet time as she wanted to yap away, but I was just too tired. And, of course, Pollyanna eventually found other people on the bus to listen to her.

 An Off Day

Traci's Diary Entry
November 12th, Qiadong bound en route to Shanghai

We decide to tour the country by train, heading south, stopping in random towns along the way to grab a meal, catch an attraction, or see a landmark. We arrive in Qiadong after a very uncomfortable nineteen hour overnight train ride and I'm very irritable today! Amy is so bossy sometimes and has to have everything her way. Only another year to go with her! Whoohoo! Somebody shoot me now! On top of getting my period, my back hurts from lugging around my now 50 pound backpack. I have searched everywhere for a chiropractor and no one has ever heard of one! After a week of scouting phone books, clinics, and asking hundreds of people, I finally find one. After getting snapped, crackled, and popped, just like at home, this doctor explains that being a chiropractor here is a self-taught career. Not only has he taught himself to be a Chiropractor, but he has taught his two sons as well. I ask him if he will write the word chiropractor for me in Chinese so I can find one faster and easier next time, but he says that I might have better luck going to a massage therapist as many of them have been trained to "move the bones." What a clever idea! A massage therapist who does chiropractic adjustments for ¼ of the price!

On top of it all, it is laundry day and I have drawn the short straw. It seems we have to communicate everything by playing charades here. By using hand-gestures and pointing to my dirty clothes, I ask the hostel attendant if they have laundry service. She nods a firm NO, so I ask her where the washer and dryer facilities are and she motions for me to follow her. She takes me into a dingy room and hands me a plastic basin from the floor with some laundry soap and then sticks out her hand to collect my money for the rental fee. After week one of wearing the same dirty clothes, I have no choice but to hand-wash them, wring them out, and lay them all over the room to dry. It is chilly here and our room has no heat, so some of the articles of clothing are still sopping wet, after drying for fourteen hours.

We go to dinner tonight and ask for an order of tofu and mixed vegetable stir fry. We are informed that they aren't allowed to mix the vegetables together. They even bring out the manager to confirm that they cannot mix the vegetables together in one pan. So they bring out five separate dishes: a tofu dish, a broccoli dish, a carrot dish, a green veggie dish, and a plate of peanuts. They stand there watching us in complete amazement and talking in Chinese with one another as we combine all the ingredients into a stir-fry and eat. Cost for five plates of food with beer is 15 RMB or $1.88 total and tipping hard working staff is not accepted. So far we have had mostly positive experiences with the food as far as tastes go, but in terms of ordering our meals, well, that's another whole story! Qiadong was an interesting layover. Good night and good riddance! Tomorrow is going to be a better day.

On the Train to Nannjing – Last Stop Before Shanghai
Amy's Diary Entry
November 14th

This twelve hour train ride was better than our previous ones so far. We had learned that it is better to spend a few extra dollars to upgrade our train seats. Our first train ride to Qiadong was in an overnight sleeper train. We bought the cheapest bed available, which was the top bed in a column of three beds. There were 6 beds in a compartment with no door and only about 2 feet between the columns of beds. Our bed was only a foot away from the ceiling, and we had to hoist our backpacks up there as well. There was no door on the compartment and thus no privacy. We slept in our clothes and pretty much stayed lying down for the entire trip because the only place you could sit was on the bottom bunk, and that was someone else's bed. They paid extra for that bottom bed. The swaying of the train was really noticeable on the top bunk and poor Traci got motion sickness twice. She was a good puker though, and hardly made a sound. I was hoping for warmer weather as we traveled south. It had been really cold. We had worn our thermal underwear almost every day. We upgraded on this train trip to something called a soft sleeper I think. There were only 4 beds in this compartment and a door. There was also a table between the columns of beds. Two Chinese gentlemen had the beds next to us. One had been just sleeping on his top bed the whole while, but the guy on the bottom, I'll call him Ching, had been smiling at us and gave us a can of bean soup as a welcome gift. We tried to refuse it, but he was insistent. It smelled pretty nasty, so I pretended to take a drink, rubbed my belly, passed the can to Traci, and then refused to take it back from her. I could be so mean sometimes. We, in turn, gave him a bottle of cheap, red Chinese wine that neither one of us could stomach. I wonder if that was why he gave us the canned bean soup. Ching burped without hesitation and occasionally farted without embarrassment. We had been burping and farting out loud just as blatantly as the locals and we found our boorish behavior amusing. I had gotten pretty good at blowing snot rockets as well but Traci usually ended up with snot on her shoulder or chin. I guess growing up on a farm taught me a few useful things.

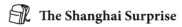 **The Shanghai Surprise**

Traci's Diary Entry
November 16th, Shanghai, China

It seems that I am always knocking into people with my bulky backpack when I get onto trains, buses, and subways. So this morning when we set out for the market via subway, I ask the woman at the front desk of our hostel to teach me how to say a few words in Chinese, and one of them is "excuse me." She writes the words "qing wèn" pronounced something like "chieng heng," and I practice and practice and am sure I have the term memorized. Sure enough, a couple hours later we embark on the subway. I knock into this poor lady with my backpack –so I quickly said "Chieng Wheng" or excuse me (so I think). She bursts into laughter and within a minute has told all the people surrounding us in the subway what I have said and they all are laughing hysterically and pointing at me which cause us to start laughing uncontrollably, and we are all laughing at each other laughing for several minutes! Not only does the lady and about a dozen others have tears in their eyes, we do as well! I do not know what I have said to her that is so funny, but I laugh every time I think about what it might have been…it reminds me of when author Tim Ferriss was traveling and mispronounced a word and mistakenly asked his host mother to "Please rape me in the morning" instead of "Please wake me in the morning."

Calf Head Market

China Vegetable Market Stand

We get lost on our way to the market today. The Chinese have been very willing, friendly, and helpful. They look at our maps and point us in the right direction or even walk us to where we want to go. One couple even closed their mini-mart in order to walk us to our destination. A smile and an attempt at a Chinese thank-you, Xia Xia (pronounced "shea shea") are well rewarded with bows, smiles, handshakes, and sometimes hugs. What an amusing day at the market! Amy and I both agree that the Chinese markets could captivate us for entire days. Never before have we seen such variety at an open air market.

Of course, there are rows and rows of stands with unique looking fruits and vegetables, but the raw meat and animal products really capture our attention. Raw meat hangs in the blistering sun for hours. Flies are so common that the meat keepers don't even bother to shoo them away. Animal

Buy Your Own Live Chicken

organs and animal hooves, feet, and faces with the texture of beef-jerky are easily recognizable. Slugs, locusts, shark fins, vertebra, scorpions, whole alligators, starfish, and other such delicacies round out the selection. Most of those selling these products are tolerant of our pointing and picture taking while we stand in front of their stands, drinking up the novelty of these common markets. In some markets cages of chickens are available for the shopper who selects

A Delicacy - Intestines With Gravy

the most desirous bird. The throat slitting of the poor hen commenced as they hang the wiggling bird by its feet and drain its blood into a jar. They seriously eat everything here! Locusts, bugs, roaches, scorpions, worms, sea slugs, maggots-you name it… they eat it!

Scan Me!

A Street Corner Vendor Fries Us Some Live Scorpion, a Delicacy in China. Cost: 7 for $1 USD
http://j.mp/l5Rif7

*Throngs of People Crowd the Alleyway
To Get Their Meat For The Day*
http://j.mp/kE5OLH

We have experienced true-blue prejudice first hand! On numerous occasions, we find a good restaurant that we can semi-communicate with by playing charades. We walk up and down the aisles of the restaurant and shop for things on other people's plates. We even walk into their grimy kitchens and pull ingredients out of the bins that we want to eat and then point to the frying pans! We feel we have a good relationship with these places, so we go back several times. Each time we return and order the exact same food but the price keeps going up and up right before our eyes for the very same dishes! One time, I ask why the price is different for us than the price on the menu. I am told that the menu has changed since yesterday and the prices are more expensive today for the specific meals I have ordered! Can you imagine the stir and lawsuits if a Chinese person came to America and ordered from the menu at a restaurant and got charged twice the price as anyone else? This is my first time of truly feeling like a minority and discriminated against. None the less, it is a whopping 30 RMB or $3.76 for both of us to eat a complete meal at the Mi Phart Inn Restaurant… and it is delicious! Today has been a great day, so much better than yesterday. Off to bed early, big day tomorrow.

*Traci Negotiates A Bite Of Food From
A Restaurant Patrons Plate*
http://j.mp/iAH0Zq

Shanghai Inflation and Bed Bugs

Amy's Diary Entry
November 16th, Shanghai, China

Shanghai hardly seemed like China at all. It was so very modern and Westernized. Once again there were English signs everywhere.

I knew it wouldn't last when we ventured out to rural China so I enjoyed the ease of communication while I could. I knew our hostel had bed bugs as every morning I woke up scratching like a flea ridden

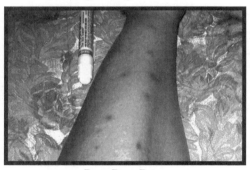

Bed Bug Bites

dog. Traci had a few bites here and there but nothing like mine. I told her it was because I was so much sweeter and she said it was because I'm so much fatter and had more for them to chew. We complained to the hotel staff, showing them the 20 bites I had on my arms alone. They grabbed a spray bottle from behind the desk and sprayed the mattress before putting on clean sheets. The next day I woke up with just as many new bites and again showed them to the front desk, but this time she just nonchalantly shrugged her shoulders and ignored my pleas. Since we were both too lazy to move to a new hostel I guess I will just suffer. Traci and I spent the day apart today. I insisted on what I call sanity days because I needed my alone time. I told her I would need these days regardless of who I was traveling with, but she, of course took it personally and became morbidly morose. Oh well. She eventually got

Nanjing Street

over it. My intention was to find this particular market, but of course I never found it. Instead I just walked around the city streets, not really knowing where I was going. There were a lot of big public parks here just like there were in Beijing. I love that about this country. Unlike our parks in America the parks here were always filled with people. There were ping pong tables set up and usually groups of people will be practicing tai chi or dancing to music that was blaring over boom boxes.

Others would be jumping ropes or trying to fly kites. Some set up their music stands and played accordions or flutes. This old guy spotted me and shouted out a "Hello" and waved me over. He welcomed me to China and told me through an interpreter that he wanted me to enjoy this beautiful country. Traci and I had been telling any local person that asked that we were from Canada. I guess we thought that being Canadians would be safer than being Americans in the wake of 9-11. Everyone seemed to love Canadians. I wondered if they would have the same reaction if we did actually say we were from America. He hugged me before sending me off. I did not expect the warmth that we've received from so many people here.

Traci Eating Crab On A Stick For 10 Cents

Houseboat On The Bund

Amy Shares A Moment With Chinese Musicians
http://j.mp/iAgWM5

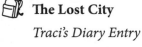 **The Lost City**
Traci's Diary Entry
November 18th

Well, we seem to have the hex of near misses of our departing trains, breathlessly running with our 40# backpacks and boarding with only minutes to spare. So today we decide to set an alarm clock early so we can leisurely make our way to the train station, which is an hour bus ride away. Imagine our surprise and chagrin when the train attendant finally makes it clear to us that we are early all right... an entire day early! Our overnight sleeper train doesn't depart until tomorrow! As a result we have an unexpected excursion in a place we enjoy. We have breakfast at a dingy little local place called Mi Suns Dung Café and share a plate of dumplings and breakfast bread of some sort for 4 RMB or 50 cents. They still use good old fashioned cigar boxes for a cash register here and in the smaller towns or rural areas.

We stroll through local neighborhoods and get invited to share a slice of watermelon with a store owner and his family on the sidewalk neighboring his shop. We don't speak a lick of each other's language, yet we have a meaningful and intimate experience together and it is really wonderful to see how they live and be included in their lives, even if only to share some watermelon. We see a shop owner trying to kill a rat the size of my shoe by chasing it out into the street and spilling boiling water on it. Someone joins in the crusade and finally kills it by repeatedly whacking it with a handmade broom. The woman then picks up the dead rat from the curbside and takes it into her shop. Guess that's tonight's dinner.

In sharp contrast to life in the developed world, life in China is lived on the sidewalks and in the public parks. Sidewalks are often used as an extension of one's living quarters. Clothes lines are strung up on the sidewalk to hang out laundry, underwear included. Entrepreneurs set up mobile stores to sell their services or wares. It is not unusual

Sewing Machine Woman

for a woman and her sewing machine to work on the sidewalk all day or for a portable barber shop to appear next to a busy city street. Child-sized tables and chairs set up on the sidewalks play host to dinners and impromptu card or board games. It is expected that you will walk around their activities. Napping occurs anywhere anyone has the desire to nap. Public parks host hundreds of activities, including dancing, playing badminton or ping-pong, jumping rope, flying kites, exercising

Men Eating Lunch On Child-Sized Table

with tai chi or yoga, playing card and board games, singing, and performing church-style concerts. Many of the parks, especially in Beijing, are gigantic by American standards. It is not unusual for the parks to encompass several miles and house lakes, forests, and historical monuments. Going to the park is so entertaining that we decide to visit one in each city that we go to from now on. We see people carrying their pet goldfish around in plastic bags with water (for luck) along with their caged birds, locusts, and rabbits. Yes, pet locusts are a big hit here, adorning the counters of their business. All cages we have seen for every pet so far are so small that the animal can barely turn around. Even dogs and cats have no slack in their chains or leashes when tied to a post all day long.

The other big thing we notice is that people urinate and defecate in public here. We actually saw a child defecate on a piece of cardboard

Men Napping

as he squatted by a curb. This was a busy street lined with stores and food carts. He wipes himself off with a piece of the cardboard and walks it over to a garbage can. They give tickets for that in America. Come to think of it, they give tickets for everything in America!

Discoveries, Fun Facts, and Useless Tidbits

- Everything we have bought in China so far has fallen apart in the first week. Purses, backpacks, key chains, clothing, sunglasses, and umbrellas.

- Ice is a rare commodity. Whenever we go to a restaurant, we have to ask for ice with our beverage, and most times we receive a single ice cube or two or three if we are really lucky.

- We always have to ask for napkins everywhere we go to eat. Again, we are usually handed a couple of super small squares or some toilet paper. Often times we are charged 10 cents on our bill for the napkins.

- Black pepper is hard to find here. Whenever we ask for pepper, we are given Tabasco sauce.

- We rarely see people in blue jeans here. Even labor workers wear slacks/trousers!

Largest Park in Beijing Host Hundreds of Activities, Including Dancing, Singing, and Performing Church-Style Concerts.
http://j.mp/m5tZyn

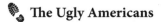 The Ugly Americans

Amy's Diary Entry
November 19th

Last night we certainly gave the Chinese every reason to label Americans as ugly, and I was so ashamed of our behavior. I lost sleep over it and that rarely happens. We walked into this little Chinese restaurant that held at most maybe 30 people. We ordered a chicken dish from the menu. Traci tried to specify that we wanted only white chicken that was skinless and boneless. She always did this and it drove me crazy. If you wanted skinless and boneless white chicken then you should probably stay in America as I suspected that most people in Asia were just happy to be able to eat any chicken at all. The waitress who took our order smiled and shook her head in the affirmative, as if she knew what Traci wanted. Twenty minutes later our plate of chicken arrived and consisted of primarily chicken wings complete with skin and grizzle. In Traci's eyes, and mine too, this was inedible. I didn't even like chicken wings in America when they were loaded with breading and delicious sauces. We attempted to send it back, but they wouldn't take it. Our waitress eventually brought us our bill, but we did not think we should have to pay for this atrocious meal that sat untouched, and Traci tried to explain this to the owner. He, of course, felt there was nothing wrong with our dinner and started to yell at us in Chinese. We tried to quietly leave without paying that portion of the bill, but he blocked the doorway. There were other diners who tried to broker the situation, explaining our viewpoint to the owner and vice-versa but the owner remained adamant that we were paying the bill. After twenty minutes we settled on paying a reduced amount for the meal we never ate and left the restaurant. What a bunch of self-righteous bitches we were!! Almost everywhere we had been in China so far people had been nice to us, often letting us walk into kitchens to point out what we wanted to eat. People would walk us to our destinations after we tried to ask for directions by pointing out on a map what we were trying to find. And what did we just do in return? We threw hissy fits over a measly $4.00 plate of chicken! I just could not leave that city without trying to rectify the sour impression we had left. I returned to the restaurant by myself the next day and found a patron who could again serve as a translator. The owner was at first a little standoffish and did not want to accept my money, but this time I was adamant. I pointed repeatedly to the word apologize in our Chinese phrasebook, put my hand over my heart, and bowed before him. He eventually smiled as well and shook my hand. I hope I at least partially erased a bad memory, but maybe he just wanted me out of his restaurant once and for all. I vowed that I would never do such a thing again.

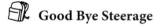 **Good Bye Steerage**
Traci's Diary Entry
November 20th

Okay. We not only make our train today - we make a huge discovery. We find that our first class train tickets come with a first class seating area called soft seating waiting area! After a first class train jaunt to our next couple of destinations we discover that we have been waiting to board our train in the hard seating waiting area, also known as steerage. We have been foregoing all of the first class luxuries such as elbow and sitting room, real leather couches, a western style toilet and just plain cleanliness. As we sit in steerage, thinking we are in first class we can't help but wonder what the third class accommodations are like, as we don't think they can possibly get any worse! I'll bet you can guess what the first sign that we will look for from now on is... Our first class train tickets bottom sleeper (25 hour jaunt) costs 250 RMB or $31.25 each. What a deal! Riding the rails is my favorite means of travel. There is just nothing better. I love meeting people and making friends and seeing the world's countryside. During the day Amy keeps her nose in a book as usual and I socialize and teach some people how to play King's Corners. We sip warm Chinese beer and share snacks. The language barrier is tough at times, but that is what makes it fun to me... playing charades and looking up words on our lingo translator in order to communicate.

I later meet a young girl named Arbilla. She is Chinese and speaks Chinese and perfect English. She is an exchange student in California and is going to visit her family for the holiday break. What a treat to have someone else to talk to for a few hours besides Amy, who is by now sleeping during prime friend-making time. Arbilla is very nice and she is pretty but she has a big mole on her face with three really long, black, hairs growing out of it. They are 3 inches long! Amy and I notice that every person we have met here who has moles have really long, black, coarse hair growing from them. We wonder if there is some sort of significance to this or a reason why they do not just trim the unattractive looking hair.

I ask Arbilla to write a bunch of English food items and terms for me in Chinese characters into my Chinese language book. "I want vegetables with sauce." "I am a vegetarian." "I like tofu." "No MSG (monosodium glutamate)." "Not too spicy." "We want to eat our food at the same time, so bring both dishes together instead of one at a time." "No meat please," etc. The 'no meat' phrase was added after we were served a plate of small chicken pieces, complete with bones, skin, veins, and grizzle. Somehow skinless, boneless broiled chicken breast has been lost in the translation. The seafood restaurants have tanks of fish, crabs, oysters, snails, turtles, frogs, snakes, and eel, all alive, from which people choose. No, we have not braved that yet.

Abrilla also translates the news and newspaper stories for me. It seems there is never any bad news to report in China. Daily reports affirm how happy the people are, how the government is meeting all its financial goals, the factories are meeting or exceeding all of their production quotas, and the quality of life for all Chinese people is improving significantly. The worst story in the paper is that some young gang member has been convicted of murder and is going to be publically executed. I'm all for public executions and think they should be done daily from 9-5, with a mile of convicts standing in line chained together waiting their turn to be thrown into a wood chipper! I think if we had real consequences and made daily examples of the murderers, child molesters, and rapists, we would drastically reduce the number of innocent people that are getting murdered, raped, and sexually abused AND reduce the number of useless pieces of shit taking up space and air on our beautiful planet. I've heard the argument that it costs more money to execute convicts than it does to keep them alive, but I would do the job for free! Not only would we save billions of tax payer dollars but everyone in the world that I know would sleep deeper, breathe easier, and feel safer. You can see that I am still working through some anger issues. I'm troubled by the injustice of my own abuser walking free while I still feel damaged and chained to my past.

👣 Suzhou - Traci's Enlightenment

Amy's Diary Entry
November 21st

Traci could be so naïve sometimes. Yesterday we took a train to Suzhou with Keanna, our new black African American friend from Australia. We didn't get half the brazen stares that she did but she just smiled back and said "hello." When we arrived in Suzhou, known as the Venice of the East, Traci negotiated with a taxi driver to drive us around all day for only 60 RMB, or $7.50. He didn't put up much of an argument, so Keanna and I were already suspicious of his motives. He drove us to the Silk Museum where before we were even out of the car, another Chinese man told us that the Silk Museum was closed for the day. Well that was a blatant lie as I could see other people at the ticket counter buying their tickets for the museum. He lured Traci instead into being taken to the Chinese Silk Research Institute, a much bigger and better silk place. If we agreed to go to this other place he would be our personal tour guide for free. Keanna and I knew what was going on here but we indulged Traci and agreed to the new plan. This bigger and better place had about 3 silk looms set up and after a brief explanation lasting all of 5 minutes we were taken immediately into a large store filled with expensive items made of the silk that was produced in the shop next door. Yeah right. Traci ended up buying some inexpensive underwear, much to the dismay of our tour guide. I'm sure he was hoping for a big commission on a silk quilt. We got back into the taxi and now our friendly tour guide wasn't quite as smiley and nice as he was before. They took us to our next stop and informed us that sudden business had come up and they wouldn't be able to take us to any more places. Well Traci could hardly believe that but Keanna and I just shook our heads and gloated in our astuteness. We demanded part of our money back from our all day taxi driver, and he grudgingly complied. We explained to Traci what had just happened and she was incredulous. Back they went to the train station to lure other unsuspecting tourists into their scheme. We visited a few more places in Suzhou and found the exact same items that were being sold at the Silk Research Institute for half the price. It would be really easy to get mad at these people for trying to scam us, but really, how could you? We have so much in their eyes and even though we were counting our pennies because we felt our funds were limited, we probably had as much as they hoped to make in the next 10 years. Being here has made me appreciate what we have in the United States.

Amy & Traci's Wal-Mart Adventure
Traci's Diary Entry
November 22nd

Amy comes storming out of the bathroom, yelling at me for using up all the hot water in the shower. It takes three days of her griping at me and our hotel attendant for having to endure cold water showers before she finally figures out that the Chinese hot and cold nozzles are reversed from the American style. No wonder I always get hot water whether Amy showers first or second. It seems that Ms. Smarty-Pants isn't so smart after all.

What an exciting day! Whoever thought hanging out at Wal-Mart would be so much fun. Not only is there a Wal-Mart here, there is also a store called Wu-Mart, which is the exact same thing as Wal-Mart, only cheaper. Amy and I get a massage at Wal-Mart. Yes, a massage at Wal-Mart! It costs $10 USD for 60 minutes and two older women come out in their little white nursing skirts, white pantyhose, white nursing shoes, and white old fashioned nurses' hats and escort us into a room with three massage tables. My massage is wonderful but Amy keeps trying to tell the massage nurse that hers hurts. She eases

Bulk Rice

up for a few minutes and then Amy tells her again it is too hard. This massage junkie will be visiting Wal-Mart in every city from here on out and not just for the $10 massages, but for the sheer entertainment and amusement of what we will discover next.

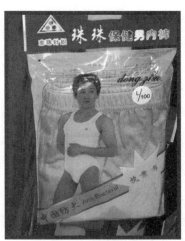

Anti-Bacterial Dong Holder

They also have a pharmacy that offers many ancient remedies and herbal cures. They have these foot reflexology sandals for $10 USD, so I try one on but can't even walk because the pain is so great. The Chinese believe that your feet are the roadmap to your body; you tell the pharmacist your health ailment, say you have diabetes, chronic fatigue syndrome, or kidney problems, and they will custom make you a sandal with different sized rocks glued to the sole that are supposed to press on the point and eliminate any flare-ups.

They have everything there! We find close to 100 different flavors of potato chips, suckers, popcorn and popsicles. No joke! Corn flavored, pea flavored, lychee flavored, milk flavored, apple flavored, corn flavored, red meat flavored, beef granule flavored, chicken bouillon flavored, Italian chicken flavored, BBQ steak flavored... the corn and pea flavored popsicles are so bad that they

Cock Soup

go into the garbage after just one bite! And, yes, they actually do taste like corn and peas. Popsicles cost about 15 American cents.

Chopsticks

Beef Candy

The best is their beef department. They do not have 1# packages for sale but instead pieces of raw beef just sit in bins. Hundreds of people literally manhandle the meat, tearing off the sections they want, bagging it and carrying it up to the register for purchase. Chicken and pork sit on insulated mixed meat tables in the middle of the store and are divided by ears, feet, hooves, faces, legs, wings, tails, ribs, and innards.

Mixed Meat

Ducks

Rib Cages

Pig Faces

Meat Sits On Insulated Tables In The Middle Of the Store and Is Divided By Ears, Feet, Hooves, Faces, Legs, Wings, Tails, Ribs, and Innards.

http://j.mp/l5zjDo

Most dairy products are not refrigerated. Milk is sold in bags or boxes and sits on a shelf, next to the eggs, yogurt, cheese, etc… and you can buy things like whole alligators,

Alligators

snakes, frogs, tarantulas, pig faces, and locusts, just to name a few.

We end up spending a lot of money here. We each buy cute little silk Chinese pajamas for $5 USD but when we are leaving the department we are stopped and told we have to go and pay the pajama department cashier. Next we buy a badminton set and again, we are stopped and told we had to pay the sports cashier, and our groceries are paid for at the main checkout. We discover some very unusual items on the stands that line the checkouts. Rather than the candy, gum, and magazines commonly found in the stands at American checkouts, they have feminine hygiene items, condoms, lubricant, batteries, and adult battery operated devices.

Here are some costs of items at Wal-Mart:

- Local large bottle of beer (640 ml): 6 RMB or .75 cents.

- Milkshakes: 6 RMB or 75 cents.

- Tri-pack of Nabisco chocolate chip cookies: 12 RMB or $1.50.

- 4 pack of Ramen noodle soup: 1.20 RMB or .63.

- Multi-serving instant oatmeal: 5-9y or .63-$1.13.

- Can of soda: 2.5 RMB or 30 cents.

- 100% acrylic, bulky, high neck sweater: 88 RMB or $11.00.

- Roll of 10 pack toilet paper: 4 RMB or 50 cents.

- 2 oranges: 3 RMB or 25 cents.

- Banana: 1 RMB or 10 cents.

- Carton of fresh strawberries: 10 RMB or $1.20.

- Teva sandals: 120 RMB or $15.00.

Check Out the Potato Chip Flavors at Wal-Mart in China
http://j.mp/l36sd4

Huangzhou

Amy's Diary Entry
November 23rd

I loved Huangzhou, a beautiful city. I have been frustrated because so many of these cities are so big, and I was sure we have been just scratching the surface. Although we didn't have the time to stay in each city as long as we should, I guess it was better than not being here at all. Our hotel was right across the street from a popular lake. Two mornings I jogged on the path along the lake. There sure weren't many joggers around here. I got a lot of stares and a lot of people yelled "Hello" and waved to me which was really cool. I was cooling down on a bench when 3 young girls shyly made their way over to my bench and started talking to me in halted English. We talked for about 30 minutes and they asked if they could treat Traci and me to dinner that night as they wanted an opportunity to practice their English with native speakers and to learn more about our home country of "Canada." I readily agreed and am so glad that I did.

These 3 college students, who looked like they were all of 15, were 21 years old and have taken the Western names of Ping Ping, Lily, and

Our New Friends

Amani. When we arrived at the restaurant that evening they asked us what kind of food we liked and we rattled off about six different dishes. We thought they were just making conversation, not realizing that they would order every dish for dinner that we had just named. As a treat for dessert they ordered a Chinese delicacy of fish soup, and since it was a special occasion, 3 beers to share among us. They did not really like beer and only took a few sips, but we had no difficulty finishing their share and ours, as we had grown to love and even crave Chinese beer. But as for the fish soup... one taste was more than enough as it tasted as bad as it sounds. As tokens of friendship from their country, they gave us symbolic Chinese gifts that were to bring us happiness and health wherever we were to go in life. They were as fascinated to learn about our country as we were to learn about theirs, but unfortunately we made very poor Canadians. They probably thought that Canada is a lot like the United States. They asked us about a well-known Canadian pop band, but of course, we had never heard of them! Then they asked us to name a famous Canadian college, but we couldn't so we told them they were all public colleges. I hope we didn't give them too much misinformation. They may have known more about Canada than we knew ourselves but were too polite to correct us. These young girls were refreshing in their naiveté and such a contrast to most American girls of the same age. They had never been on dates with boys, never tried cigarettes, and did not like the taste of any alcohol. They liked fast food, but their parents told them not to eat a lot of it or they would become fat. They lived in a dorm room with three other girls that had no heat or air conditioning. They were concentrating on their studies for the next several years and would date after they graduated from college. After they graduated from college! Their comments were interspersed frequently with the phrase "My parents say..." It was remarkable the influence their parents still held over these 21 year old girls. They all said they would love to travel as we were but could never be away from their parents for that long as they would miss them too much. After buying us dinner and showering us with gifts, Traci decided to give them each a pair of the silk underwear that she had purchased at the Silk Research Institute in Suzhou as a token of appreciation and thanks. But they vehemently refused to take our underwear offering. What were we thinking? Why would anyone ever want our underwear, new or not? We are such idiots sometimes.

 **Hong Kong**

Traci's Diary Entry
November 25th

Hong Kong is expensive! We've been averaging $75 dollars a day instead of our more typical $18 dollars a day in the rest of China. Hong Kong is even more international than Shanghai and has less of a Chinese flavor. I don't really like it. There is a lot of pollution here, and it is so humid our clothes don't even dry completely after a hand-washing. We've done a lot of the typical tourist things like Stanley Market, Victoria Park, the tram to the top of the city, etc. but I'm left with

wanting more of the real China. I can't believe we've only been traveling 3 weeks. It seems like 3 months. It is Thanksgiving today but of course no one here recognizes this very important

Pedicure On The Street For $3

American holiday. Instead of a turkey dinner with my family, I'm

eating Chinese spaghetti with Amy, which turns out to be Chinese noodles with ketchup squeezed over the top of them. She has curried vegetables. Needless to say, my fork wanders over to her plate. We're stuck here for awhile since Ms. Planner demanded that we pre-purchase our train tickets to go to Guang-zhou and Yangshou, and now we don't like it here and want to leave early, but they will not change our tickets for us.

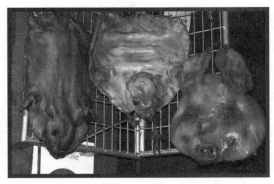

Jerkied Rabbit, Chicken & Pig

A Stroll Through A Market In Hong Kong. Every Kind Of Food Imaginable Is Here
http://j.mp/lwFwNL

Speaking of tickets, the taxi drops us off at the train station where we are going to purchase tickets. We have all the pages marked in our English-Chinese conversion book and are trying hard to make it clear that we want two first class train tickets, lower bunks, leaving tonight. The 1st attendant shakes her head "no" and motions us to another window. This isn't unusual as at times there is a ticket agent who can speak enough English to get us through, but the 2nd and 3rd attendant also shakes their heads "no" and motion us away, and now there are no more windows to go to. Frustrated customers behind us intervene trying to help and keep making flapping motions with their arms, laughing, and speaking in Chinese to each other. We think that they are just mocking us "waigoren" (foreigners) or being rude, but we are not leaving the train station without our train tickets. Finally, a woman who speaks a little English hears what is going on and makes her way towards the front of the line and informs us that we are at the airport, not the train station. Aye Aye Aye! Onto Guangzhou, via train.

Leaving Guangzhou
Amy's Diary Entry
December 8th

Guangzhou was not our city. This was our 2nd stay in the city, and I didn't want to write about it the first time. I thought the 2nd time would be better, but it wasn't. The people weren't very friendly at all compared to other places in China. It was really hard to find anyone who spoke even a little English which, of course, made it much more difficult. Our hostel there the first time was awesome with fluffy, white comforters, a TV with one English channel, a private bathroom, hot water, and it was clean. Well, this time they demanded 100 RMB more for a security deposit even though there was a huge sign on the front desk where it said in English that the security deposit was 200 RMB, not the 300 RMB we were being charged. Of course we tried to point this out for about 15 minutes, but the staff wasn't budging so we had no choice but to pay it. Not a big tourist city, hostels weren't easy to find here. Our room this time was on the other side of the hall and was hot and stuffy. Plus I woke up again with bed bug bites, so we tried to explain to them that we wanted a different room on the other side of the hall because this room was so hot. Instead they just opened up the secured window, hesitated, shook their head in the negative, closed the window, and left the room. We finally got a new room. Then when we were checking out trying to get our 300 RMB security back they would only give us 200 RMB. When we tried to remind them that we had to pay 300 RMB they pointed to the sign where it said the deposit was 200 RMB. Well Traci became irate and threw her backpack up on the counter and then hopped up there and sat and insisted that she wasn't moving until we got the whole amount back, shaming them with her two fingers. I was pissed too but didn't think that would be the best approach to take and was even worried about Chinese police coming in and taking us to some Chinese jail for such outrageous behavior. I finally talked her down from the counter, and we left without getting any our 100 RMB bogus deposit back. We bought some food from a little stand on the sidewalk as I saw people biting into what looked like a potato, but when I bit into it, it was nothing but a piece of fat. It was so gross! Traci's meal wasn't any better, so we found what looked like a homeless guy and gave it to him. We've done that a bunch of times now. To make the whole situation worse the guy in the stand tried to give her change for a 5 RMB note instead of the 20 RMB note she had handed him. One day when we were walking down the side-walk this little girl who looked to be 5 or 6 years old came up to Traci and handed her a rose and told her it was because she was so pretty. Traci, of course, thought that this was one of the most beautiful gestures and she was touching her heart with her hand and thanking the little girl over and over. I was rolling my eyes, knowing that there was more to come and I couldn't believe Ms. Pollyanna was still so gullible. Of course 25 feet later the little girl was tugging on Traci's jacket and holding her hand out because she wanted money for the beautiful flower. Traci tried to give the flower back, but she refused to take it back. Instead Traci set it gently on the sidewalk, and we walked away. Then we went back to the only store we had found that sold really cold beer, but this time we were charged 10 RMB a bottle instead of the 4 RMB that we were charged the first time we were there. We were on our way to the train station to leave this miserable city anyway, so we shamed them with our fingers and made the purchase. We snuck our way into an air-conditioned waiting area at the train station, but an attendant found us and walked our butts into the steerage waiting area. To top it off the backpack that Traci bought for $2.00 on our way to the train station burst at every seam as soon as she had it filled up. This town had soured our opinion on China and its people. At least we had the bottom berth for our train trip to Guilin for a day and then a bus ride to Yangshou. Goodbye Guangzhou!

Guilin & Yanshou – The Screen Savers of My Mind
Traci's Diary Entry
December 13th

Guilin is famous for its spectacular limestone scenery. There is the popular saying "Guilin shanshui jia tian xia," which means Guilin's mountain and water scenery is the best under heaven. Two crystal clear rivers flow through the city, encircled by mountains with unusual and bizarre rock formations and caves. We enjoy a picnic lunch of tomato, cilantro, and cucumber filled baguettes in the folds of this new heaven.

Traveling in the south and southwest of China and spending more time with English speaking locals has exposed a different side of this beautiful country. We have met some very beautiful and kind-hearted human beings who are equally interested in learning more about us and how we live as we are of them. We are really getting off the tourist track and going into the villages and meeting the people. One incredible encounter is with a local woman in Yanshou, in the Guangxi province. This woman's Western name is Wendy and she

becomes our personal guide of the country-side for several days. Amy misses out on day one of the tour because I actually need a day away from her, which doesn't happen very often with this easy

Our Guide Wendy

rider. This time she really pisses me off good. She yells at me loudly in the middle of the restaurant for spending "unnecessary money" on a second order of food! I don't like my $2.00 plate of grizzle, guts, and

$2 Raft Ride

fat, so I shove it aside and order a plate of broccoli and nuts with fish sauce. I have to inform her that we are not a couple, and I am paying for MY meal with MY money, not "OURS"! Funny how it's okay for her to spend 50 cents on a can of Diet Coke every morning, but I'm bad and wrong for spending another $2 on food, so I don't go to bed hungry for the third night in a row. Anyway, Yanshou has been by far the most enchanting city in China with limestone pinnacles jutting up from the countryside, rivers, and lakes. This place serves as the setting for so many of the classical Chinese paintings. Wendy walks us through fields of rice paddies, grapes, chestnuts, oranges, peanuts, sweet potatoes, and fruits, some of which we have never heard of before such as pumello. A pumello has the shape of a large pear, with an orange type skin that tastes like a bland orange. The fields are cultivated as they have been for hundreds of years, either with water buffalo or by hand. She points out

one plant that people use different parts of for tea, medicine, and mosquito repellent. Even the crops are multi-functional, with nothing discarded as garbage. The left over parts are cooked and used as feed for the pigs. We are taken through a rural village called Chicken Feet and some of the locals invite us into their homes. The homes are unheated concrete structures with maybe a bench or wooden chair to sit on. The only thing hanging on the wall is a calendar. The kitchen is in a separate concrete room and contains a fire pit and, if fortunate, a single hot plate. They make dinners from garden vegetables and maybe meat bought at a local market that morning as there are no refrigerators in the homes. The only store bought products in the homes are soy sauce, peanut oil, and monosodium glutamate (MSG). After a bamboo raft ride and a look at local burial plots, we have a short tour of an elementary school, where children lack basic school supplies such as paper, pens, or textbooks. The playground is devoid of any recreational equipment, but does have the errant chicken or dog meandering through. Only 10% of children in rural China achieve test scores high enough to qualify for high school. The parents must pay tuition at all levels of school, which for the Chinese farmer can be almost impossible to earn. If local schools are not available and if they earn high enough scores, they will attend boarding school in nearby cities, coming home only on the weekends. It is a no brainer; this is the first school and village we will "adopt." My parents will be tickled to receive the photographs we just emailed them of their new third-world "family." I know they love

Moon Feet Village School

Unheated Classroom

following our adventure and vicariously going on the journey.

Hours after our tour begins we arrive at Wendy's home in Moon Village, population 500. Here she prepares a dinner of 5 or 6 different dishes, all of which she creates using nothing but vegetables, herbs from her vast garden, and a little pork. To keep us busy and make us feel like we are contributing she has us peel chestnuts. By the time we finish peeling 2 dozen chestnuts, she had cleaned, peeled, and diced the food for all of the other dishes. Dinner is wonderful. Wendy is a remarkable woman. In the early morning before coming to the city to find work as a guide she will work in the fields or wash clothes using a washboard. After guiding tourists for most of the day, she comes home to make dinner for her family. In her spare time, she knits slippers and sweaters, also for herself and her family.

Limits on the number of children a couple can have, remain intact. If a couple's first child is a boy, they can have no more children, but if the firstborn is a girl they can have another child. Hopefully their prayers will be answered, and their last child will be a son. Two children are the limit for any family, regardless of the sex of the second child. If a couple exceeds their limit, the government imposes a substantial fine of 20,000 RMB or $2,500.00. If the couple is unable to pay this fine, the government may seize their home and sell it to satisfy this fine. Despite this strict policy, there are more babies born in China each year than the entire population of Australia. It is also this policy and the emphasis on a male heir that leads to abandoned baby girls. Wendy herself is raising one of these little girls as her own, after

Bathing Baby In A Bucket

finding her on the roadside when the little girl was a mere 2-3 months old.

Seeing firsthand this poverty and impoverished living is an entirely different experience than reading about it. It must be demoralizing for the people that regardless of their incessant labor, factors beyond their control, such as government restrictions on relocation and scarce and often poor quality of education, etc. limit their ability to improve their lives. It has given us a renewed appreciation for our country. China continues to be fascinating and multi-faceted. Sometimes we must remind ourselves to put our western standards of acceptable aside and be non-judgmental of this ancient and encompassing country. By the time we leave we will have spent twice the amount of time in this country than initially expected, yet we will leave with the feelings that we have missed so much.

In several cities we must have screamed naïve to the taxi drivers, and they take full advantage of it. Taxi drivers pick us up and nod their heads in understanding as we point to our desired destination on the Chinese map. Instead of taking us to our intended destination they will stop at a nearby but completely different tourist sight and wait for an attendant to come out to our taxi and escort us inside. We, of course, don't know the difference and fall prey to being escorted inside where our purchases are anxiously anticipated. We finally become wise to this charade, and the taxi drivers that attempt this in the future lose out on any fare that they may have earned if we had been dropped off at the correct place the first time. They don't argue too much about it, which proves to us they knew all along what they are doing. On one occasion we had hired a taxi driver for a 30 minute ride back into Beijing from an outlying region. Fifteen minutes into the ride our taxi driver, who knows only a few words of English, hails another taxi while driving. They both pull over to the side of the road and begin speaking Chinese. A moment later we are shooed from the cab we were in and passed on to another driver. We have no idea the reason for this. One minute we are in a nice, clean, air-conditioned cab, and the next minute we are climbing into an old, dirty cab with no air conditioning. A couple of other times the driver pulls into the petro station and shoos us out of the cab while he fuels it up. CRAZY!

The Contrasts of China
Amy's Diary Entry
December, 14th

China put a smile on my face almost every day. Whether it was the storekeeper who smiled and said "neehow" (hello), the unexpected

friendly encounter in the park or at the train station, or as we tried to order a meal, the Chinese people repeatedly made us feel welcome. Yes there were incidents where a few Chinese had tried to pick pocket us, but many more

Whole Fish

people had gone out of their way to help us purchase tickets or find a bus station. China was an up and coming powerhouse in the world, but our contacts in China were with the working class and often the poor. I loved seeing the workers in the rice fields, the old farmer plowing his field with water buffalo, or the Beijingers riding their bicycles in all kinds of weather. It was selfish of me to hope that these ways of life never ceased to exist. Seeing it in a history book would never be the same as witnessing it in the flesh, but I'm sure that the rice worker who spent much of his life bent over would have preferred a method of rice planting that didn't involve an aching back. There were sides to China that I was happy to leave: the pollution, the littering, and the beautiful caged dogs waiting to be butchered.

Memories of those that will do backbreaking work all of their lives and never get any farther ahead would stay with me, as would the sharp contrast between the generations apparent on city sidewalks when the old

woman carried her vegetable with her shoulder yoke was passed by a young, beautiful woman with long black hair dressed in fashionable Western clothes and talking on a cell phone.

Those contrasts would not last very long and I was thankful I had this opportunity to witness this in person. China had been a great country to start our travels as it forced us

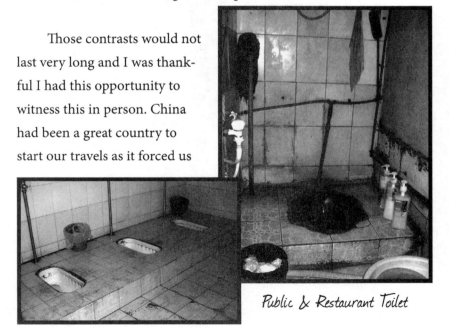

Public & Restaurant Toilet

into a world completely foreign to us, which had been exactly what we were looking for. China had set high standards for the rest of Asia, and I hoped Vietnam could meet those expectations.

Yangshou, China

Amy's Diary Entry
December 16th

Yangshou is the most beautiful city I have ever seen! Words could not adequately describe the tranquility of the river, the fields, and the limestone peaks that jut out of the ground. I rented a bike the other day because Traci needed a day alone and biked out into the country past rice paddies flooded with water and other fields that were being plowed by water buffalo. Farmers were walking their one or two cows along the side of the road, and others were hauling carts filled with coal. I rode by a blacksmith shop that looked like it was right out of Little House on the Prairie. I watched him for awhile putting a piece of metal into the fire and then taking it out and pounding it with hammers. There were old, leather-faced women carrying their grandchildren in baskets on their back, people playing board games in front of their homes, and a lot of skinny dogs running around the streets. I had a hard time with all the litter in the countryside though. We've seen people come out of their house, walk across the street, and throw their garbage over a fence before walking back into their houses. We had seen other people walk on the sidewalk, unwrap a candy bar, and just throw the wrapper on the ground. There were piles of smelly rubbish next to houses or at the edge of a town, and I wished they would be nicer to their animals. We had seen a dog that was tied up being beaten because it had barked and also seen them sold for butchering at the back of a market.

We were definitely singled out more in the rural areas. Beggars found us pretty regularly. The other day we were walking around in the town confines and came to this open city square area. There were two or three guys with monkeys putting on a little circus show. We watched like everyone else did and then one of the guys came around with a cup looking for donations. He stopped right in front of us and wouldn't move on, like he did with everyone else. We hadn't even taken a picture of the animal act and did not feel like we needed to give him money since no one else had put anything into his cup. At one point he even gave Traci a little push on the chest so we just walked away. People set up all kinds of little shops on the sidewalk. There was a guy who made keys and another who fixed bicycles. One woman was sitting on the sidewalk with a sewing machine, sewing. We were getting better and better at bargaining though. We learned that we had more power if we waited and shopped after the Japanese tour buses left. The shop owner would give us a price for something and we ultimately paid about a third of their asking price. We finally had purchased so much stuff that we were going to ship a box back home so we found two boxes that we could use and scrounged a bunch of newspapers and magazines for packing. When we took them to the post office they told us we had to use special boxes that we had to buy from the post office, and we could not ship any Chinese newspaper out of the country. It ended up costing us $70 USD each to ship our boxes home and who knows if they will even make it. Not many boxes would be sent home at that price.

Dali

Amy's Diary Entry
December 17th

Traci got taken for another little ride again in Dali, which has a whole area that is set up entirely for tourists. We wandered a few cobblestone streets with nothing but restaurants and stores before trying to decide where to eat and what to buy. I pulled out a map to figure out our next destination and while I was studying the choices this old lady who was squatting on the sidewalk grabbed Traci and

Lying Old Lady

started pointing at her shoes which had holes in them and seemed to be held together by strands of thread. The old lady then pointed to a store, a shoe store of course, and then back at her feet. Traci was led to the slaughter as soon she was in the store with the old lady. She bought her a brand new pair of shoes. Funny though, the old lady didn't put them on. She walked out with them in a bag but Traci left with a good feeling in her heart that she made this old lady's life better and shared her good fortune with others less fortunate and blah blah blah. Pollyanna didn't appreciate it when I told her that she had just been scammed again. My suspicion was confirmed by Marley, the owner of a popular tourist hangout, who said this lady lived in a nice house in the country but pulled this scam day after day with kind-hearted and gullible tourists. Store owners were complicit because after the stupid tourist left, the shoes were returned and the store owner split the money with the old lady. The old lady also got tourists to buy her clothes and coats. This lady's kids did not want her to do this, but she got a kick out of it. This was the kind of stuff that made me question everybody's intentions.

Eating Lunch Squatting

Water Buffalo & School Kids

Discoveries, Fun Facts, and Useless Tidbits

- We had seen many billboards/posters in the shopping centers with older looking models. It was funny to see that 80% of the advertisement models are Caucasian, not Chinese.

- Frivolous lawsuits are rare in china; china expects one to use common sense. If a person falls into a large hole in the middle of the sidewalk or slips on a wet floor it is the person's fault for not watching where he is going or what he is doing.

- Children go to work with their parents or worked the streets themselves. If a parent has to do something without their children, only the in-laws are allowed to care for them.

- Nursing homes are only for elderly who have no children to care for them. It is always the responsibility and honor (not obligation or inconvenience) of the son to move his parents in with his family when they could no longer care for themselves.

 The Dali Karma

Traci's Diary Entry
December 19th

Tourists and locals alike are attracted by Dali in Yunnan province. It beams with ancient customs and history. We gradually make our way to Yangren Street or "Foreigner Street" which is full of Western tourists inside of Dali City. I can't help but smile at everything and everyone. I just love this travel experience. Dali has both a modern city and the ancient walled city that the tourists love to visit. The locals have found a way to capitalize on the tourists, causing it to lose some of its integrity and allure in the process. Despite all this it is still beautiful and sadly, one of the few old cities that has been maintained in this province. We stroll through the town and admire the San Ta (three pagodas) of the Chongsheng Temple in Dali and then through the markets, where we see a huge pile of pigs' feet, which have been rubbed with something to keep them fresh a little longer. On a nearby spit are pig entrails, chicken stomachs, hearts, and innards. I'm going veg for the rest of the trip!

We save a small cat from getting whipped with sticks and stoned to death by a group of local boys who have the poor thing cornered. I know it isn't worth our lives if the boys had turned on us, but we can't help it. Instinct and adrenaline take over. I personally cannot stand back and watch someone harm something or someone who is defenseless. The boys flee the scene after we begin yelling at them and we scoop up the trembling kitty and bring her back to our hostel for a good meal and a safe place to sleep. We have no idea what we are going to do with this cat. I want to bring her with us but Amy will not let me.

Thank God we met Marley, the owner of Marley's Café. She has a cat named Mi Mi who acts as the café mascot and Marley gladly accepts our cat, which I have named China. Marley renames the new cat Mi Mi, which I have discovered means cat in Chinese. It turns out that most Chinese people call their cats "MiMi."

I walk past an old lady who looks to be in her eighties, squatting on the sidewalk. I smile as I walk past and she tugs on my pant leg and folds her hands in prayer or please position. I squat beside her and we share a long stare with no words. Then she points to her shoes, which clearly cling to her feet by just a few strands of thread. She points to a store and then back at her feet, so I pull her up and we walk arm in arm across the cobblestone path to the store. I'm excited to let her pick out a new pair of shoes and she seems excited to receive them. We smile and embrace. She is happy, and I feel good inside. Amy keeps picking on me and telling me I have been scammed, but I let her facetiousness run off me like water on a duck. Later, Marley confirms Amy's beliefs and the teasing increases. While I don't appreciate being scammed, my karma and who I am as a person lies in the act of giving, and the old woman's karma lies in the act of taking and lying and cheating kind-hearted people. We all have to meet our maker and get cooked in the baker in the end. I know that I will sleep well tonight, and I know that what we put out in the world, good or bad, will return back to us, tenfold.

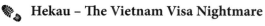 Hekau – The Vietnam Visa Nightmare

Amy's Diary Entry
January 5th

What a nightmare this had become. We took a grueling over-night sleeper bus trip from Kunming to Hekau in order to cross into Vietnam. Our visa for Vietnam was dated for January 6th, but we were assured by the officials at the Vietnam consulate in Hong Kong that we would be able to cross into Vietnam a few days early. The officials at the border were not okay with this plan of ours, despite our pleading and almost downright begging. Our Chinese visas expired on the 4th, but we figured we would just pay the fine for leaving the country late since we obviously weren't getting into Vietnam before the 6th. The Chinese officials told us that we would not be allowed to leave China until we had an extension that carried us through to our departure date, and to top it all off, the closest place to get this extension was in Kunming, the place that we had just left the day before. We argued with them as well, and finally the agents pulled a higher ranking official out of his office and he opened up his rule book and pointed it out to us. It was clearly written in Chinese! Traci thought that if she just stood there and didn't move that they would eventually give in but I had no such pretences. Rules were rules to the Chinese and you just didn't break them with-out repercussions. Well the bus ride from Kunming sickened Traci as it was on narrow, winding roads which of course, left her throwing up and nauseated all day. So I was back off to Kunming by myself on another 14 hour bus ride. Once there I had to wait several hours for the visa office to open but got my extension as soon as the office opened. Then I left the premises and changed clothes, put my hair in a ponytail, donned a cap, put makeup on, and went back to the visa office, pretending to be Traci so I could get her an extension too. Well the officials thought it was pretty funny that two American girls needed visa extensions on the same day; they even told me about my earlier visit to them. The disguise worked as now Traci's passport was stamped with the same extension as mine. Maybe we all looked the same to them. Fourteen hours later I was back in Hekau and it was then that I read on the back of our hotel door that said "Chinese visa extensions are available at the Hekou Public Security Bureau just around the corner!" The stupid border agents should have known that. Traci did her best to hide the sign from me.

After 2 months I was definitely ready to leave this country. We had a few more bad experiences in the rural areas with people trying to cheat us or charge us more for things. I didn't like all the pollution and the seemingly disregard for the environment. I felt very bad for the cats and dogs and some of the infant girls born here. The poverty was staggering yet the people seemed to have iron clad resilience to it. They worked so hard and seemed to reap so little for all of their back-breaking work. But then again I read a statistic that over half of all the world's suicides occurred in China and that more women than men killed themselves here so not everyone had that resiliency. I could totally understand a woman's desperation here. They did seem to work harder and shoulder more responsibility than a lot of men. Of course, this was just an observation since our conversation with local people was limited due to the language barrier. But when a couple was walking down the sidewalk together, it was often the woman that was carrying the shopping bags and the child while the man walked next to her, carrying nothing and smoking a cigarette. Life in the country was a lot different and harder than life in Beijing appeared to be. I figured, if we had traveled through this country than we could travel through any country. Traci and I have been getting along fairly well except for our big argument on New Year's Eve, which was a result of too much wine and her not knowing when to shut up and stop going on and on about the same thing. She was pushing my buttons intentionally, and I had had enough. By the end of the night she wanted to venture off on her own, and I told her to be sure and leave my airplane tickets. Well she didn't leave and by the next morning after all the alcohol had worn off it was soon forgotten. Even though I was not real keen on traveling by myself, I was stubborn enough not to try and stop her from walking out the door if that is what she wanted.

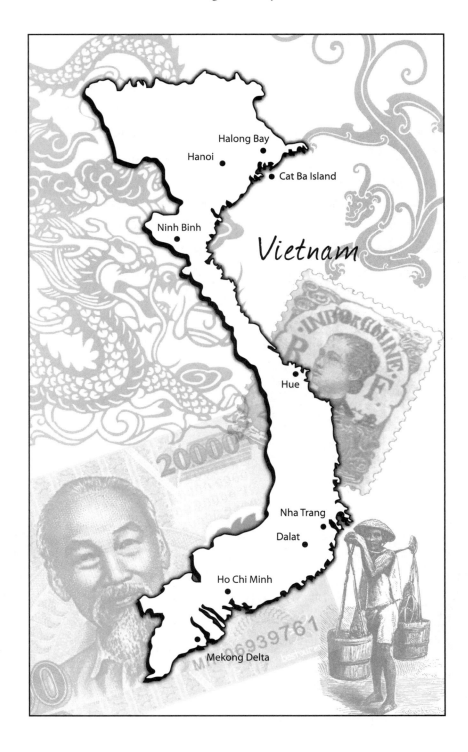

Halong Bay

Hanoi

Cat Ba Island

Ninh Binh

Vietnam

Hue

Nha Trang

Dalat

Ho Chi Minh

Mekong Delta

Vietnam

*"The real voyage of discovery consists not in seeing new landscapes
but in having new eyes." - Marcel Proust*

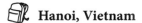 **Hanoi, Vietnam**
Traci's Diary Entry
January 11th

Amy and I are getting along better after our little blowout last
week. After twenty games of cards and two bottles of wine, we had
gotten lippy with each other, and I remember threatening to continue
on without her, but of course, by morning, the red-wine fog and day
old animosity disappear as quickly as the scent from my newly purchased bottle of Obsession perfume. We both apologize for our parts
in the button-pushing session. It is tough being with someone 24/7
for months on end, with no real break from each other, but then again,
she is the only person I can imagine sharing this kind of adventure
with, so maybe I should try a little harder to make it work out.

Life is very different in Vietnam, much different than China and
certainly much different than any other place that I've ever been. After
nearly a half century in isolation, Vietnam remains one of the poorest

countries in the world. Many things run scarce here, much of which I have once taken for granted. There is nothing in a can, nothing frozen, and no toilet paper, yet the people smile and greet us with warm affection. The touts are a little too persistent. While that Ground-hog Day routine gets old and irritating every time we step foot out the door, I understand that this is their survival. It has been a challenge for me to be kind to the pushy venders after the 200th "No Thank You" as they follow us halfway to our next destination, shoving their goods in our faces. Being rude or even mean just isn't my nature, that's Amy's job.

The exchange rate is 15,000 dong to one USD. WOW! What a feeling it is to walk around with 3 million dollars in your pocket at one time. Too bad it isn't 3 million in American money. There are 100,000, 50,000, and 10,000 dong bills, which can become confusing. Tipping is not accepted here either. We have even had servers chase us down the walk to return the few coins we leave on the table. Several times, we inadvertently overpay the bill by ten times and the clerks point this out and return our money. Considering we are new at this and how poor they are, they could have easily ripped us off. Their honesty on these occasions is admirable.

On our first day of arrival, Amy and I are approached by male prostitutes offering us "great pleasure" for 30,000 dong or $2 USD. I tell them that the only "dong" I'm interested in from Vietnam is money. They didn't think that was funny. Both are young teenagers. One says to me, "I may be a bit too short for you but I think we can still make it work." When we say no, they lower their prices to 15,000 dong or $1 USD. If he would have looked as good as John Stamos I might have taken him up on it, but in all seriousness, when does a girl ever have to pay for sex? All she needs to do is walk into a bar at closing time and bat her eyelashes. It is baffling. Do these boys seriously get business?

The plan is six weeks in Vietnam, beginning in Hanoi and ending in Saigon. I purchase backpacker bus tickets from Hanoi to Saigon for 435,000 dong or $29.00 each. They are open seats on a first come, first serve basis, getting on and off at the location of your choice. It should be fun.

🥾 Hanoi, Vietnam
Amy's Diary Entry
January 13th

Walking across the border into Vietnam was rather anti-climactic as it consisted of walking through two wooden shanties, paying money, and getting at least five different stamps in our passport from five different officials standing behind five different counters before we could step foot on Vietnamese soil. At least there were no baggage

checks or body searches. I wouldn't blame anyone for not wanting to search us too thoroughly as we rarely had any make-up on and the most we did with our hair was to put it in to a ponytail and then usually put on a

Hanoi Street

hat. We were some real lookers on this trip. It was really weird though because as soon as we walked over the border, the people looked different. The housing was a little nicer and even the stray dogs

appeared to be in better condition. We still had to hang out for 6 hours in that first town, Lao Cai, before jumping on a train to Hanoi. Hanoi was our first official destination in Vietnam and I was convinced it was the noisiest city I had ever visited. In Hanoi the majority of residents (70%) seemed to have a motorbike, but everyone, whether riding a motorbike, driving a car, pedaling a cycle, or lumbering along in a dump truck had to blow their horn every 15 seconds. The streets were very narrow and the sidewalks were not functional for walkers. They are either used for motorbike parking, as store extensions where merchants displayed their wares, or dining rooms, complete with plastic table and miniature chairs occupied by a variety of foods and their diners. This seemed to amplify the noise to ear-splitting levels, so now we wore earplugs during the day while walking in the city to block out the noise rather than at night. It seemed like every 20-30 seconds someone approached us and tried to sell us donuts, baguettes, oranges, books, etc. Anyone on a motorbike seemed to also work as a taxi as we were constantly getting asked if we wanted a ride somewhere. It got a bit irritating, but I had to remind myself that these people were only trying to make a living and how would I feel if I were in that position? We politely declined and most of them accepted the first refusal.

We saw the great Ho Chi Minh's body. He died in 1969, and despite his implicit desire to be cremated, which was outlined in his will, the Vietnamese government instead has displayed his body since 1975. It was in a specially built grandiose mausoleum. His body had just returned from Russia where he was sent for three months each year for refinishing, touch-ups, re-embalming, or whatever they must do to someone who has been dead for over 30 years. It was kind of funny because first we had to pair up and then walk in a straight line to the sarcophagus. Once inside we had to walk single file by his corpse. The line had to keep moving at all times.

Another interesting historical site was the Hoa Lua prison, better known in America as the Hanoi Hilton. I had read John McCain's book about his time in this place and was really looking forward to seeing it firsthand. They demolished most of the prison in 1993 to make room for an office and apartment complex but part has been renovated to serve as a historical public attraction. The handouts and picture captions focused on the repression and torture of the Vietnamese revolutionaries by the French as they fought for their independence, but it didn't mention the torture that our servicemen suffered at their hands. The prison, built by the French in 1896, had housed far more Vietnamese prisoners than American prisoners. At one time it held close to 2,000 Vietnamese revolutionaries. The only pictures of our servicemen that were displayed were pictures of American fighter pilots, preparing their own meals in the clean kitchen, meeting with foreign dignitaries, and receiving packages from family abroad, all while neatly dressed, clean, and shaven. I doubt that their recollections of their personal experiences in this hell brought back memories of such favorable conditions.

So far most people here seemed very honest. Both of us had inadvertently given cashiers a 20,000 dong note instead of a 2,000 dong note, and they returned

it and pointed it out to us. They could have easily shortchanged us and we wouldn't have even noticed. We had laundry done by our hotel staff, and I had accidently left 30,000

Workers In Rice Field

dong in the pocket, which was also returned. That left us with warm feelings toward the Vietnamese people.

We were heading out in two days to go to Nihn Bihn, Halong Bay, and Cat Ba Island.

The Ear Plug City
Traci's Diary Entry
January 14th

The next stop was Ninh Binh, which does not offer much as a city, but the surrounding countryside is the authentic Vietnam. Rice paddies in various stages of production with their mandatory laborers are everywhere. Women normally do the backbreaking work in knee-deep muck and water. What is worse is that they do this planting and harvesting process two and sometimes three times each year.

One of the more pleasant cities in Vietnam so far has been Hue, pronounced "Way." It is large enough to fulfill one's needs but small enough to remain friendly and relatively quiet. Hue is a popular place for tours of former military sites. The Vietnam War can still be a controversial issue in the United States, but it is worth remembering that not only did more than 58,000 Americans die while serving there, but the war also killed more than 1 million North Vietnamese soldiers, over 220,000 South Vietnamese soldiers, and either killed or injured 4 million civilians. War is horrid

Hanoi Highrise

regardless of which side you are on. The effects of Agent Orange and napalm are still evident in large areas where the native vegetation is sparse and unable to recover. Because of this period, we wonder if there will be lingering hostility against America or American tourists. We ask several Vietnamese this question directly and the response is similar in that they view the U.S. government and the American people

Covered Woman On Street

as separate entities. They still see America as a land of opportunity and the people as generous and friendly. While the government had fueled the fighting, the American people actually helped to end it. The

Vietnamese that we ask are less than 35 and college educated. Sentiments of those who actually experienced the war may be different.

Street Shoe Market

Our hotel owner, De and his wife Ahn, of the nice Thuy Ahn Hotel in Ninh Binh ($10 USD per night) said, "You are very lucky to live in America. I am very unlucky to live here. Here I work very hard and am only this big, but if I lived in America I would be huge." He uses his hands to emphasize the differences in size. This has come from someone who, by most Vietnamese standards, is doing extremely well.

It is so loud here that my ears constantly hurt! Sometimes it is so piercing, I feel nauseated. I'm wearing ear plugs almost 24 hours a day. In fact, Amy snapped at me earlier today because apparently I have

Dog On A Platter

been talking too loud for her comfort. With my earplugs in I can't hear how loud I am talking. There is a polite way to ask someone to tone it down. People and motor bikes are everywhere. There is no rhyme or reason to the direction of traffic, and it seems like everyone has their horns wired so they stay on all day. It is very interesting to see families of four, five, and six piled on a moped, with a child on the handlebars or hanging on to mom piggyback style. No one wears helmets.

On our way to an open market we befriend a big black bear in a cage that is so small he cannot even stand or walk. We bring him a ball from the market, hand feed him crackers daily, and pay special attention to him at his home in the middle of a busy and noisy sidewalk. We learn that this bear has been in captivity since birth and will remain there until his death. Every 6 months they extract his bile and use it as medicine. My heart just breaks over this type of animal abuse. If we can treat innocent animals so inhumanly, then why can't we treat the human animals  that murder, rape, and sexually abuse children just as inhumanly? I just don't understand.

 Cat Ba Island / Ha Long Bay Vietnam
Traci's Diary Entry
January 17th

And then it HITS! Every traveler's nightmare has arrived in full force. Montezuma's revenge… the Hershey squirts… bacterial diarrhea. It virtually shackles me to the hotel room where a toilet is only five steps away. Limited to bread and stale soda I linger for five days. Actually, it is not very funny as a 102-degree Fahrenheit fever with severe stomach cramps can be quite serious. I wish several times for my mom to be here to rub my back like she did when I was little. It is a good thing that we have brought along that small medicine chest as a double whammy of meds finally has me back on my feet. The only thing we can think of that may have been the culprit is a glass of not so hot water used for a late night snack of oatmeal. I'm fastidious about avoiding grime, dirt, and meat. I use my hand sanitizer as if it is an obsession. Amy has been short and irritable, even while I have been rotting away for days on a filthy bathroom floor but at least she has checked in on me and brought me food and juice in between her comings and goings.

Boat Ride

I brave a three-day excursion to Halong Bay and Cat Ba Island. It is a welcome retreat from the noise and commotion of Hanoi. Halong Bay is similar to Yanshou, China, with limestone peaks rising from calm, blue waters. It takes 4 hours by slow boat to arrive at the island, but no one minds as the day is sunny and warm. Along the way, we see fishermen in simple sampans. Some have covered houseboats. They practice their trade wearing

Lake Homes

conical hats with their pants rolled up to their knees and no shoes on their feet. At various interludes, there are mooring clusters of homes with their transportation vehicles, usually rowboats, tied to the front. Children, yes children, beginning at age five, man boats by themselves and go fishing. Seriously, I've never seen anything like it, but it is common here. In addition, these homes are not just 4x4 shacks, but have porches, hammocks, clothes hanging on clotheslines, and areas for children to play with each other and their pets.

Kid In Boat

We see small children of five and six using a cleaver to chop fruits and vegetables outside on a stump or a blanket on the ground. In America we don't even let five year olds play outside by themselves or earn an allowance at that age, let alone take a boat out and go fishing, help pluck rocks in the field, collect cans and bottles, or just beg tourists for money. These people may be poor and under-privileged here, but they certainly have more smarts and aptitude about them than many Westerners I know. I agree that age five is too young to be put to work but my gosh, I know twenty-five year olds who still live in the nest, don't know how to pay bills, do their laundry, cook a dinner from scratch, host a dinner party, send a thank you card, change a flat tire, save or invest money, or make it in the real world without the help of Mommy and Daddy to pay for their gas, insurance, and going out money. In my opinion, that is a greater travesty and failure of parental guidance or duty. At least the parents here are actually teaching their children how to be self-reliant and self-sufficient.

We are staying at a cheap government hotel. A tout leads us to this gem which charges $7 USD, which isn't bad. It has simple beds and blankets, heat, a fan, a Vietnamese TV, a private bathroom, and so far, no bed bugs.

Trapped in Hanoi
Amy's Diary Entry
January 20th

The differences in our traveling styles were certainly becoming glaringly evident. I thought maybe once we got here Traci would take a little more interest in reading about where we were going or what there was to do, but that hasn't happened and as usual I was the one who did all the reading and planning, just like I had done for the entire year before we left for this trip. Half the time, I didn't think she even knew what city we were in or where we were going to next. For the last several mornings I had asked her what we were going to do that day or what were some of the things we could do, and her pat answer was always, "I don't care Amy" or "I'm open to anything." She had waited her whole life for this trip and yet she had no initiative in planning a day. I certainly didn't expect her to do much, but something would be nice. And then the other day she got mad at me because I had to tell her again, like for the 4th time, to take her ear plugs out when she went into a restaurant or our hotel so she wouldn't sound like an idiot as she yelled at everybody. I didn't tell her nicely enough, so her feelings got all hurt. Really? You're how old? I had been irritable with her lately and it was escalating. She had had some stomach cramps the last several days before she got really sick with diarrhea and a fever.

She was confined to our room and I had been bringing her food. We finally resorted to the antibiotics that I brought along. I was glad we were close to a beautiful lake that had a walking path around it. I spend hours reading and people watching and then wandering through some more markets. While I was sure it wasn't easy for her traveling with me either of course, I was only aware of my frustrations. I criticized her a lot for stupid stuff. I was a bit bored with this traveling. While what we were doing was cool, I liked to have a focus and a purpose. I took my frustrations out on her because she was always there, and I sure did not think traveling would be this tiring. It was hard carrying everything you owned on your back and unpacking and repacking every couple of days because you were off to a new city. Each time we arrived we had to find a new place to stay and figure out how to get there, all the while hauling a now 45# backpack around. And I felt like I was doing it all. Maybe I just needed to vent. Hopefully I just needed to vent.

 ## The Battle Grounds

Traci's Diary Entry
January 24th

Emotional day! As I continue trekking on I am not certain if this experience is more enlightening or detrimental to my mental health, my spirit, and my hopes of peace in humanity. Vietnam has been a completely different experience for me than China. It is more beautiful and sad at the same time. It is one thing to read and hear about stories of impoverished living, but it is an entirely different experience and gut wrenching feeling to see it and see them living it. People live in one room clay and straw houses with no heat, beds, or blankets and use water buffalo to plow their fields. My eyes and my heart meeting theirs has catapulted a collage of minor epiphanies for me and introduced me to new levels of anger and ignorance that I did not know I had. It is impossible to endure an experience of this magnitude and return home the very same person as when I left. After extending the distance between me and my native land and culture and the power it has held over my thoughts, beliefs, political position, value sets, religion, and social tier, it seems that I am rebuilding the foundation of who I am and what I really believe, as I go. I had no idea of how pre-fabricated and cemented my ideological paradigms and singular world views really had been until arriving here. This malignant piece of history has stretched itself into the remotest parts of my being.

Amy and I walk through these miles and experiences together, yet alone. It is the first hour of the first day in another new place. We sit quietly in front of a filthy and lifeless riverfront watching the villagers bathing and laundering their clothes. We both think separate thoughts about what our eyes see and hearts cannot understand. We share the occasional grin or stare that is simply filling in the space for words that are not there.

I sit and wonder if these human beings have hopes and dreams of something more than their next meal or a blanket. I wonder what their purpose in this life is. Are they only here to suffer? Is this their Karma? Is this where the old saying "Hell on Earth" comes from? I wonder if they have more hope for their lives and futures than I do for them. What is it that I can truly do and contribute to make their lives better, different, and more? I feel helpless. What am I supposed to do? Perhaps the answer is something as simple as: ALL THAT I CAN!

We visit what is left of the Thua Phu Prison, the hell where revolutionary soldiers and patriotic people were imprisoned, tortured, gang raped, sodomized, and murdered. There is something notably different here in the swirls of stale air and energy of these places where we have been. I do not have words to describe how eerie it is and how it feels or smells. It reeks of death, of hatred, of sorrow, and of a pain that I swear I can feel!

I visit an outdoor War Museum, now home to modern war weapons of the U.S. that were once manned with American and puppet soldiers, then captured by the Liberation Army from the enemy in the Thuan An Port on March 26th, 1975. I was five years old and didn't understand anymore then I do now, three decades later. How can brother hate brother, father hate son, or man hate man? I remain convinced that it all comes down to humans' need to control, dominate, and conquer. It is all a battle between pride and ego. Ego cannot survive when we are in spirit, just as darkness cannot survive with light. When I am in my ego, I am pro-death, and when I am in my spirit, I know that the only way to dispel darkness is with light, and the only way to cure hatred is with love. I too have a long way to go in my own personal war of ego vs. spirit.

There are a couple dozen rusted and decaying carriers and weapons laying to rest in that cemetery museum, including: The "Battle Field King" which is also known as the anti aircraft M48 tank. There are numerous crane tanks and 105, 122, 155, and 175 MM artillery units. Though this is an outdoor museum, a very specific smell lingers about and clouds the air. Each decrepit carrier smells like an old musty basement or dusty attic inside. Many carriers or units are half blown apart or are burned, rusted shells, barely recognizable, at least to my eye. Few look barely damaged and one impaired vessel is still expelling infrequent sweat beads of oil, keeping its faded, blackened headstone beneath, dark and slick even after all of these years. I cannot help but wonder the fate of its soldiers. There are no signs, no traces of their life or their death.

A nearby glass case houses large displays of captured flags, I.D. cards, dog tags, badges, patches, medals, and torn and tattered military uniforms. As I look at each picture of those young soldiers' faces, young men from and representing my home country, my eyes fill with tears. I record each of their names in my notebook, but for what reason, I do not know. I wonder where they are now… if they had made it home. I wonder how their lives have changed as a result of their experience in this place that I stand.

The fields are full of emptiness, but life continues. It seems that people here are being born and die every day, but no one is really living. Everything related to the war seems to remain untouched as they have no money to tear down or rebuild. Houses, buildings, schools, churches, structures, once bombed, still stand, but they barely hold remains of what once was. Not many things seem to have been demolished or rebuilt. Still, life and jungles grow and live on amongst it all. The smell of burnt rotting soot is even more prevalent after a fresh rain. There is no doubt that a cloud of malignancy still hangs on 28 years after war's aftermath. The silence here in these fields is so deafening that it is piercing my soul. Is this silence in the air the silenced voices of lives lost or just the silence of what once was? Is this the sound of victory or defeat? I wonder.

Hue

Amy's Diary Entry
January 25th

We arrived here a day later than expected because neither one of us could stomach the mislabeled backpacker bus from Ninh Binh. We were the last 2 passengers on the 10 PM bus. We were only the third and fourth backpacker on the entire bus as the other thirty passengers were locals who had crammed the aisles with suitcases and boxes, which was pretty typical. We climbed over the obstacles in the aisle and finally sat down in the only seats remaining, which were across from each other. We absorbed completely the odor of wet socks and stinky armpits. It was so hot in the bus that I was already dripping with sweat before I got to my seat. Half of my leg room was being taken up by a tall French tourist and half of Traci's seat was being taken up by a rotund French woman, but at least she had on some nice perfume and smelled pretty. This had all the makings of a miserable trip and it was scheduled to take 12 hours. We looked at each other and asked, "Do you want to get off?" I think we were both afraid the other one was going to say no. We yelled to the driver to stay put and we climbed back over suitcases, boxes, and people and escaped into the fresh air. The train ride here hadn't been the most comfortable as this time our hard sleeper meant what it said. It consisted of a woven straw mat put over a metal bench. We tolerated that for about six hours and then snuck into a compartment with soft, cushioned beds. The attendant came by and tried to make us leave, but we feigned ignorance as to what he was trying to tell us and just smiled and laughed and kept shrugging our shoulders. Eventually he gave up, and we were left in comfort for the rest of the trip. But that train sure beat that bus.

War remnants seemed to be everywhere in this country, whether in the form of a cemetery, a famous bridge, or a burned-out church. Maybe they viewed their war remnants like we do the historic sites of the Civil War, important memorials to soldiers who died for an important cause. As Canadians, we asked some Vietnamese how they viewed American tourists in light of this recent war, and the general consensus was that they were grateful to the American people who they felt helped to end the war by their demonstrations and protests. They felt the war was started and continued by the American government.

I was touched by Sun and Muong, two little girls who I will remember forever. We had seen them before as they were regular

Sun And Muong

beggars on the popular tourist street that was lined with restaurants catering to tourists. Our first encounter wasn't so pretty as we tried to offer them cookies instead of money for their outstretched hands. The older Sun was happy with that, but little spitfire Muong slapped it away. What sympathy we had for them soon vanished with that display. The next day Traci and I were having a solo sanity day, and I was having breakfast when I spotted them again. Sun motioned hesitantly that she wanted my aluminum can so I signaled them to come closer to my table. They soon were sitting at my table, devouring my breakfast scraps. I ordered them each a meal and watched them gobble that up as well. Ann, a young Vietnamese woman who spoke pretty good English, joined us and was able to tell me a little about these precious girls. They lived by the river and their parents were fishermen. They were 9 and 13 years old, but they were so small I would have thought they were only 5 and 7. They came to this street frequently by themselves to beg for food and money. This was known and accepted by their

Lunch With The Girls

parents who were very poor and likely had other children to feed. Sun and Muong were dressed in ragged clothing, and I arranged for all of us to go to a market where I bought them each a new play outfit and also a traditional Vietnamese outfit, as well as shoes, hats, and sunglasses. We then went to Ann's home and bathed the girls and dressed them in their new outfits. Ann was the only child of laborers and lived in a concrete home with 3 rooms. The furniture was sparse. Her parents had devoted themselves to earning money for Ann to attend college, which she did. She had graduated with a degree in accounting and English but could not find a job, so she was trying to start her own

Home In Sun's Village

business. Sun, Muong, and I walked back to the same popular tourist area. We were all holding hands, and the two little girls were engaged in their own conversation while giggling and frequently looking up at me and rewarding me with genuine smiles of delight. I bought them dinner before disentangling myself from them and went back to the hostel to find Traci. The following day we arranged to be taken to their homes and again were left in wonder as to the conditions that some people were forced to live in. Their homes were on stilts, and the walls of their one room homes were of tarps. A few of the homes had 1 or 2

Kids At Sun's Village

of the walls made of plywood. A few plastic chairs and maybe a table were the only furnishings, along with various kitchen wares. There were kids every-where, all surrounding us as I'm sure the word got out that we had bought food and clothes for Sun and Muong. Some other mothers brought their kids over to us and pointed to their children's feet, which of course were shoeless, or to their ragged clothes or to their mouths. Other little boys would run up to us with out-stretched hands and say "one dollar, one dollar, one dollar." That was a bit disturbing. Muong's mother was 32 but looked at least 10 years older. She had had her 6th child several months earlier. Her oldest child was 13. I asked Muong where she slept, and she pointed to the bridge that crossed the river, and Ann confirmed that many people slept under the bridge. Muong wouldn't let go of my hand and stomped on other kids' feet if they encroached on her new possession, which was me. I looked at pretty little Sun, with her long dark hair. She was just starting to develop breast buds, and I wondered how long it would be before she was trapped in this same life leading nowhere. They found us the next day while we were eating at a restaurant, and who could blame them? If I were hungry, I would look for the people who bought me food too. For maybe the first time in my life, I felt a motherly urge to care for these little girls. I wanted to take them back to America with me and offer them a better life. Their futures seemed bleak and predictable if left here to fend for themselves and there were so many other children just like them. We left the next day, and my heart was truly sad as I knew I would probably never see either one of them again. I still think of them when I'm lying in bed at night and wonder how and where they are. Traci's mom is shipping them a goodie box from America.

 **Hell's Kitchens**

Traci's Diary Entry
February 1st

We unfortunately have witnessed several kitchens in Vietnam that has changed our menu preferences to tofu and veggies, at least temporarily. A bathroom break during a 12 hour bus ride from Hue to Nah Trang found the waiting line for the single toilet weaving through the kitchen of a local restaurant. While waiting, we and a number of other passengers, found ourselves entranced by the black flies that perched on the chicken carcass until they were disturbed by the cook who examined the carcass, searching for scraps of meat to pick off and place in the next patron's order. Like any consummate chef this one freely nibbled from the carcass before throwing the pieces into the pan. She did not have gloves or a hairnet on while working in the kitchen nor have we seen any workers ever wash their hands after using the bath-

Kitchen At Bus Station

room. The leftovers from another customer's uneaten dinner are scraped into a kettle that does not appear destined for the garbage. What really captures our attention are the 3 full grown, well-nourished rats that scurry across the floor and disappear under the cupboard. When we finally make it through the kitchen, and into the toilet, there are dirty dishes piled onto the floor within 2 yards of the squat toilet. It appears they are going to be washed as there is a faucet and dish soap nearby. Sometimes it is better not to see the kitchen but just enjoy its results.

Happy Lunar New Year. Today is the biggest event of the year. It stretches into a 4 day celebration. It is a new day in a new place. I am half buried in the velvety sands of Vietnam Beach with a cold Saigon beer in near reach. You can openly drink anywhere that you go here. I swear if it wasn't for the Vietnamese music playing in the background of the nearby street, I would believe that I was back in Hawaii. When I close my eyes, I feel my first sense of peace here on this beach. It's a nice reprieve and I'm happy to be greeted with such tropical beauty. The whole beach is mine for this moment and right now I feel like so is the whole rest of the world. But soon this majestic sun will set and the mystic moon will rise, and it is hard to imagine that this is the same sun that warms my face as when I am at home. The same moon mesmerizes me no matter how many times I have seen it. When night finally falls, I make my wishes on the same stars, a million miles and hours away, as I did back home when I was five, dreaming big dreams on those stars.

It all seems so strange to grasp that nothing is different as much as everything is. This earth seems so insurmountable yet so tiny. We all come from one earth just as we come from one mother, and when we destroy a piece of it we are ultimately destroying a piece of our selves. I don't believe that we have to carry the torch of past generations. I believe it's time to learn from their mistakes and hit RESET!

Discoveries, Fun Facts, and Useless Tidbits

- Mom is usually seen reaching through dad's arms as he drives, gripping onto the child he is balancing on the handle bars.

- Once a relationship becomes sexual couples are expected to marry each other.

- It is common to see people openly urinating outside on the streets or sidewalks.

- The Lunar New Year or Tet Nguyen Dan, is the most important day in the Asian calendar. The holiday officially is 3 days long but most people celebrate it for an entire week. New Year's Day falls on a different day every year.

- They still operate the safety guard arms at the railroad crossings manually.

- Each table at a restaurant receives one menu despite the number of people at your table.

❧ The Lunar New Year

Amy's Diary Entry
February 3rd

This New Years fell on February 1st. The entire home and graves of family members must be cleaned before the New Year celebration can begin. All the food eaten during the 3 official days of the celebration must be made ahead of time. During the holiday no one would work, touch a broom, sew, swear, become angry, or show rudeness. Debts are paid, faults are corrected, and wrongdoings forgiven. Everyone started the year with a clean slate.

The Vietnamese believed that at midnight on New Year's Eve, 3 spirits returned to the earth and are welcomed back with fireworks and as much noise as possible. The noise not only served as a welcome to the gods but also to ward off those evil spirits lurking everywhere. All problems from the previous year were left behind at that momentous minute. The first visitor to the home on New Year's Day held dire importance, since it would have a major impact on the entire next year. The visitor that supposedly brought the best fortune was a wealthy, married man with children. Blacklisted visitors would be anyone who had lost a job, had an accident or death in the family during the previous year, were single and/or middle-aged women. Needless to say we were not invited to anyone's home on New Year's Day!

We were in Nha Trang for the Tet holiday. During the day the streets would be relatively peaceful. Families and friends could be seen gathering inside homes, sharing tea and finger foods, and talking and laughing with each other. The ancestor altars or Buddha shrines were resplendent with fresh fruit, roasted chicken, white rice, and other food items unknown to us. The aroma of incense permeated the air. The streets returned to life at dusk with everyone out in their holiday outfits. Bicycle vendors cruised up and down the street selling large, red balloons, inflatable animals, ice cream or popcorn. Sidewalk restaurants sprang up within minutes, roasting lobster, crab, or shrimp over red hot coals. One kilogram (2.2#s) of your choice cost 50,000 dong or $3.25. Ample beer or wine was on hand to help welcome in the Near Year.

There was a carnival with what had to be the slowest Ferris wheel that could still be called a ride; it was moving so slowly the riders could leave the car and new ones enter without the wheel ever having to come to a complete stop. Further down the street was a stage with live performers. Instead of bleachers or benches everyone parked their motorbikes in front of the stage and used them as chairs for the duration of the concert. Both young and old wished us a 'Happy New Year.' Our waiter tried to teach us the Vietnamese translation, 'Chuc Mung Nam Miu.' but in our ears it sounded more like 'choke your mama.' On the way home a boy, who may have been around 9 or 10, tried to grab my breasts. I managed to get a hold of his hand and wanted to hold on to it so I could twist it to the point of pain, but he managed to slip free. Maybe that was another tradition of the New Year. It was a real joy to see and be a part of this celebration.

 **Nha Trang, Vietnam**
Traci's Diary Entry
January 30th

We take one of the much hyped tours to Monkey Island where
monkeys roam freely. We are left thoroughly disgusted by this attraction. First is the "show" where muzzled black bears are encouraged by
either wooden paddles or leather straps to walk around the floor in a
circle while in an upright position, carrying signs over their heads and
wearing tutus around their skinny middles. Then the bears are forced
to pedal in circles on bikes, carried by the momentum of the initial
push from the trainer. One bear falls over after the initial momentum
dissipates and despite attempts by 2 handlers to force the bear back
onto the bike, the bear who appears to be scrambling for his life, manages to make his way under the railing, through the audience, and out
to the grounds, where he is chased by a throng of workers. Another
bear is pulled on top of a barrel and expected to balance on a piece of
wood that is set on top of a ball. This poor bear is not able to perform
this balancing feat and attempts to jump off the barrel several times,
only to be forcibly held in place by the handler. Finally the bear does
break free and jumps to the floor where a tussle ensues between the
bear and the trainer. The bear at one point wraps his arms around the
legs of the trainer until he is hauled by his collar back into the holding
area, beyond the view of the mostly enthralled Vietnamese audience.
Both of these bears are obviously beaten to perform and would probably be beaten with more vigor after this day's performance. This all
occurs in the first 5 minutes of the show, and we cannot force ourselves
to watch anymore, so we leave to wander the grounds and find the
monkeys. That does not take long.

The rest of the grounds seems like Planet of the Apes but with miniature primates. Within 30 feet of leaving the bear arena, a monkey approaches us and, of course, we think it is adorable at first. Once a cracker is thrown to him and a food source is identified, an eruption of monkeys ensues and we are soon surrounded by 10-15 monkeys, all wanting their share. These monkeys walk towards us on their hind legs, screeching with their open mouths revealing well preserved teeth. They have no qualms coming to within 8 inches of our legs. We walk backwards, trying to create distance between us and an approaching monkey, only to bump into another one creeping up from the rear! One monkey jumps onto the arm of an adolescent boy trying to seize food; it results in a scratch along the boy's arm. These monkeys are out-right aggressive, and we are scared. We escape to safer ground, content to watch others feed these malcontents. The monkeys are not to blame as they have been conditioned to accept this bizarre life as normal.

There are several other instances of animals being mistreated. A visit to the Botanical Gardens in Dalat, Vietnam, would have been delightful except for the appalling sight of 2 beautiful birds fighting to their death in a bamboo cage, while 30-40 visitors encircle the cage in either a crouched or standing position, riveted by the gruesome battle. We are also witnesses to cock fights, and monkeys, bears, and wild cats kept in cages so small and with so little stimulation that they continuously walk in circles until they stop to pull more hair off their already naked arms and legs. It makes us just sick.

Today we are taking the day off from each other. Nothing is wrong, just a mental health day to keep our friendship intact. In fact, we are getting along quite well and having some real fun together. I know I've said this before, but travelling with someone 24/7 for 2 years has its challenges, especially because nothing is routine. Every day is a new adventure to a new place, with having to find a new bed, new transport to figure out, new activities to plan, and new chores to keep. It takes a strong relationship AND both people need to be relatively open-minded and agreeable. There is little escape, and it can be challenging to find or stay in balance. Even though I'm a free spirit and Amy is a planner and sometimes that gets in the way, there is no one else that I could see myself sharing this adventure with than her.

A shoe shine boy keeps bothering me to shine my shoes. I am wearing sandals so I keep telling him no. He finally leaves and I sit on the beach catching up on my diary. The boy returns and asks me one more time if he can shine my shoes, and I finally yell "NO! My sandals don't need cleaning!" He drops a fistful of cow dung on them that he has been hiding behind his back and says "How about now?" I am totally speechless and stunned. How can I not give the boy some business with his determination to earn a few cents? The sandal shine cost me 25 cents, but to him, it was a full day's wage.

I stroll up and down the unbelievably noisy streets just people watching, window shopping, and sampling the street vendor food. The "Ground Ants with Tomato Sauce" catches my eye, so I decide to order them. They are surprisingly good for 5,000 dong or 70 cents. Next, I order an ice cream sandwich for 1,500 dong or ten cents. The ice cream vendors place scoops of local ice cream in a sliced baguette, giving a literal meaning to the ice cream sandwich. After two bites, I pass it off to a beggar, who is delighted.

Other menu items are:

- A fresh baguette with jam: 1,500 dong or 10 cents.
- Pork and bamboo shoots: 10,000 dong.
- Fried veggies with tomato & egg: 7,000 dong.
- A western candy bar: 6,000 dong or 40 cents for the large size.
- A cheese & tomato omelet on a baguette: 15,000 dong or $1.25.
- A spaghetti dinner with garlic bread and glass of wine: 25,000 dong or $1.50.
- A bottle of Vietnamese fruit wine: 20,000 dong or $1.40.
- A 40 oz. bottle of beer Tiger, Saigon, or Lao: 8,000-12,000 dong or 60-80 cents.

Next, I stroll down a few mazes of bazaars that the Lonely Planet guidebook suggests. Funny, there are vendors selling the Lonely Planet books for $3.00 each; we paid $35.00 for ours, back home. That is just not right!

A massage in Vietnam is certainly unique and worthwhile at $3.00 an hour. Walking in the massage area and seeing a ladder suspended from the ceiling above the mat ensures that this is to be a once in a lifetime experience. Never before has a masseuse straddled me on the table, nor has anyone manipulated my back with their feet and toes so perfectly that it feels better than the touch of hands, all the while hanging onto the monkey bars above the bed. It is difficult to fully relax, yet it is awkwardly pleasant. Truly this is the most unusual massage I've ever received. Massages in Vietnam are called "medical massages." The masseuse goes to school for 6 months and is taught chiropractic techniques and methods of adjustments by doctors at the hospital instead of by teachers in the classroom. It makes you wonder what is studied during the rest of the 4-6 years of chiropractic school in America.

Well, I finally break down after being the victim of numerous stares, chuckles, and raised eyebrows to my overgrown leg and armpit hair. Yeah, being the germ phobic and anti body hair person that I am, I cannot believe that I have made it an entire year without shaving! I have my legs and pits "threaded" by a local masseuse on the beach of Nha Trang. After applying a powder to my leg, this woman uses a spool of thread, keeping the reel in one hand and wrapping the thread around her other hand, while she also holds part of the string in her mouth. She smoothly and quickly maneuvers the thread like a scissors, pulling out about 10 hairs at a time by their roots. Both legs take about 20 min and cost $2. What a cool experience, and I feel like a girl again.

A table of people are chuckling and pointing to me or to the fact that I am eating with my left hand on the tour lunch today. I'm left-handed, so of course I'm going to eat with my left hand. Someone then informs me that the Vietnamese consider it uncouth to eat with your left hand because the left hand is used to wipe oneself after using the bathroom. Another note about the toilets, toilet paper is rare, so

Saigon Traffic And A Stroll Through A Village
http://j.mp/jHdmlr

all bathrooms either use a sprayer attached to the toilet or there is a bucket of water next to the toilet for one to clean oneself with; one must pour a bucket of water into the toilet in order to flush it.

🥾 Leaving Vietnam

Amy's Diary Entry
February 12th

Vietnam seemed a country surrounded by its memories and attempting to break free of them at the same time. The war memorials documented an evolution of a country that has now grown beyond the possibility of another civil war. It was important for me to see the Vietnamese side of this drawn out conflict, but it didn't take long for me to

tire of another war memorial, and I had now had my fill. I wanted to see other parts of Vietnam, those that didn't have to do with turmoil, death, and destruction. Vietnam was refreshing as there was so much optimism and energy in its people. I was amazed at how drastic the change was from China to Vietnam by walking only a few feet over

a man-made border. It did not disappoint, and I am glad I was able to see it at this point in its history and look forward to see what it will become.

Our last stop in Vietnam was the Mekong Delta, known as Vietnam's bread basket. This area produced enough rice to feed the entire country as well as a sizeable surplus. Travelling in the delta required a small rowboat as many of the canals that lead to small villages or homes were only wide enough for 2 small rowboats to meet.

Just as in other parts of Vietnam a large number of people lived in houseboats on the water. Many of these houseboats had small fish farms under their homes. The fish farm was composed of nets or wire to contain the fish and every 6 months, the fish was sold to a processor. The most common fish raised was the catfish. In the back of one houseboat was even a floating pig pen, housing 3 full grown pigs. Unfortunately raw sewage and industrial waste dumped into the Mekong River before it empties into the South China Sea make this waterway very polluted, but that didn't deter the chil-

Mekong Pig Pen

dren from swimming in its cool water to escape the mid-day heat. The delta, though extremely smelly in certain places, was an impressive finale to six weeks in Vietnam.

Discoveries, Fun Facts, and Useless Tidbits

- Vietnamese women value pale skin as a dark complexion implies that one must work as a laborer in the fields. As a result, women always wear hats, cover their faces with either masks or towels, and wear long gloves that extend to the upper arm.

- Women are pitied if they are not married and do not have children, especially at our advanced age of 30+. People frequently ask if we are married, so rather than be objects of sympathy, we make up perfect husbands who are waiting for us in America.

- Early model garbage trucks arrive in your area or village blaring music that sounds the same as that of an ice-cream truck in the states. It is your responsibility to carry your garbage to the place of the garbage truck and then you stand in the long line until it is your turn to deposit your trash into the truck. They also recycle trash here, only it is done a bit differently than in the states. They pay a group of individuals to rummage through every trash bag pulling out chopsticks, cans, bottles, plastic etc. We are not certain what happens after that process.

- The locals seem to answer and say yes to anything and everything, pretending to understand our questions even when it is obvious that they don't. We have ended up at several wrong places after showing our taxi driver a map or an address. Now we hand him the paper upside down and if he says "yes" without flipping it over, we know to find another taxi driver.

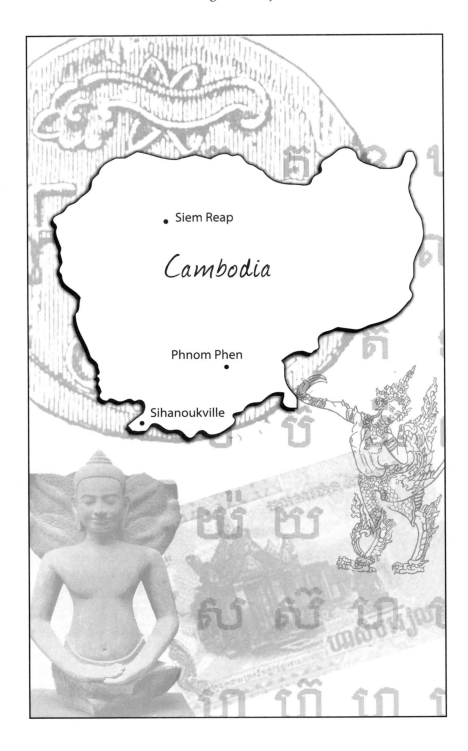

Cambodia

"The world is a book and those who do not travel read only one page."
— St. Augustine

 We Survived

Traci's Diary Entry
February 16th, Phnom Phen Cambodia

Vietnam already seems like a lazy and blurry dream that I have not fully awakened from, and I can barely remember the feel of China, but her memory is forever branded into my being. Time is so deceiving. It seems like just yesterday that I was only dreaming of going around the world and we have been traveling for days now.

We ended our travels in Vietnam with a two day overland and water tour of the Mekong Delta and cross into Cambodia using a variety of means: a large tug-style boat, a canoe-style boat paddled with one oar, and a speed boat. Cambodian speed boats are row boats with an outboard motor. The final leg of the crossing is in a van packed with 20 people and their backpacks, instead of the 12 people it is designed to transport comfortably. We never quite know what to expect when booking tours or transportation in Asia, but at least we always know it will be interesting.

Cambodia looks different almost immediately as well, exuding a distinct Thai sway rather than the Chinese influence evident in Vietnam. It just amazes me how the whole flavor can change in just a few feet. The wats here are reminiscent of Hinduism rather than the

Cambodian Palace

Buddhism predominately practiced. The Cambodian people have much darker complexions, prominent brown eyes, and wider faces with defined features. The currency in Cambodia is called riel and its 4,000 R to $1 USD and again, there is no tipping here. We score with our hostel. For $12 dollars we have 2 double beds, a refrigerator, cable TV with several English channels, and air conditioning. This is by far the hottest country we have been in so far. The heat is overbearing, and it wears me out. After being outside for 3 hours, it feels like 8 hours, and I'm drenched in sweat. I'm so glad we have air conditioning.

We've passed some very interesting names of hotels and restaurants today on our way to explore a new village.

The signs read:
> Twatt Motel - Feel free to come inside. Pre-pay required.
> Phart Inn
> M'e Hung Long Café
> Phat Diner – Good eats here!
> Mi Sons Long Dong Café

Mi Dung Café - Good eats here!

Phu'ssy Café - Good eats here!

I received a nice email from mom today. She says they just got confirmation that their packages to the Chicken Moon School and Moon Feet Village have arrived. They have a system; Mom does the shopping and Dad takes care of the shipping and handling. They send paper, pencils, crayons, coloring books, jump ropes, and balls to the school and miscellaneous household items directly to Wendy's home. Dad finds it a bit ironic that every item Mom buys at Shopko is made in China and he is boxing it all up and shipping it all back to China to help their needy people, when they can get the same items there for pennies to our dollars. While I can see his point, I still feel happy in knowing that we put a smile on someone's face that truly deserves it and doesn't have those extra pennies to spend. Good karma lies in the act of giving.

The Killing Fields

Amy's Diary Entry

February, 16th, Phnom Phen, Cambodia

The heat was overbearing here. I had to come back to the hostel for awhile to cool off and shower for the second time. A few hours in the heat felt like a day. Although parts of the city were modern and clean most roads were unpaved, made of red clay, dirt or gravel. Two large rivers converged into one at the

Cambodian Woman Bathing In River

riverfront. The first time we came down here to sit by the river we watched as a few local people bathed and washed their clothes in the river. Traci shared her sandwich with a shy little Cambodian girl that came and sat about 5 feet from us. She only had shorts and flip flops

on. She never held out her hand expecting more to be put in it, but just sat there quietly, accepting whatever was offered. The boulevard that wound along the river was lined with palm trees and all kinds of national flags. The crowds arrived at about 4 or 5 PM, once the sun cooled down, because it was too hot to be outside before that. Sidewalk restaurateurs opened up for business at the same time. They brought big kettles of various foods, washable dinnerware, and plastic stools arranged so their customers could dine in comfort on the sidewalk while others sold balloons and toys to the kids. There were a lot of restaurants set up for the tourists, and they had "special" pizza on the menu, which meant it included marijuana as one of the toppings. We saw elephants walking up and down the boulevard a couple of times each day. The streets stayed busy until 10 or 11 at night. Cambodia was by far the hottest country we have visited thus far and I was miserable

because of it. We had yet to see a McDonalds or KFC, which was nice on the one hand but we missed the inexpensive ice cream sundaes. There was not the incessant blaring of horns here but there

Elephant On Cambodian Street

were a lot of people with missing arms and legs. We were told that this was still because of all the land mines that dot the countryside and was a remnant of the Vietnam War. Most of the amputees were adults because the landmines outright killed the smaller kids that stepped on them. They seemed to hang out by touristy sites and beg. I was sure it was their best bet for a decent meal. It was hard to refuse them, and we did share our coins, but if we gave money to every outstretched hand, we would soon be on our way home. It was very sad.

We visited the Killing Fields and Security Prison 21, both of which were morbid and gruesome. How could they be anything else? Thousands of skulls that once held a human life were displayed in a glass case or remained buried undisturbed in fields. There were only 3 or 4 other people at the Killing Fields, and it was about 15 minutes outside of the city, so it was very quiet and eerie. Once again some lunatic man was able to convince people that it was okay to kill and torture their neighbors, friends, and other countrymen. They did not quit until over 2 million people had died. What a waste.

Steps At Killing Fields

Killing Fields

We were heading to Sihanoukville tomorrow. Beautiful beaches give it its nickname, Fort Lauderdale of Cambodia. I would be happy if it's just a little cooler there.

Sad Video Footage Of "The Killing Fields" In Cambodia
http://j.mp/laltFU

Phnom Penn Markets
http://j.mp/juUFbO

🎒 The Crooks of Cambodia

Traci's Diary Entry
February 26th

Okay, I got taken today and it's all Amy's fault because she needed her weekly mental health day. I hire a cyclo driver named Kiren to show me around, and in conversation, he tells me he lives with his parents and eight siblings, so I ask him if I can pay him extra to go to his home and meet his family and video tape their home and life. He excitedly agrees. After a friendly homestead tour, a nice visit with six of the eight siblings, and a wonderful home-cooked local meal prepared by his ailing mother, he invites me to his favorite watering hole to see how the local people live it up in Cambodia. I agree, and we have a wonderful time singing karaoke for a couple of hours and sharing a single pitcher of Cambrew beer. Dozens of smiling, local people come up to our table, welcome me, snap my photograph, shake my hand, toast my glass, thank me for entertaining them with my singing and dancing, and ask me what America is like and how I like their country. I must admit that I am amused by their extreme excitement and this rock star treatment. That was until the waiter comes over and tells me that Kiren has told all of his friends and the barkeep that all the drinks for the night are compliments of his "rich friend from America" and hands me a big fat bill! When I argue the bill, Kiren bolts out the door and leaves me stranded. Suddenly everyone in the entire facility forgets how to speak English and they ignore me.

The local patrons had ordered a bottle of 750ml bottle of Stoli vodka for $6.25 USD, a 750ml bottle of Belvedere vodka for $8.50 USD, and dozens of 40oz bottles of Cambodian beer at $1.30 USD each, and these are just a few of the itemized listings added to my bill. It cost me $50 USD and another cyclo ride back to my hotel. What a disappointment! His family had been so wonderful, and I have them on film for gosh sakes, but I am told by the hotel staff that reporting it will do no good and will probably cost me more money for them to investigate. Rather than comforting me, Amy is quick to remind me of how trusting, gullible, and naive I am. JERK! You win some and you lose some! That is how you get out in the world and meet the real people. So what if it doesn't work out 100% as expected 100% of the time. The majority are good and fun and are in my favor! My attention and focus is on meeting good people everywhere I go, and, more times than not, I meet good people everywhere I go. It is still fun hitting the town local style, meeting Kiren's family, and sharing an authentic Cambodian meal. That is worth $50 to me, though he has now cheated his family out of being our next adoption recipient.

Discoveries, Fun Facts, and Useless Tidbits

- If a woman does not bear a son within the first 3 years of marriage, the man has a legal right to leave her and any daughters they may have and marry another woman.

- Everyone turns a year older during the Tet holiday. It is not until someone is considered really old that he or she celebrates his or her own individual birthday. Really old begins at age 50!

- Children are given red envelopes with lucky money instead of gifts during the Tet holiday.

- Cash registers are non-existent. Hand held calculators are used if necessary to calculate any charges. If a large bill is used to pay, many times the clerks will have to take change from their purses or go next door to break the bill into smaller denominations.

- Names are written in reverse to what we are accustomed to. For example for Vo Tri Tai, Vo is the last name, Tri is the middle name, and Tai is the first name. A person can change the middle name if he or she chooses.

- When a family member dies, the family chooses the coffin, transports the coffin to their home, places the body inside the coffin, and takes it to the cemetery for burial, after digging the grave themselves.

American Beached Whales

Amy's Diary Entry
February 27th, Sihanoukville, Cambodia

After a week here it was getting old. There wasn't a whole lot to do around here except enjoy the beaches, which we had been doing. It still climbed into the 90's during the day. Little girls, around age eight, ply the beach all day long. They carried baskets filled with fruit on the top of their heads and carved pineapple with very sharp knives as if they were professional chefs. We asked them why they weren't at school. One of them brushed a strand of dirty hair away from her empty eyes and told us that her parents couldn't afford to send her to school and she had to work so that a brother could go to school instead. We bought unwanted fruit from so many of them because of their plight and our pity. Who knows… maybe they had found a jackpot of a story that guaranteed tourists would buy from them. I hoped that was the case. This area seemed to have a lot of potential for development, and I'm sure one day it will be ruined, but maybe what I think of as being ruined will lead to more jobs for the locals and a chance at school for more little girls. Everywhere we went there was just so much poverty. People had nothing. It was depressing. I had been missing my family a lot lately. I wanted to call home, but I was afraid that would make it worse. After almost 4 months of living solely out of a backpack, I was beginning to understand why not many people chose this type of travel.

Discoveries, Fun Facts, and Useless Tidbits

- Dogs recognized us as potential threats as they would often growl and bark at us if we ventured too close to the front of their homes. The local Cambodians walk by unnoticed.

- January is the coolest month in Cambodia when temperatures average around 86 degrees. The hottest month is April when temperatures reach 104 degrees! Needless to say it is miserably hot here.

- Eighty percent of Cambodia's exports are in the garment sectors, including international brands such as Columbia, Gap, and Calvin Klein.

- The average salary in Cambodia is $260.00/year.

- Foreign aid constitutes more than half of the government's annual budget, but unfortunately entering politics in Cambodia (like other countries) is more about self-interest than national service.

Amy Continued

February 28th

We were on our way to Siam Reap on a supposedly fast boat. Well this fast boat looked like a silver bullet with a walkway around the sides, and so far it hadn't been all that fast. We thought that we were going to be sitting inside the silver bullet, but that was where our luggage went. We were herded to the top, and now all of us were sitting on top of the silver bullet. If you were traveling with someone, you could use them as a backrest. We had no chairs or even cushions or an overhead canopy to block the searing sun. It wasn't bad at first as it was still pretty cool since we left at 7 AM, but now the sun was out and it was getting really hot. We were out in the middle of a big body of water and I couldn't see any shoreline. I didn't feel especially safe. The top of this boat had become extremely hot. This was like traveling on top of a city bus instead of inside the bus as it rolled along for 5 hours. Once again we just looked at each other and shook our heads. We would never have imagined that this would be our boat ride because we were imagining an open-air boat with cushioned seats. We went by all kinds of wooden houses that were up on stilts. Some looked pretty sturdy, but others looked like a strong wind would blow them over. Most of them had hammocks strung up under them, and already people were lying in them. Maybe they slept there and hadn't gotten up yet. Kids were swimming in the water and there were hundreds of men fishing from their boats. We were told that fishing wasn't very good right now because it was the dry season. Cambodia may be poorer than Vietnam but it did feel authentic. The food hadn't been as good as in China and Vietnam and the bed bugs continued to find me and replenished their bellies with my blood every night. I wished they'd munch on Traci instead of me for a night. She seemed to get only 5 or 6 bites but then complained about them incessantly while I had 20 on one leg alone. People looked at me like I had leprosy and I knew it was gross. Being so hot and sweating over them seemed to make the itching worse.

Siem Reap

Amy's Diary Entry
March 3rd, Siem Reap, Cambodia

Our hotel in Siam Reap had several enclosed pens and pools for alligators. The adult crocodiles were kept separate from the baby croco-

diles or else they would become lunch for the adult crocs. There were
about 9 adults, 40
adolescents, and 30
babies in the complex.
I'd always assumed that
crocodiles were rela-
tively silent reptiles but
they had their own
vocabulary and when
they spoke, they spoke

Alligators At Cambodian Hotel

loudly. They loved to scream right before sunrise, so every morning
we were awakened by these opinionated reptiles. Even with this added
attraction our hotel was only $8.00 USD per night for double occupancy.

It was a nice room, with nice entertainment, but the hotel's cleaning standards were not up to par with our comfort level by U.S. standards. We had the same sheets on our bed since we arrived, though we
asked several times for them to be changed. We had even taken our
sand infested and orange stained sheets off of our beds and handed
them to the cleaning woman directly, only to find that she simply
remade the beds with the same unwashed sheets. Nor had she ever
cleaned our bathroom or provided ANY toiletries. We had to pay extra
for the air conditioner and paid each day for the room, no tabs or end
bills. It was miserably hot and we were only able to withstand short
excursions before we had to return to our room and rest beneath the
one life-saving air vent.

Siam Reap, which means Siamese Defeated, was a rather small
city built on both banks of the Stung Siem River. Tourists flocked to
this city since it was the gateway to the temples of Angkor, one of the

architectural wonders of the world. It was impossible when trying to describe a sight of this stature to find words that truly conveyed its historical majesty, but I'll do my best. We spent the days alone at the Angkor Temples. We set the alarm for 5:15 AM and our moto driver, Fiat, picked us up at 5:30 AM. He was at our beck and call for three days

Angkor Wat

through the Angkor Wat Temples for a meager $21.00 USD. We arrived just in time for the sunrise, which was pretty to see, but one morning was enough. The temples were incredible. Most were over 1,000 years old and were still standing strongly, sometimes three stories high. The arches, called false arches, were made by overlapping huge rocks. Some weighed a ton by themselves. The stairs were steep and scarier to walk down than up. There were Buddhas set up in almost all the buildings or at least an altar for that purpose. The aroma of incense permeated the air and there were ever present altar-keepers or children seeking a handout. Passageways were wide enough for 2-3 people to walk side-by-side, and the carvings were everywhere. Many of the temples were surrounded by high walls and often a moat. The bas reliefs (carvings into the stone) were so intricate, detailed, and intertwined. Each told a story and had a beginning and an end. Most were about various battles. We spent 5 hours there before going back to our hotel for lunch and a nap. Our driver picked us up again at 2:30 PM and we spent the rest of the day there and did the same schedule for the next two days as well.

We rented pedal bikes and tooled around for 4-5 hours, exploring the streets and sights that this fascinating place had to offer. We stopped

at a rehab hospital for amputees where a number of them were walking on steps, sand, uneven rock type surfaces, and parallel bars. We were the only visitors. Inside the hospital there were technicians making and grinding prosthesis with old and out dated hand-held tools. Cambodia had the highest number of amputees in the world, one out of every 275 people. An estimated 150 people still stepped on landmines every month! Most children who stepped on landmines

Child Selling Postcards At Angkor Wat

were killed but adults usually survived with loss of limbs, yet America still continued to manufacture 37 different types of landmines, having the 4th largest arsenal in the world with 11.2 million mines. It cost only $3.00 to make one and about $1,000 to remove one. Sad, sad, sad! Afterward, Amy went back to the room to take a nap, and I hired a cyclo driver to take me through an unexplored village.

Traci Explores a Poor Village
In Siem Reap
http://j.mp/l0LUOZ

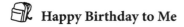 Happy Birthday to Me

Traci's Diary Entry
March 5th

Mom just sent me an email that several of my relatives and close family friends have made birthday deposits into my bank account today as they want to be part of our school/village "adoption" program. Another handful of friends have emailed us asking for addresses to send packages themselves. I feel so lucky and blessed to have such wonderful family and friends in my life. If I had millions of dollars, I would have no greater joy than walk around the world again and give it away to people like these. This is a Happy Birthday!

My birthday just got better! Amy says she will treat me to anywhere that I want to go for dinner, so we take a cyclo about twenty minutes into town and walk the strip until I find a place that looks upbeat and fun. It is called Ecstatic Pizza; I read somewhere that it is known for its Western-Style pizzas and Happy Hour specials – that sounds good to me! It's the kind of place where you walk in and place your order and then go sit at a picnic table and wait for your food. We order a medium "Pizza of the Day" and two Angkor Wat beers and make our way to a table beside some Western-looking travelers. How nice to finally converse with others who are on a similar journey as ours and have been to some of the same places! Conversation is not only engaging, it is enthralling! What a treat! But then the pizza comes and I dig in. Amy is so engaged in conversation with the travelers, she doesn't mind that her half is getting cold. All of a sudden, I begin to feel warm rushes of dizziness pour over my body. Something is seriously wrong! I feel strange and light and airy. All of a sudden, out of nowhere, I begin laughing so hysterically that tears were falling off of my face, not dripping, falling! I am laughing so hard that I can barely catch my breath. Amy keeps kicking me under the table, pinching my leg, and giving me dirty glares. At one point she spins her head around so quickly, with an evil look, in a demonized tone, and snarls how rude I am being. It reminds me of the scene from the Exorcist. I double over and begin laughing even harder. Within moments, I am no longer laughing, I am crying, real tears! Everyone is staring at me. Amy is so embarrassed and irritated by my rash behavior that she apologizes to our new friends and begrudgingly shoves the leftovers in a box and hails a rickshaw to take us back to our hostel. She doesn't speak to me the entire ride back as I vacillate between hardy laughter and funny tears. While I am washing up and calming down in the bathroom, I hear a loud crash in the sleeping area. Oh great, I think, she is so pissed now she's throwing things. I peek my head around the corner to see what fell, and it was Amy. She has fallen out of bed and she is lying between the nightstand and her bed with pizza smeared all over her face, shirt, and the floor. She is laughing so hard she can't pick herself up, but she has enough wits about her to laugh-out the barely understandable words, "THIS PIZZA HAS POT IN IT!" as she points to the empty box now covering the floor. That is the closest thing to an apology that I have ever gotten from her! We both scurry to scoop up the leftovers from the floor and laugh for hours and hours, drinking our warm beer in our air conditioned room and reminiscing on the fun times of our journey and years of friendship! It is a true surprise party with a real "Happy" ending! The next day we go back and order another one!

Discoveries, Fun Facts, and Useless Tidbits

- Most homes have either their own water pump in the front yard or a large well in between two homes for shared use.

- The garbage trucks broadcast a myriad of tunes as they cruise the streets picking up garbage. Favorites seem to be 'The Happy Birthday Song' and 'It's a Small World After All.' When cars are backing up they also play tunes.

- There have been numerous times when we have found ourselves surrounded by 6-10 children who are content just to watch us write in our diary or stretch after running. Personal space is not a priority here as the children think nothing of being close enough to touch you.

- We are still waiting for both of us to be served and eat dinner at the same time.

- Divorce results in a woman being stigmatized for the remainder of her life. Her chance of remarrying is virtually nil, so great the shame.

Cambodian Market

The Meat Market – Fly Infested Raw Meat Hangs In The
Heat All Day

Sacks Of
Cockroaches,
Beetles &
Grasshoppers

Amy Eating A Deep Fried Tarantula

Cambodian
Gas Pump

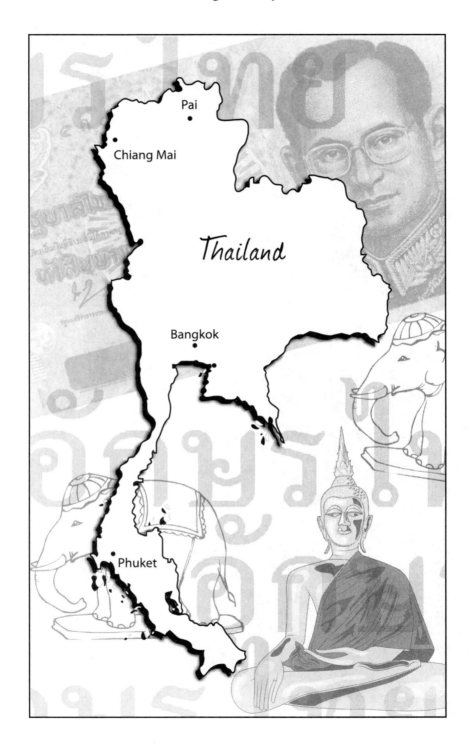

Thailand

"Not all wanderers are lost"
- H.M. Jacks

🥾 Thailand Civilization

Amy's Diary Entry
March 12th, Bangkok, Thailand

Well we were back in civilization once again. We purchased
tickets that were supposedly going to take us from Siam Reap, Cambodia, all the way to Bangkok but when
we cleared customs at the Thailand
border, our ride to Bangkok didn't
exist. There were about 20 of us all in
the same predicament, and we were all
ticked off. Some of the people were
yelling, but once again what choice did
we have? We had been scammed, and
there was nothing we could do, and no
one was willing to help us. There were,
of course, Thai drivers with vans that

would now be more than happy to take us the rest of the way to Bangkok. I swore they were all in on it together, and they got together to come up with new scams to screw the tourists. So for $8.00 each we

hopped into a van with no seatbelts that was designed for about 8 people, but we managed to cram 15 people inside like canned sardines. The driver was crazy as once again he was passing indiscriminately on narrow roads, all while the rain was pouring down and making it hard to see well.

We were staying in a hostel at the end of Khao San Street, an area devoted to the backpacker crowd as there was nothing but block after block of stores, restaurants, travel agencies, and hostels. Everyone seemed to speak English, so bargaining was easy. All the backpackers looked like each other with long, dirty dreadlocks, tattoos, and baggy shorts or long skirts. I found it funny that they all were trying to be unique and express their individual personalities but they wound up looking like exact replicas of each other. Probably just my age, because I'm sure I was probably the same way when I was 21 or 24. Kudos to them, I guess, for having the guts to travel around the world at such a young age as I wouldn't have even dreamed about something like that when I was 23. At first I found all kinds of things that I thought I just had to have, but now that I have walked through the area a couple of times my desires lessened. I eventually remembered that everything I bought had to be hauled around for awhile. The food was disappointing so far. Their salads were typically made of cabbage with a couple of green beans and a slice or two of carrots on top. They used pita bread as pizza crust, as a burrito shell, and also as taco shells. None of the restaurant staff had been all that friendly, but why should they be? They knew that backpackers only stayed for a couple of days. The other day Traci was served beer in a glass with a pretty big chip on the rim, and when she showed it to the waitress, she was told, "You be careful now." It was pretty funny.

This was a pretty cool city as there were temples and wats everywhere but also a lot of trees and greenery. We went to the Forensic Medicine Museum, the Snake Farm Institute, the Temple of Dawn, the Royal Palace, and Wat Pho. Wat Pho held a huge reclining Buddha, but a reclining Buddha was the same to me as one standing on his head. There was definitely more to do here. We had been in so many wats and temples and palaces in China, Vietnam, and Cambodia that they were all starting to look alike, and we decided to avoid them for awhile.

There were a lot of beautiful people, some with obvious cosmetic enhancements. This also appeared to be a transvestite haven, but no one seemed to pay any more attention to them than they did to the daily news-

A Beautiful Man

paper. We were told that a sex change operation only cost $3,500 here which was why people come here from all over the world to have it

Transvestite At A
Cabaret Show

done. We went to a real movie theater for the first time since leaving the states and even though there were only about 20 people in the entire theater, we still had to pick the seats that we wanted to sit in when we bought our tickets. Before the movie started, they played the national anthem and everyone stopped eating, drinking, and talking and stood until the music stopped.

There were pictures of the king and queen everywhere in Bangkok, but none of them were riddled with hand drawn mustaches or horns sprouting from their heads. I thought of what would happen if pictures of our president were plastered everywhere in our country. They'd be destroyed. It was nice to see the respect that the Thai people had for their monarchy.

I finally received my package from home that I had asked my family to ship. It was filled with everything we had requested that was unavailable in Vietnam and Cambodia, but was now readily available here in Thailand. I didn't think I'd share that with my sister Wendy, who went shopping for my goods and took the time and expense to ship it here. The best part was the card and letter from her and Mom. I even got a little hand-written note from Dad, which may be the first one I had ever received. My niece Tammy had another little boy while I was gone. He was going to be so big already when I got back that I'd completely miss him being a baby.

Discoveries, Fun Facts, and Useless Tidbits

- The Thai Government began a major war on drugs on February 1, 2003. Since that time more than 2,000 people believed to be involved in drug trafficking have been killed and 240,000 addicts have turned themselves into police custody for rehabilitation.

- The literacy rate in Thailand is 93.8%, one of the highest rates in mainland southeast Asia.

- "Saving face" in Asia means avoiding confrontation and embarrassment at any cost. However our interpretation of "saving face" has become that an Asian person can never admit that they don't know an answer to a question, that they were ever wrong about anything, and that every question is ultimately answered with a "yes" and a smile.

- A sign reads:
  "Yellow fever is the syndrome of a Caucasian man leaving his Caucasian wife/family for an Asian woman, typically one much younger and much more accommodating to his every personal need." It is very common here to see older Caucasian men with very young Asian girls.

- Birds, squirrels, and other small animals in Vietnam, Cambodia and Thailand are captured and stacked in small cages; you can purchase one for its release for $10.00 USD.

 Civilization Alas

Traci's Diary Entry
March 17th, Bangkok, Thailand

Alas, civilization in Thailand! What a change, even from just 100 feet past the border crossing. Sadly, we are welcomed by a scam! Despite me suggesting that we buy our bus tickets over the border, Ms. Pre-planner insisted we purchase our transportation for Thailand, in Cambodia. When we arrive, our "Welcome Wagon" doesn't exist, so we have to pay all over again for our transportation into town. It's funny how Amy never says anything when she falls prey to a con. And I never say "I told you so" or point out how her pre-planning has failed us again.

It is nice to again see familiar products from home. The ride to Bangkok from the Cambodian border is a bit frightening as the driver of the van passes every car in sight, seemingly undeterred by the tor-

Public Transport

rential rain. Despite the downpour, it is obvious we are back in a developed country as there is a 7-11 store every few miles. Once we arrive in the city proper, their frequency increases and now they can be found every few blocks until we are in the heart of the backpacker district where there is at least one and sometimes two 7-11 stores to every block and an ATM on every corner. The civilized world is revisited as we take advantage of the authentic salad bar at the Pizza Company, the English edition of the Bangkok Post, and the latest Jack Nicholson movie About Schmidt. One super cool thing that I really like is that all the hostels and even some bars and restaurants post their free "movie of the night" on the sign outside, welcoming visitors. There are bean-bag chairs scattered all over the floor awaiting the next movie watcher to sprawl out and have a drink, dessert, or a meal. We never see the same movie name posted at any other of the facilities, but the Carpenters and ABBA play over and over and over again in stores, restaurants, and cafes.

After the two day back-breaking journey from hell from Cambodia to Thailand, I go to find a well-deserved handmade banana milkshake (10 cents USD) and a massage while Amy unpacks and relaxes. There are massage parlors on every block, so I just randomly chose one. I am greeted by a friendly, older woman who asks if I would like 60 minutes or 90 minutes and if I want a plain massage or the house special; I order the 60 minute house special and pre-pay my $15.00 USD. The woman takes me around back, and I get to choose a masseuse from a group of seven young men. So of course, I pick the strongest and most handsome looking one. It is a superb and professional massage until he gets to the inside of my thighs and hits the most southern point of my torso head on with his fingers! I spring-board up and gasp "What are you doing!" and he nervously yanks his hand away and answers, "No worry! No worry! I no poke you! I no poke you! Only fingers! Only fingers! I so sorry! I so sorry! You order 'Happy Massage.' " And as it turns out... I had, not knowing that the "House Special" includes a happy ending, a service I thought was for men only. I guess when they say "Full Body" massage in Thailand, they mean FULL BODY massage! ...So what did I do? The world will never know!

Restaurants here, like most in Asia, are open from 7 AM to 11 PM, 7 days per week. They are usually run by a single family. Thai food is one of my all time favorites so I'm in seventh heaven here! But we've already had some interesting dining experiences. For lunch we ordered a pizza. It turned out to be pita bread with cheese and ketchup on top, and, oddly enough, no one ever heard of "Thai Pizza." They also use pita bread to make their tacos and burritos, and the "salsa" they use is diced tomatoes with red pepper flakes or Tabasco sauce in it. If you order sour cream on your taco or burrito, you are given plain yogurt. All I can say is yuck! Many restaurants in Asia when serving fish as an entree, will serve the entire fish, including the head, tail, scales, and guts. Amy told the waiter that she wanted a fish filet, not a fish with a head. He nods in understanding or so she thinks, until he brings out her dinner, an entire fish and tail again, but with the head cut off. At least the eye is not staring back at her like on the fish she ordered in China. I order spaghetti and garlic bread and am served a plate of spaghetti noodles with plain ketchup squeezed over the top and a piece of toast with garlic salt sprinkled over the top. It looks exactly like the meal I had in China on Thanksgiving Day and nothing like the meal showcased on the menu. We will stick to eating Thai food and not succumb to our cravings for the long lost foods of home. We also notice that if the restaurant staff messes up your dinner order or if it just didn't taste good enough to eat, you must still pay for it, even if you end up ordering another entrée. You are charged for both. At least we finally receive all of our meals simultaneously after 5 months of eating in shifts.

People we meet everywhere keep telling us how cheap Thailand is. All I can say is that they must never have been to China because every place since has been expensive to us. Sure it is not as expensive as home, but when you start out visiting the cheapest place in Asia first, everything thereafter just seems expensive. One thing that is cheap though is fake I.D. cards. They have every kind of profession imaginable and make them, photo intact, in a matter of minutes, right in the street. I buy a phony travel journalist card for $10. Amy thinks it's a waste of money and wrong, but I am certain it will help protect us against scams, at least some of the time.

Is This Where the Term "Ring Your Neck" Comes From?
Amy's Diary Entry
March 20th, Chiang Mai, Thailand

It was just as hot here as it had been in Bangkok. We searched this city for an hour before we found a hotel with air-conditioning, a necessity now instead of a luxury. This was a city that seemed like it was built around the 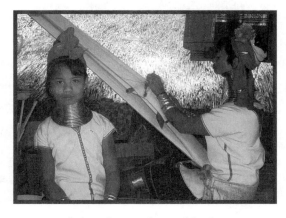 tourist. Three to five day treks in the mountains of Thailand were very popular from this outpost, however I could barely stand to walk around in the heat of the day for 2 hours much less 6-8 hours. Every sign said that their trek would take you to "untouristed" hill tribes. What did that even mean anymore? Once they had been visited once or twice they were no longer untouristed.

Elephant treks were big here as well. We decided to take an organized day trip in an air-conditioned van to visit 2 hill-tribes of sharp contrasts. The first village was the Karen "long-neck" village, which consisted of approximately 65 people who had sought refuge in Thailand 3 years ago after life under the harsh regime of Myanmar (Burma) became perilous. The women of this tribe started wearing gold rings around their necks at age 5 and each year more rings were added until the maximum number of 21 was reached. This added 10 pounds to the women's weight, all being carried by their necks. The

maximum number of rings varied, depending on the person. The rings were worn continuously, except for periods of time totaling about 2 weeks per year when the rings were removed to allow the irritated skin underneath time to breathe and heal. The original purpose of the rings was to prevent tigers and lions from carrying the women off to the jungle. This village now earned its living from tour groups going through their village and buying their handicrafts. My inherent cynicism thought they only wore the rings for 20 minute periods throughout the day, putting them on when they heard the commotion of the tourist throngs and taking them off as soon as we left. Like that had never been done before.

Inside The Karen Long Neck Village
http://j.mp/jcQbmp

A Hmong village was the other stop on this tour. A bus full of people were dropped off at the side of the road and told to start wandering around this village that consisted of several blocks of dirt roads and wooden shacks. Many of the residents were sitting outside on chairs, watching their naked, dirty children play in the dirt while they cleaned vegetables or defeathered dead chickens. There were several gatherings of men around active cockfights, which sickened most of us. Children surrounded us with their palms turned upward, waiting for handouts.

Cocks Fighting In Village

I understood they had nothing compared to us, but such blatant begging and expectations of rewards no longer produced as much sympathy from me as it did earlier in this venture. The five foot radius satellite dishes on top of some of the shacks didn't help matters.

We signed up for a 2 day Thai cooking class, beginning tomorrow.

 Thai Cooking Class
Traci's Diary Entry
March 24th, Chiang Mai, Thailand

There is no better way to get inspired by Thai cuisine than to take a cooking class, and Chiang Mai, Thailand, reigns supreme. For just 900 baht or $30 USD, the 7 hour class includes just about everything a cooking class should: tour of the market and farm, individually selected appetizer, soup, curry, stir-fry, dessert, garnish course, and a printed book with every recipe on the menu including those not prepared. Our adventure in culinary arts begins with round-trip transportation from our hotel to the school. Our first stop is a local market where we get an education in produce, rice, coconut milk, curry, seasoning, and learning Western substitutions for some of the more uncommon items. We are given an hour to browse vendor stalls that carry everything from ginseng to carrots and pig's faces to innards.

From there it's about a 20 minute ride through the countryside to the farm. We are welcomed with a refreshing drink, before taking a guided tour of the farm. Here we pick the remaining ingredients necessary for preparing our meal. Once we are in the open air terrace and in our assigned groups, in our appointed cooking stations, everything is set up for us. The only chopping and cutting we do is in learning how to make fancy garnishes out of carrots and tomatoes.

Of course the best part of Thai cooking is relaxing and eating the fruits of our labor. This remains a highlight of Thailand.

Here are a couple of fast and easy recipes for you to try from our cooking class:

Bananas In Coconut Milk (Kluai Bod Chii)

Serves 2
Preparation:15 Minutes

Ingredients:
1 Cup of coconut milk
1/2 Cup of water
1 Tbsp. of sugar
2 ripe bananas
a pinch of salt

1. Steam the bananas in their skins for about 5 minutes (or boil for 2 minutes) until the skins starts to break. Peel and cut each banana into bite-sized.

2. Put the thin coconut milk and pandanus leaves into a pan. When it is boiling add the banana, palm sugar, sugar and salt. Bring back to the boil and add the thick coconut milk. Simmer until the sugar has dissolved (about 3 minutes)

Notes:
1. If you want the sauce to be thicker then add 5g (1 teaspoon) of tapioca flour to the coconut milk.

2. Once the thick coconut milk has been added do not boil for too long as the oil will separate out and the bananas will be too soft. The bananas should be slightly hard.
3. It can be served hot or cold.

Papaya Salad (Somtam)

Serves 2
Preparation Time: 5 Minutes

Ingredients:
1 Cup of shredded green papaya (Peel the papaya and rinse under running water. Remove the seeds and shred the flesh with a grater)
1-2 Thai hot chilli
2-3 peeled cloves of garlic
1 Tbsp. of lemon juice
2 tsp. of sugar
1/3 Cup of chopped long beans (chop about 3 cm long)
1 tomato, cut into 6 pieces
2 Tbsp. of peanuts
1 Tbsp. of fish sauce or soya sauce
1/4 tsp. of salt

*Green papaya can be replaced by cucumber, cabbage, carrot or ' Granny Smith' apple.

Directions:
Put the garlic, chilies and long beans into a mortar and pound roughly. Add the papaya and pound again to bruise the ingredients. Then add the dried shrimps, fish sauce, lime juice and palm sugar and stir together using the pestle and a spoon until the palm sugar has melted. Add the anchovy sauce and tomatoes and pound to combine. Then add the peanuts and mix together. Serve with sticky rice.

*The taste should be spicy, sweet, sour and a little bit salty.

📖 Prescription for Diarrhea

Traci's Diary Entry
March 30th

We are on our way to an elephant ride in the jungle (another birthday gift from Amy) that is a two hour bus ride away. Since I have such a strong history of motion sickness, I decide to play it safe and go to the pharmacy to get some prescription meclizine. You can purchase almost anything that you want without a prescription, including pain meds, insulin, birth control, and medicated cast strips for casting your own fractures. I explain what I need to the pharmacist and he assures me that the pills he gives me, which I have never heard of before, will prevent motion sickness. I have no choice but to comply with his knowledge as it is not printed in English. Shortly after taking the

The Elephant Ride

motion sickness pill for the tour bus I am about to board, I suddenly get a bout of diarrhea and am unable to leave the bathroom, let alone go on the elephant trek. Amy later finds out that the pharmacist has sold me something for constipation, not motion sickness. We are both disappointed, but are rescheduling for tomorrow. Corporate drug companies will never survive here.

I've always wanted to learn how to give a Thai massage in Thailand, and today is the day I get to cross it off my bucket list. That's right! I'm officially enrolled in a Thai massage certification course. My class is from 4 -7 PM for the next week and costs less than $100 USD for the whole program, including my internship which consists of getting a critique from three other teachers on my skills and knowledge. I will use my new found talent for personal use as I've already checked that my real Thai Certification, from a real accredited Thai Massage School, in the country of its origin will not be valid in the good ole overly-regulated U.S. of A., or like some of the Asians call it, the United States of Assholes, or the United States of Arrogance! Hearing those conversations makes it easier to be a Canadian and laugh along with them, especially knowing that I've lived up to both of those names.

Discoveries, Fun Facts, and Useless Tidbits

- In Thailand if you purchase something from a chain store and want to return it, you must return it to the original store of purchase.

- After you board city buses and secure your seat or standing place, a travelling ticket attendant walks around and collects your fare.

Phuket, Thailand
Amy's Diary Entry
April 9th

I couldn't believe I was such an idiot. We were scrambling to get all our stuff together to jump off the train at this stop, and I forgot to grab my glucose meter. It was sitting in its little bag right above my sleeping berth, so now I had hundreds of useless strips and no way to check my sugar. Diabetes is always there hovering, and I hated it. I always had to have sugar available, no matter where I was or what I was doing. I couldn't leave the house without insulin or a meter. Traci worried that I would go low and die and I obsessed about my sugar going too high, blinding me in 20 years. Without a meter to check it was a complete guessing game as to what my sugar was, and I have had some bad guesses in the past. I walked all over this city looking for replacements and I couldn't find any meter anywhere. Seriously did no one have diabetes in this city? I wanted to just take my chances and hang here for a week and just try to stay on the high side, but Traci insisted that we go back to Bangkok right away. This was one of the places I was looking forward to the most! It had some of the most beautiful beaches in the world, and I wouldn't see them. I was so mad at myself and my crappy fate of even having this disease. At home I could rationalize it and tell myself that it was not as bad as multiple sclerosis or cancer and while that was true it still sucked. I went 37 years without a medical problem and then was cannonballed with Type 1 diabetes. It was a pain having to carry around a thermos of insulin and a year's worth of supplies. If Traci would have done something like that, I would be all over her, making her feel guilty and as stupid as I could, but she never once condemned me or made me feel bad. She was more concerned about my health and was willing to forego this tropical paradise to find me a meter. We were going to at least hang out at the beach while we waited for our bus to Bangkok, but then found out the closest beach was 30 minutes away and would cost us each $10 one way. Too cheap to pay $20 for an hour at the beach, we talked about leaving for India early.

Back in Bangkok
Amy Continued
April 11th

It took me awhile and a lot of walking, but I found a glucose meter that worked with the thousands of strips that I had. Hopefully that won't happen again. Diabetes has not only been a disruption in my life, it has aged me prematurely. I sometimes don't feel good after seeing my reflection in the mirror. I contacted Traci's former employer today and inquired about having plastic surgery. I am seriously considering it when I return home. We decided to head to India a bit earlier than we had planned, so instead of hanging out in Bangkok for another week Traci got our tickets changed to leave tomorrow. Once again our visas were going to expire in a day or two and we learned that we would have to leave the country in order to get an extension, so instead we just left. Tomorrow was the first day of Songskran or the Thai lunar Festival. The Songkran festival celebrated the lunar New Year in Thailand. Monks and elders received the respect of younger Thais by the sprinkling of water over their hands. Everyone else, especially tourists, were soaked with either high powered water guns or buckets of water poured over their head, all for "good luck." There was no escape being drenched by Thai kids having a great time. We would miss the big New Year's celebration but since we had already witnessed the Asian New Year in Vietnam we don't feel too bad about that. Many travelers rave about Thailand, but it was my least favorite country thus far. Neither one of us knew what to expect from India. We had heard other travelers rave about how great it was and then just as many had horror stories about their time there and getting scammed. I cannot imagine it would be any hotter there than it was here. I was going to see how India went but I didn't think I still wanted to go to Africa. I had not told Traci yet that I was questioning my desire to continue our adventure. I was sure it wouldn't go over very well. I was thinking the best opportunity to leave was when she went to the ashram.

Discoveries, Fun Facts, and Useless Tidbits

- Tour buses always end up making unexpected stops. Once aboard the bus we usually drive around for another hour picking up additional passengers, and then we must stop at the gas station to fuel up because obviously no one knew that the bus was going to be used for a tour that day! Along the way we stop and pick up/drop off locals heading the same direction and sometimes drop off /pick up bags of mail at the post office.

- The most popular drug in Thailand is a methamphetamine, better known as Yaa Baa or "crazy drug." It is estimated that 1 in 10 adults are addicted to this drug, even though it was unknown until 5 years ago.

Thai Toilets

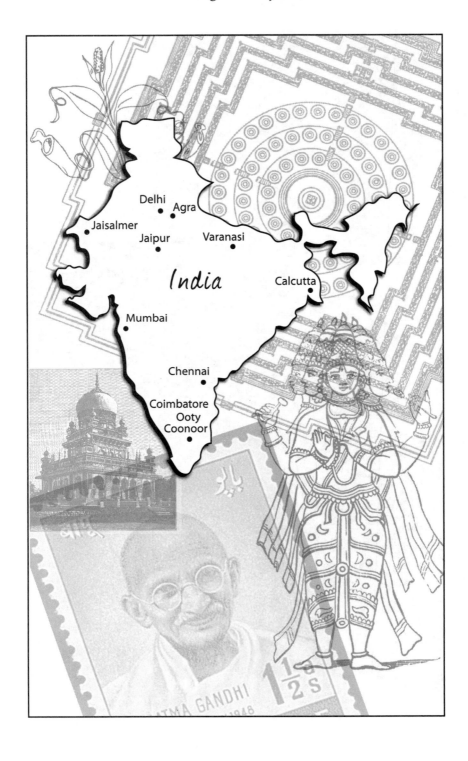

India

"Go forth on your path, as it exists only through your walking."
- Saint Augustine

 Welcome to the Land of Karmageddon
Traci's Diary Entry
April 13th, New Delhi, India

We both make our first phone calls to our parents in 6 months to let them know we are alive and kicking, from the airport leaving Thailand. We make sure we call late in the evening to insure everyone will be home. They are each thrilled to hear from us and reiterate what a joy it is receiving our weekly emails, photos, and updates to our website and seeing who we are sharing the bounty of their birthday and holiday gift money with. Everyone back home is happy and healthy. The five minute phone call seems like five seconds. It is hard to say goodbye.

Wow what a different place India is and has been from the minute we stepped out of the airplane. Since we are arriving at night we make a hotel reservation online while still in Thailand to free ourselves from walking around at night in a new city trying to find a place to stay. This hotel reservation supposedly includes a pre-paid taxi to bring us to the hotel as taxi drivers in India are notorious for telling tourists that their reserved hotel has either closed down or burned down in order to take them to a hotel that the taxi driver knows will give them a commission for each guest they deliver. We go to the two taxi booths at the airport, but of course, neither one of them knows anything about this pre-paid taxi but they have a taxi that can help us out for a fare that is 3x the expected amount. We make another call to our hotel and this time we

Our Taxi

are told to pay for our own taxi, and we will be reimbursed after checking into the hotel. It doesn't take long for us to question India's integrity. One of the first peculiarities that sets India apart are the elephants on the highway, ambling amidst the heavy traffic, paying no mind to the blaring horns of the cars that are trying to weave around them. The white-knuckle-ride to the hotel is filled with near misses of side-swipes and rear-end collisions as the driver makes no attempt to look toward either side or behind him as he switches from lane to lane. All of a sudden driving in China doesn't seem so bad. He finally pulls up in front of our hotel, the Jyoti

Hotel Scaffolding

International Deluxe, and the front of it is hidden behind 3 stories of wooden scaffolding. The rooms inside are complete with stained sheets, unflushed toilets, and a layer of dust that covers everything. At first we think this must be just the basic room, so we ask to see the deluxe room, only to find out we are already in the deluxe room. The currency is called rupee and it is 47 rupees to $1 USD. The hotel is going to try and charge us 1700 rupees ($36.00) for a room when the 800 rupee rate ($17.00) is clearly posted both on the door of the hotel and on the brochure sitting on the hotel check-in counter. They are only willing to lower the price when we walk out the door and down the dark street to find a more acceptable hotel. We do find a much nicer hotel with a better rate and an attached restaurant within several blocks.

It is just as hot here as in Cambodia. We spend the first day here just walking around, trying to get our bearings in this new, strange place. Delhi is the capital of India and is home to 14 million people. It has so much air pollution that every day spent breathing the air in the city is equivalent to smoking a pack of cigarettes. As a result, vehicles greater than 8 years old are banned from the city's streets. Bulls, cows, goats with their kids, sows with their piglets, donkeys, dogs, and the occasional water buffalo roam the streets freely. People spend more time in the streets than in their homes.

Streets Of India

There are snake charmers, markets, hawkers, pan handlers, touts, beggars, and homeless people. You always hear about this but it is

Working In India

entirely different when you actually see it. An article in the Hindustan Times, Delhi's daily newspaper, reported that residential owners of cows will soon face fines if they release them into the streets after milking them. They do this so the cows can fill their bellies on Delhi's greenery. I imagine it's a lot cheaper than feeding them.

Holy Cow

Charmed By Snake Charmers, A "Dying" Profession
http://j.mp/jR1FUs

Excerpts from India Newspapers

- Delhi has one of the worst ratings for the quality of its drinking water at 120 out of 122 cities around the world. It also ranks poorly for water availability at 133 out of 180.

- Some neighborhoods in Delhi only have access to water once per day when the water tanker arrives in the neighborhood. The truck is empty in 7 minutes.

- Some schools in Delhi have no drinking water. The kids drink from the puddles in the yard or playground where pigs and dogs roam freely.

- Two out of three women in Assam, a state in India, justify wife beating. A whopping 44% percent of women believe that wife beating is justified if the wife neglects the house or children. Another 41% justifies it if the wife shows disrespect for her in-laws or goes out without informing her husband, and more than 30% believe the wife should be beat if she does not cook properly.

- In today's paper, 150-200 people died from heat exhaustion. It sounds like a lot, but out of the billion person population, it's just a drop in the bucket.

🐾 The Land of "Impossibilities"
Amy's Diary Entry
April 16th, New Delhi, India

The street hawkers were quite persistent here. Traci expressed mild interest in a high flying helicopter toy and the vendor followed us for 10 minutes. Within a minute we were also being hounded by a purse salesman and another guy selling whips! We weaved in and out of traffic and walked close to parked cars in an attempt to eliminate their walking space but they would always reappear. Several times we were approached by pairs of young, well-dressed men who would welcome us to India and then initiated a pleasant, seemingly innocent conversation complete with travel tips and warnings about other louts. Within the first several minutes of the conversations we would be reas-sured by comments such as, "We do not want anything from you" or the familiar "We do not care about money," or "Money is not important to us." Eventually the purpose of this encounter would come to light and always included a visit to a silk shop or a travel agent or a café for drinks or tea. I had read about how some of these encounters led to drinks being laced or large bills left for the victims to pay, so we knew enough to refuse right away. Initially we tried to be polite when we refused them, but since politeness usually led to more pleas or a pro-longed conversation that led nowhere, we soon had no qualms about forgoing the politeness and just saying "No" immediately to everything and anything offered. In fact, "No" may be the word we had spoken most often since arriving in India, while their most spoken word is "Impossible." Everything we have asked for is "Impossible" to get or have. Several times men's hands seemed to get caught on our breasts as we weaved through pedestrian traffic, but interestingly enough, this was never a problem for women's hands.

The food is incredible! I ordered paneer tikka and murg malai kabob at the restaurant of our hotel while Chicken Little, otherwise known as Traci, ordered spaghetti. Seriously. Spaghetti??? So I implemented a new rule. If she was going to order Western food then she had to eat it, and she only got one bite of my excellent Indian food. My dish was so good that she tried to keep eating and eating it, but I put an end to that. "Eat your spaghetti fraidy cat." The waiter offered to wrap up our leftovers and bring them to our room. Of course we were expecting little cardboard boxes, but ten minutes later he was knocking on our door with our leftovers, which were on the same dishes except now they were covered with napkins and placed on a tray.

👣 Babu
Amy Continued
April 17th

We met Babu, a tuk-tuk driver, only a couple of days after arriving here. Babu refused to negotiate a price with us the first day we hired him but instead told us that we could pay him at the end of the day if we were happy with his services. If we were not happy we did not have to pay him. He repeated the line we had already been told

Touched By The Hand of Gandhi

many times by others here in New Delhi. It caused us to become instantly suspicious of anyone who spewed it out, "Money is important to others but not to me." Yeah right! Money seemed to be the only thing that was important here, and the game seemed to be how to get the most out of stupid tourists. Babu carted us around to many of the popular tourist attractions, which included the site of Gandhi's assassination and where his cremated remains were entombed. We seemed to get more attention at the tourist sites, and just as we did in

Ghandi's Final Footsteps

China we were asked to pose for pictures with family after family. We cheerfully posed every time we were asked.

Babu then took us to a Sikh temple that enclosed a large square bathing pool that equaled the size of several Olympian swimming pools. There were people several rows deep on each side of the pool where members were waiting to immerse themselves or their children. A communal meal was made by volunteers for all the congregants. We were invited for the meal, but when it came time to actually eat, we were put by ourselves in a hallway, outside of the main dining

Blessings At Sikh Temple

area. We could see inside the main dining area, and others could watch us while we ate. We now wondered if we weren't being used more as entertainment or amusement for the temple members. Utensils were

not provided as the meal was supposed to consist of finger food, but rice and beans were a little difficult to eat gracefully with our fingers. We used our flatbread chapattis (Indian bread that resembles Mexican tortillas) as a utensil but Babu soon scolded us and told us to eat like we were in India, not Ethiopa, whatever that meant. So we instead scooped the food onto the chapattis and made make-shift Indian burritos.

Prepping Communal Meal

We Are Left In The Hall Alone

We spent several days with Babu visiting the Lotus Temple, Connaught Circle, the Gate of India, the Parliament House, the

National Museum, the Old Fort, Secretariat buildings, and many others. We were dressed in shorts and tank tops the first day because it was hotter than Hades here. Babu told us that we were not dressed

appropriately for women, and that was why so many people had been staring at us. We just figured it was because we were white. He insisted that we should be wearing saris like other Indian women so we would

blend in more. Maybe he hadn't noticed that we were pasty white when compared to the native women and that a sari was unlikely to make us blend in any better, but we were game. Of course he

Sari Shop

took us to a store owned by one of his friends and within 20 minutes we were adorned in saris that definitely covered every square inch of us. The store owner asked Traci if she wanted to try on a Kashmir outfit, as they were supposed to be of higher quality, but she retorted

*Posing In Our New Saris
With Babu*

"Cashmere?! I don't even like cashmere, and it's way too hot to be wearing cashmere in India!" I then had to explain to her that it was Kashmir, an Indian State, and not cashmere. The real kicker was when he was showing us some scarves and told us that they were special because they were hand-made by Sikh people, and then he pointed to some other items and also mentioned that those were hand-made by Sikh people. Traci asked him what was wrong with them, and he said "Nothing is wrong with them, what do you mean what's wrong with them?" She asked, "What kind of illness do they have?" I had to inform her that the items were made by the Sikh people, not by SICK people. Then she got it! Boy did we all get a good laugh out of that one.

Those outfits lasted only a couple of hours because these saris made the unbearable heat even worse, but we were sure his friend and Babu himself made a nice little profit from us. Besides we continued to receive just as many welcoming and unwelcoming stares, so they definitely weren't making us blend in any better.

Foreigners were charged triple or more the admission price of local Indians at popular tourist sites. At the Red Fort, Indians had to pay 5 rupees to enter while we were charged 100 rupees. We were also asked to pay to get our sandals back when departing some tourist sites, even though Indians were handed their shoes back without a demand for money. We soon refused to pay this sandal fee and instead made a little scene or just grabbed our shoes and walked away. I had mixed feelings about this blatant discrimination. Our income was appreciably higher than most Indians and if it weren't set low for Indians, most would not be able to afford to see some of the historic sites in their own country, but 20x higher

Red Fort

seemed a bit much. Most times the difference amounted to a couple of dollars and as little as 25 cents to get our shoes back, but on the other hand, if such blatant discrimination was displayed in America, the lawyers would have had a field day wallowing in their settlements.

Discoveries, Fun Facts, and Useless Tidbits

- In all parts of Asia, they seem to eat heavy and full dinner meals for breakfast.

- We have not been very lucky receiving wake-up calls from our hotels as they promised. Even the 5-star hotel we treated ourselves to ceases to deliver the early morning request. We are late in meeting our new Indian friend for breakfast.

- Cash registers are still a rarity.

- Power outages happen on a regular basis here. Only the biggest and best places seem to afford generators. We learn the hard way to hit save on the computer every few minutes!

- We purchase new packages of batteries and all of them are dead. They have expired 5 years earlier.

- Many Indians eat with their hands, rolling their food into balls. The belief behind this is that they are sending cosmic energy through their hands into their food.

🐾 Amy Continued
April 20th

We needed to buy train tickets for Agra and Varanasi and we convinced Babu that we were going to buy our own train tickets at the train station rather than purchasing them from a travel agent and paying the agent a commission. We had been traveling for several months now and thought we knew by this time how to buy our own tickets. Babu tried to talk us out of it, but what did he know? He had only lived here all of his life, but he finally let us have our own way. He directed us to the queue for ladies and we were almost to the counter when he reappeared and asked us where our reservation form was. We, of course, did not have any reservation forms, so he found them for us, and we hastily filled them out. We got to the counter and were told there were no tickets to either Agra or Varanasi tomorrow and it would be days before any tickets were available even though all the while we were talking to the clerk other Indian customers were shoving their forms and money in front of us. She gave them their tickets while she continued to tell us there was no availability. We looked at each other like "What the hell?" The travel books said it would be easy to get next day train tickets. Babu was 30 feet behind us with a smirk on his face. We finally gave up and returned to our tuk-tuk where Babu informed us that overnight tickets would have been available if we had slipped the attendant a bribe. Babu told us, "This is India. It's not like the West. Everything costs extra money here." We ended up at the travel agency where we were able to purchase train tickets to our next 4 destination cities without difficulty.

Before we left Delhi Babu invited us to spend an evening at his home with his wife and 3 children. His home was a 2 bedroom apartment with cement floors throughout. One of the bedrooms held a double bed and also served as the family room. There were 2 metal chairs, a small coffee table that served as the dining room table, and

Babu's Family

a 12 inch TV that sat atop a large oil barrel in this bedroom and blared Hindi music. The 3 children slept in this double bed. The other bedroom was rented to an adult male relative. Babu and his wife Lexan slept on a folding cot in the

entryway. The kitchen was about 3 feet by 4 feet and held a 2 burner stove that sat on the floor. The bathroom was a hole in the cement floor and mold covered almost every wall. Babu, the children, and Traci and I shared several beers and some snacks in front of the TV that was always blaring. After 2 hours we asked to help his wife Lex prepare

Traci's Cooking Lesson From Lex

dinner as the time was starting to drag, and we had run out of things to talk about. It was amazing what she produced with this 2 burner stove, handfuls of spices, and staples such as rice and legumes. Lex served us and Babu dinner instead of eating with us, as is customary in the Indian household, but we weren't especially comfortable with this. We asked her to eat with us and then asked Babu if she could eat with us, but our request was politely

declined. When we finished eating she fed the children. After dinner
she dressed us in elegant saris. We were hesitant to put them on

because, of course, it was hot and the apartment was not air conditioned. I was in my
usual sweaty state without even a fan to
stand in front of and cool off with but Lexan
insisted. She even adorned our foreheads with
the traditional red dots or bindi. Overall it was
a nice evening, but then Babu asked us to help
him pay for the education of his children.
We wondered if this was his standard modus
operandi with all of the tourists that he met,
but after seeing the conditions that most

*Lex Dressing Amy
In Traditional Sari*

Indian people live in who could blame him? If you didn't ask you
would never receive. We decided to make Babu and his family our
next "adoption," but instead of mailing him a package from America,
we instead granted his wish and gave him American cash. At the train
station the following day Babu left us with the warning "Remember
this is India. Do not trust anyone." How right he was.

*Inside of Babu, The Tuk-Tuk,
Driver's Home*
http://j.mp/miAp1P

Discoveries, Fun Facts, and Useless Tidbits

- We were passing observers of a wedding and the bride never even looked at the groom when he placed the ring on her finger. One Indian husband said of his arranged marriage, "I have never told my

wife that I love her, or she to me. But she knows it because I gave her my seed that bore our son, and I know it because she delivered him to me."

Happy Wedding Day?

- Driving school in India is every day for a month including hill driving, market driving, night driving, and sudden stop and starts.

- Food orders are not taken a minute early. If the lunch hour begins at noon and you arrive ten minutes early, you will have to sit and wait

until exactly 12 to get the menu.

- Our waiter farted really loudly while serving us our dinner and never said excuse me or apologized.

- The chef at our luxury hotel was seen picking a booger out of his nose and then resuming his bread kneading duties.

Lunch Time

 **The Taj Mahal**

Traci's Diary Entry
April 21st, Agra, India

A visit to Agra and its infamous Taj Mahal turns out to be another comic adventure. We arrive in Agra on a Thursday morning and plan to leave on a night train the following day. Since the Taj is closed on Friday, the visit to see this temple of love has to be made on Thursday. In an attempt to decrease the number of tourists visiting the Taj

Taj Mahal

Mahal, the Archaeological Survey of India has raised the admission price to 960 rupees or $21.00 for foreigners and to 20 rupees or 40 cents for Indians. Yeah! Let's do that with all of our American attractions to all of our visiting and illegal foreigners! Despite hearing numerous stories of fellow travelers being stricken with food-borne illnesses while visiting India, Amy is determined not to miss out on mutton and other Indian meat dishes, but within hours of arriving in Agra a legitimate reason merges to consider avoiding them. Her body decides to purge these local specialties from her system in a most violent manner, confining her to the hotel room on the only day available to see the Taj and causing her to swear off meat for the rest of their travel in India, much to my chagrin. But I do manage to refrain from saying "I told you so!" as she of course would have said to me! I spend an hour rubbing her feet until she falls asleep and another hour walking the streets, stopping at every little shop along the way, looking for anything to help or comfort her. I return with crackers and white soda. She has a high temperature, and I don't want to leave her, but she convinces me not to miss the opportunity to see the grand Taj Mahal. When I arrive, they ask for 1,000 rupees to get in, not the 960 that the sign says. I begin shouting at the ticket attendant and tell him I am done being scammed and I will not pay the overage! As I am walking away, a local man who over-hears my plight offers to take me through the back entrance for just 100 rupees. After I barter him down to 50,and make him look me in the eyes and pinky-swear that he isn't scamming me, we set off on the 30 minute journey around the compound. There are all kinds of little one room shack homes hiding

One Room Home

behind this gorgeous temple. I peer my head into a few open doors and ask if I can see their home and ask how many people live in the small confines. His general answer ranges from 4-6. Everyone is kind and friendly, but every one of them asks for a couple rupees for answering my questions. Then we get to a few areas where we have to bribe the gate attendant with my money to get into

Swamp In Back Of Taj Mahal

the restricted areas. And wouldn't you know it, we get all the way to the back of the temple and the guard wants 1,000 rupees to enter the back door. All of the sudden my guide can't speak English and he splits! But I still refuse to succumb to the bribe over principle. I snap plenty of photos of the outside and made the trek back to the temple entrance of the compound alone, but not before getting invited into the home of some local people I meet earlier for a meal. They are more than thrilled with their 10 rupee tip and the opportunity to snap a few photos with me. That makes it worth it! That is the kind of stuff I love to stumble upon.

An attempt is made to change our departing train tickets to Saturday night but despite the hotel staff's valiant effort there are no Saturday train tickets available. However after missing our train on Friday night miraculously those same unavailable train tickets now become available, but only after flashing my travel journalist card and paying a palm-greasing fee of $3. It is the Indian way.

Discoveries, Fun Facts, and Useless Tidbits

- The religion Sikhism began as a reaction against India's caste system and attempted to fuse the best of Islam and Hinduism.

- Mother Teresa did not open her new order, the Missionaries of Charity, until she was 40 years old. Gandhi did not take on the fight for India's independence until he was in his 50's, proving the age-old adage it is never too late.

- In 2001 the literacy rate for Indian men was 76%, and 54% for women, a 14% improvement from 1991.

The Chicken That Flew The Coop

Amy's Diary Entry
April 21st , Agra, India

We were already on our way out of Agra without seeing the infamous Taj Mahal. We arrived here yesterday morning and had planned to leave tonight on a night train for Varanasi. Since the Taj was closed today, we had to see this temple of love yesterday, the day of our arrival. We got here nice and early and found a hotel to stay at. We were in the room for 30 minutes, and the smell of urine got stronger and stronger. We couldn't stand it. We called the front desk twice. Each time we were told that someone was on their way up to our room, but they never showed, so finally Traci went down to the desk and told them we were either leaving or getting a new room. Finally they moved us to a different room, but tried to tell us we had to pay a cleaning fee for the first room. Traci eventually got that straightened out. Within an hour my stomach started to gurgle and hurt, and I felt horrible. I was soon running a fever and spending a lot of time in the bathroom. Good thing it was an American toilet. So far this trip I had been lucky, eating pretty much anything and everything while Traci was nervous about putting anything foreign or fleshy in her mouth. I ordered meat dishes that came with great sauces and she would sit there with her tofu, vegetables, and rice and want to take all my sauce because her meal tasted like crap. Not only was Traci playing nurse and feeding me, she hired a couple hotel attendants to come up to our room and check on me; one of them was rubbing my head, the other, my back. I knew the three of them meant well, but I just wanted to be left alone. After a couple of hours of wanting to die, I gave in and took one of my antibiotics and was feeling so much better by this morning. But I couldn't believe I missed the Taj Mahal! I just wasn't well enough to leave the room yesterday. Traci did manage to refrain from saying "I told you so!", even though I knew it took considerable effort. I finally convinced Traci to leave the hotel and go the Taj Mahal but because the admission price was 1,000 rupees instead of the posted 960 rupees or $21.00 for foreigners, she refused to pay the difference, so she didn't get to see it either. Instead she took as many pictures of the outside as she could find. Now we're off to Varanasi and the Ganges River.

When we got on this train it took both Traci and I to hoist our backpacks onto the luggage rack above our seats. I was still feeling a little weak and even with both of us lifting we still struggled. There were numerous men sitting and standing on the train and do you think that one of them offered to help us? Nope, they just watched. We could not believe that not one man even offered to help us lift and guide the backpack to

Sleeper Coach Train

Our Berth

Our Train Toilet

safety. We had been feeling like we were the Indian passengers' tourist show ever since getting on this train. Our sleeping berths were at the end of the train, so instead of having 2 other people across from us, our berths faced a wall which we considered a bonus. For awhile it seemed like every person that walked past our compartment would stop and just look at us for 10 seconds like we were so strange. Ten seconds may not seem very long, but when someone was staring intently at you it felt like an eternity. We were tired of being the weird side show, so we pulled our curtain closed to enclose our berth and then used string to eliminate the narrow openings that remained at the curtain ends. An Indian passenger still had the audacity to open our curtain and look into our berth. After a few seconds Traci shouted, "Out!" They finally moved along, and no one else has intruded on our privacy since. It didn't leave us with a really good feeling. We've heard so many horror stories about train travel in India that we were going to sleep with our backpacks in our bunks. Who knew what they would do while we were sleeping?

Discoveries, Fun Facts, and Useless Tidbits

- The average annual income in India is $360.00.

- Half of India's children are undernourished.

- India's film industry is the largest in the world, larger than Hollywood, and has earned the nickname "Bollywood." Censorship is rigid and only recently has kissing appeared on the big screen, but established actresses still refuse to be kissed on screen.

- By 2010 India is projected to have a population of 31 million HIV positive people.

Things That Make You Go "Hmmm" Inside of Heaven's Door

Traci's Diary Entry
April 22nd, Varanasi, India

This city is like nothing I've ever seen or could imagine. Our hotel here is pretty nice, but we lose electricity frequently throughout the day. We hire Flower, a rickshaw driver, for 20 rupees an hour or 43 cents American, which is a much nicer ride than the lumber-delivery taxi that tried to pick us up. He stops whenever we tell him to. Our big purchase so far has been 4 cucumbers, 3 tomatoes, 2 limes, and cilantro, a fresh salad for 65 cents. Flower drops us off about 2 blocks from the Ganges River and points the way, and what a way it is! There are no words to describe the throngs of animals and people and vendors that are everywhere, both as we are walking down the lane to the Ganges and at the temples along the riverbank. Once we are in the temple grounds and along the river's edge there are monkeys everywhere and various shamans or what-ever they're called, in various states of meditation

Ganges River

or drug-induced hypnosis. We are not supposed to take pictures, but we try to nonchalantly snap a few photos without looking in the viewfinder to see what we are actually getting.

Varanasi or "Heaven's Door" is considered one of the holiest places in India, and if a person dies here, moksha (release) is granted. People travel thousands of miles in order to die in Varanasi. The Ganges River runs through Varanasi, and bathing in its river before you die will wash away all of one's sins. They say that 60,000 people bathe in a 4 mile stretch of the Ganges River each and every day. Ghats (wide descending steps) line the banks of the river and are used as an entry point for cremation or bathing.

Cremation along the banks of the Ganges River is for the privileged only as it can cost between $43.00 - $430.00 depending on the type of wood used for the cremation. Banyan wood is the most expen-

Ganges River, Varanasi

sive. If a family cannot afford cremation another alternative is to place a large boulder on top of the body and submerge the body in the middle of the river. We watch as several bodies are carried on the shoulders of untouchables to the banks of the river, where the body is placed so the feet of the deceased rest in the water. While the feet are cleansed by the river, the body is clothed in white but the shaved head and face remain uncovered. People then sprinkle the holy river water on the deceased's head from their cupped hands. After a certain amount of time the body is placed on a funeral pyre or bed of sticks to be cremated. Each family member lays a flower and a piece of wood on top of the body. One of the family members walks around the body a prescribed number of times and then places a burning piece of wood on the bed of sticks that are under the body. Additional sticks are added to the fire by each person. Within minutes the body is completely engulfed in flames and will continue to burn for 3 or 4 hours. Since we are only 10 feet away from one particular cremation, ashes from the pyre fall on our shoulders within minutes of the fire being started. At one point a son of this deceased woman approaches us and invites us to join the family on the elevated platform surrounding the burning body, but we politely decline. He tells us his mother had been 80 years old and had lived a long life, thus there are no tears at this final farewell. At least 180 cremations occur each day on the banks of the Ganges River. It was an unbelievable sight to see.

We hire Flower, our rickshaw driver, for another day and have him take us to a bunch of different temples and sights that the Lonely Planet guidebook recommends. We are kind of disappointed at the sights, but how can anything compare to the sights at the Ganges River? We have beggars coming up to us constantly it seems. Flower has pulled up in front of stores that we don't ask him to stop at and encourages us to shop, so he probably gets a commission if we do buy something, but we're pretty much shopped out. Then he tells us that he must rent this rickshaw for 70 rupees each day, so even though he drives it all day, he doesn't make much money to support his wife, mother, and sister. He wants us to buy him a new rickshaw for a mere 7,000 rupees, and then he will work for us. Sounds like a pretty good deal, would love to help the guy out... but my experience with the people in this country thus far makes it very difficult for me to trust him and Amy seconds the notion. We spend the rest of the afternoon driving through different areas.

See The Busy Streets Of Varanasi
http://j.mp/l1rLkC

Discoveries, Fun Facts, and Useless Tidbits

- The advertisements before the main feature in a movie theatre are played twice in a row consecutively. They also show hand-written warnings about pick-pockets in the theatre and advise everyone there is to be 'No Spitting' in the theatre. You select your seat when purchasing your ticket and the cost of the ticket is determined by this. Balcony seats are the most expensive at $2.50. There is a 10 minute intermission mid-way through the movie, and the national anthem is played before the start of the movie.

- McDonalds has no beef products here as cows are sacred animals and are not meant to be eaten. Instead of ordering a hamburger, you order a lamb-burger.

- India is the world's largest producer of milk, tea, bananas, mangoes, coconuts, cashews, potatoes, tomatoes, onions and green peas. Less than 1% of the raw commodities produced in India is processed, and the import of processed food is severely restricted.

- An estimated 72% percent of sex workers are HIV positive and each sees an average of 50 clients per day.

Needless to say India has been a unique experience, vastly different from any country we have visited, and we have only been in 3 cities so far. Stuff happens every day that causes us to sit back and laugh, but we also seem to be quicker to anger than we were when we started this trip. Even though we have only been here a few weeks, India has been more corrupt than any other country we have visited. We are both very glad that this was not the first country on our itinerary as it is easy to see how it would be overwhelming for a novice traveler.

Liquor is heavily taxed in India. An additional 12% tax is placed on each liquor purchase when ordered at a restaurant, as well as a 15% state tax on the entire bill, and a 12% service tax for having it served.

Happy Birthday to Me
Amy's Diary Entry
April, 24th, Kolkata (Calcutta), India

Well Happy Birthday to me! Five years ago I never would have thought I'd be celebrating my birthday in Calcutta, India. Traci found a chocolate birthday cake for me. It tasted terrible, so after we each had part of a piece we took it out to the street and gave it away to a little beggar girl who was carrying around one of her littler siblings. She was thrilled with it.

Amy's Gross Pawned Off B-Day Cake

Our first taxi that we hired in Calcutta to take us from the train station to our hotel looked like it was from the 1950s. There were gauges and dials that I hadn't seen since I was a little girl. We had him take us to a hostel that was listed in the Lonely Planet guidebook, but it was disgusting so we left. We found another place that initially told us they had no rooms, but when Traci pulled out her bogus travel reporter credentials, a room suddenly became available. We got to our room and there weren't any towels, so we called the front desk and asked them to bring some to our room. Well we made the mistake of tipping the hotel delivery boy so that night a guy would show up at our door every half hour with wilted flowers, a pitcher of ice water, more towels, a fruit basket, and even a second television. They would hand us the delivery and then stand there and wait for the tip. One delivery guy knocked on our door with empty hands and said "My shift is over now" and then just stood there.

This 3.5 Star Hotel Would Never Pass American Standards
http://j.mp/k5agPY

There had to be more homeless people in one block in Calcutta than any city shelter in the United States. Every evening when the stores pulled down their metal garage-type doors at closing time, the destitute pulled out their mats if they had one, and found their make-shift beds for the night. Every several feet there would be another person and at times entire families lying on the ground. In other parts of the city the sidewalk had been overtaken by entire neighborhoods that lived in plastic and cardboard homes. Naked children of all ages wandered in the streets, playing in the dirt and with plastic binding straps, empty plastic water bottles, or pieces of cardboard that served as their toys. Piles of garbage were everywhere. People lathered their bodies with soap while standing in the street and used public water spickets to rinse off.

Bathing In The Streets

There Seems To Be More Homeless People In One Block In Calcutta Than Any City Shelter In The United States.
http://j.mp/kqpcxj

👣 Amy Continued
April 26th

We were going to leave tomorrow but then ran into someone who has been volunteering at one of Mother Teresa's orphanages so we decided to join her. This home, of course, was in a very poor neighborhood that we walked to. We were told to remove our shoes before walking in as they did not want us to track in any disease or dirt with our dusty shoes. There were about 12 children at this facility, most

under the age of 7 and too disabled to even sit up by themselves. We
helped bathe and dress them, fed them breakfast, and then tried to play

Mother Teresa Orphanage Sign

with them or at least
keep them entertained.
There were very few
toys for them to play
with or for us to use to
play with them, but
there were what
appeared to be brand
new modern wheel-
chairs sitting unused in a hallway. It looked as if these children had not
been stimulated or given love for a very long time. The permanent
workers lived in the charities for free as long as they continued to care
for the children, but honestly they did not seem too interested in the
kids or overly kind to them. I questioned their genuine interest in this
charity and suspected they were there for the housing and meals that it

Mother Teresa Entombed

provided. Who could
blame them? What
would I do for a roof
over my head and clean
water if my only other
alternative was a wicker
mat on the sidewalk?
It was a very long and
depressing 3 hours, and
I will admit I was anxious to leave. Any intention we had of spending
a month at this charity quickly vanished.

We were told before coming to India that we would have to become quite rude in order not to be cheated every time we turned around, but of course, we didn't believe that it was really that bad. Little did we realize how rude we would become. Arguments with rickshaw drivers occurred on a daily basis as the drivers always tried to change their price once we got to our stop, from the price that they had agreed on before we even climbed into their rickshaw. We no longer wasted our time arguing with them but instead placed the fare that had been agreed upon by both parties on the ground in front of them and walked away, ignoring their demands for more rupees. We did not place the money on the ground to demean them, but they refused to take the money from us in an attempt to keep us there arguing with them longer. We no longer played their game. When my butt was grabbed at the train station the other day, I turned around and punched the guy standing behind me in the chest. He was quite surprised but then pointed to his friend who was standing next to him so I punched him too. If we were leered at for too long, we thought nothing of trying to embarrass them by shouting "What do you want?? What are you staring at?? Go away!" No longer did we stay silent if someone tried to move in front of us while we were standing in some line but loudly told them to move to the back, physically forcing ourselves in front of them if necessary. We were not proud of our behavior by any means, but found it necessary in this country that seemed to have no respect for women. I could not imagine having to live here amidst the dirt, the heat, the lying, and the disrespect. It was so sad, and I didn't know how long I could do this. We have been told that Africa is even worse. I was becoming more and more cynical every day and I did not like it. I had enough cynicism already and did not need any more. I was physically and mentally tired and ready to go home.

But first I was going to stop in Hawaii and have plastic surgery to refresh my aging reflection.

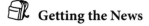 **Getting the News**
Traci's Diary Entry
May 1st, Jaiper, India

Amy just told me that she is going home and she has asked me to go with her as she has doubts that I can make it around the world by myself. I throw the covers over my head and cry. I KNEW she would do this! She's only ever been good for half of her word or the commitments she makes. The minute something gets too uncomfortable or challenging for her, she quits and moves on to the next thing. After wallowing in pity and sadness for nearly an hour, I begin recollecting all the things she has burned me with through the years… I realize that going over my mental tally sheet of her wrong doings is only making me angrier and only cementing the swaying thoughts in my head that my "Best Friend" is not a true friend. I'm not ready to go back to my $1,500 a month cocoon yet, and I haven't found the answers to my life's questions. I am staying and completing this trip, just like I had when she left me in Hawaii at month 5 of our 12 month signed and notarized contract… that she insisted upon. That decision changed the course of my life, and so will this one. She thinks I'm an idiot and won't be able to sustain or survive without her. Boy will she be surprised. My anger in knowing she feels that way just fuels my desires and affirms my conviction to prove her wrong and complete the commitment I made to myself to discover my life's purpose and meaning. Yes, my style is to figure it out as I go, and I will figure it out. I always figure it out. The issue here is not in me not knowing how to pick a place to visit, sleep, or eat at. The truth is, it has just been easier to let her steer and have things her way. I have never been bothered by going with her flow, but she mistakes my passiveness for laziness and stupidity. That bothers me. I am not lazy, and I am not stupid. What can I say? I am easy-going and smart enough to know that you cannot have two drivers and she is a bossy passenger, so she might as well be the driver! I have more perseverance, drive, and compassion than she ever will. It is a wonder why I am still her friend. I am fiercely loyal.

I tell her that it will be easier for me to part ways now, when I am feeling strong and ready to take on the world alone. As much as it hurts, I think I will grow immeasurably and find all the answers to my life's questions on my own road at my own pace. Tears are streaming down my cheek as I write this entry, but I am ready. I've come here to find my place in the world and I'll be damned if I return home without doing so. We haven't talked about her departure again, but its presence is not only evident, it's imminent.

🐾 The Conversation
Amy's Diary Entry
May 1st, Jaiper, India

I told her in the gentlest way possible that I did not want to go to Africa and barely wanted to see much more of India but that I would finish out India and wanted to leave after that. I just couldn't do much more of this. India had done its best to wear me down. I was drained of energy and had been traveling for a year and 4 months. The thought

of traveling for just one more month exhausted me, much less traveling for 6 more months. Except for Babu it seemed like every Indian
we encountered was either lying to us or trying to cheat us. Even at an
internet café they tried to charge us 40 rupee/hour when the sign outside the door was clearly marked 15 rupee/hour. When we confronted
them with this blatant discrepancy, they just shrugged their shoulders
and acted as if it is no big deal that they had just tried to steal from
us. Like Babu said to us once, "It is the Indian way." I was tired of the
Indian way and was becoming cynical and scornful of every person
I met in this country. I was starting to believe in their karma; it may
explain the unending cycle of poverty for some of its residents. I did
not want to leave my travels disliking every person and disliking this
country. I could justify it financially because I had my plastic surgery
bills from Hawaii that I wanted to pay for before I went back to Wisconsin, and the e-mail from the doctor's office estimated it was going
to be $20,000. I would already have to put that on a credit card because
when I got home I wouldn't have a car, place to live, or a job. I wanted
to give my parents a trip for their 50th wedding anniversary, and that
was only 3 or 4 months after I got back. If I continued through Africa
I would literally have only one or two thousand dollars to my name
when I got back but if I left early I would be able to pay a third of my
surgery in cash and return with three or four thousand dollars.
At least it would be something. She took it pretty well actually, just
threw a sheet over her head and started to cry. For Traci that was pretty
good. I asked her to come back with me, and we could do Africa in a
year or two, but she just shook her head in the negative. She said that
if I was going to leave, she did not even want to finish India with me
but wanted to split up before she entered her yoga retreat for a month.
I did feel bad. I was afraid for her because now she would have to do all

the planning by herself and she hasn't had to do much of it until now. I forced her to come up with a plan on a couple of days and made her figure out where we were going and how we were going to get there and tried to make her read a map. That was pretty funny actually. That was part of the reason I hadn't left already. I didn't think she could do it on her own. We didn't set any dates, and I didn't even have a timeline yet, but at least it was out there in the open.

🐾 An Honest Man in Jaipur?

Amy's Diary Entry
May 3rd, Jaiper, India

We were on our way to Jaipur on a train when we met Venay, and we were quite rude to him at first since we thought he was just another guy who wanted something from us. He was very persistent despite our initial disdain of him, and he persisted in his attempts at winning us over. Boy were we lucky that he did. We shared with him some of our negative experiences, and he then believed it was his responsibility and God's will that he show us a better side of India. We were skepti-

Venay (R) Takes Us On A Private Tour Of Raj Palace

cal of his new found belief but agreed to accompany him to a hotel that he felt was adequate for us. He ended up taking us to a brand new

5 star hotel complete with a clean, plush bed, a bathroom with marble countertops, large thick towels, a large window that overlooked the

Luxury Lunch Compliments Of Venay At Raj Palace

street, a swimming pool, fitness center, and a buffet breakfast every morning. He paid for our first night's stay, bought us dinner and drinks several times, and bargained our room rate down to less than half of the original price of 1,700 rupees or $30.00/night. The room was a slice of heaven, and we wanted to stay in Jaipur just so we could stay living in the lap of luxury. We kept waiting for some sort of demand/expectation to appear, but it never did. During one dinner conversation Venay made no secret

about his belief that there was nothing wrong with having sex outside of his marriage as long as he didn't hurt his family and fulfilled his family responsibilities. If something like that happened he felt it was

Hawa Mahal Palace – Built In 1799

part of his karma and God's will. Venay was a true gentleman and since he was in the hotel business, he left us with several contacts in other cities, as well as our promise to visit him and his wife when we were in Mumbai. Maybe there was an honest person in India after all. We didn't even care that we stuck out like sore thumbs in this 5 star hotel. Traci was wearing a sarong and a dew rag on her head, working on the computer in the business center when a man walked in and said, "Excuse me, can you direct me to the conference room?" She told him that she just arrived and did not know where the conference room was. The man replied, "Oh, gosh, I am sorry, I thought you were the maid."

After leaving the train in Jaipur there was an old woman with grey hair that was just lying on the train platform. Throngs of people would just step over her or step around her. I am embarrassed to say we did the same. We saw something similar in Calcutta as the taxi was taking us to the train station. There was another old woman who was lying in the road, alongside the curb of the road. She was just lying there, lifeless, and cars were flying by her, either not noticing she was there or not caring she was there. It was incredible.

We hired a rickshaw driver to take us around the area and sightsee. The poverty was staggering and wearing.

The Poverty On The Streets Of Jaipur Is Staggering And The Sights You See On The Streets, Unbelievable.
http://j.mp/kwWV5O

🐾 All Aboard The Red Sand Express

Amy's Diary Entry
May 6th, Jaiper, India

That was the most horrible train ride in all of our travels, and we had had some bad ones. We were in the 2nd class cars, but I couldn't imagine it could have been much worse in the 3rd class, but maybe we wouldn't have even had a seat to sit in if we were in 3rd class. There was no air-conditioning in the train, so the windows had to remain open to allow any air into the train car. Hot air was better than no air at all. We were now officially in the desert, and it was scorching hot, dry, and sandy. I didn't think it could get any hotter than New Delhi or Calcutta but it had and I hate hot weather like this. We woke up before we reached Jaisalmer, and neither one of us had slept very well. Rich, red sand covered our seats, our possessions, and us. We literally could write our names in the sand that had been deposited on the seats. Grains of sands rolled around our tongues and between our teeth.

Public Bathroom

I hadn't felt this dirty since I was a 15 year old girl and had spent all day out in the fields picking cucumbers for 8 hours. Again we looked at each other and laughed because we were just covered in sand. I thought after looking at her that she had to be dirtier than me, and she thought I had to be dirtier than her. Once again our hotel was grand and an escape from this oppressing heat. Traci's phony travel journalist card worked wonders at opening up another room that was otherwise "sold-out" and though I thought it was somewhat of a scam I did enjoy what it had brought us along the way. I'm sure it had prevented us being scammed more than we already were. This was still one country I will never return to.

The Red Sand Express. Amy & Traci Endure Sand-Burn on our 12 Hour Train Ride.
http://j.mp/kKUZtQ

The Camel Safari

Traci's Diary Entry
May 14th, Jaisalmer, India

We are somewhere in the middle of the desert. I'm sitting on our sleeping mat a little after 6 AM, the sun and I are the only two awake as she is already soaking the giant red dunes around me. By ten, we will each be ringing wet with sweat. Last night we joined up with other camel safari groups, making a little co-op of about 15 people. The thing I've noticed about backpackers is that when they meet up with

Sleeping On Top Of A Sand Dune

each other, they all try to outdo each other with their travel stories, how long they've been traveling, or how many countries they've been to. Maybe that's the difference between a traveler in their 20's and a traveler in their 30's, like Amy and me. We both feel too old for this. We all sleep on these thin but soft mats that keep us about 4 inches from the sand. All over the sand around us are thousands of footprints of sand beetles. Obviously they cannot climb, and I'm so glad I did not know they were scurrying around us all night long. It is very cool to sleep under a blanket of stars that seem close enough to reach out and touch, and it finally cooled off enough to make sleep possible, but the distant hum of highway noises did take away a little of the magic. The safari hasn't started out too promising. We are promised our own camels but yesterday when we get dropped off and the guides are

loading our camels, we notice that we are a camel short. We ask about this and are told that we will pick up a camel at the next town once the safari has started. No way are we falling for this little scheme; we didn't arrive in India yesterday. We flat out refuse to go until we each have a camel now, not in the next town. At first the guides tell us it is "impossible" to find another camel, so we continue to sit patiently on the ground. We don't yell or get angry; we just sit there and talk to each other and to Ben, our new friend from the train. When they see we are serious about staying put and catch a glimpse of my fake travel journalist card, another tan-faded under-nourished looking camel miraculously appears, forming a scrawny set.

Soon we all lurch off on our camels. Amy names her camel Mabel and I name mine Sahara Jack, after my favorite band from my high school. Getting on a camel for the first time is awkward because there is no

saddle, no stirrups, and nothing to hold onto but a thin rope that loops through their noses. Camels are surprisingly tall, much taller than a horse, and when they maneuver from their kneeling

Amy & Mabel

position to standing, they get up butt-first, and we feel like we are going to fall off, head-first. We watch each other laughing as we clumsily jar back, fall forward, and lurch in sync with our camels as they rock their way to their feet. It is a bit disorienting to be perched so high from the ground and we are already in a sweat, just from boarding our camels.

I don't know what I was expecting from a camel ride through the desert, but there is little to see except mile after mile of sand and an occasional tree. We have to keep covered at all times because, of

course, we're in the desert and it is searing hot. I now understand how people can go crazy in the desert and start to hallucinate. Riding a camel is not a smooth ride but not quite as jarring as the

Desert Villagers

elephant ride in Thailand. After 3 hours I begin to look forward to the end of the day. We are told before the safari starts that we are going to be riding through local villages. Notice the plural of the word village.

Late in the day we finally come to a village with obnoxious kids surrounding us and begging us for money. Have I written lately how tired I am of this country? We've only been here for 5 weeks and it feels

Local Children

like 5 months! After about 6 hours of riding through the desert, we join up with the other groups and bed down for the night. Today Amy makes the decision to hitch a ride into town and skip the 2nd day of the blistering heat. Ben and I press on, but after 6 hours, we too leave the safari early and head back to our cool rooms as no doubt, heat stroke was just a ray away.

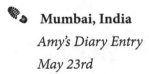

3 Day Camel Safari
Through The Desert
http://j.mp/mTgjM5

🐾 **Mumbai, India**
Amy's Diary Entry
May 23rd

    I was expecting a little more out of Mumbai, especially since Venay told us it was the New York of India. Our bus from Ahmedadad dropped us off along the side of some freeway, and we had to find our own way to the Colaba Causeway, but we were no longer surprised by this. We were still surprised that the bus driver wanted to charge us for putting our backpacks in the storage area under the bus, yet not one Indian person was asked for this storage fee for their

Streets of Mumbai

luggage. We just shook our heads no and put our backpacks in the storage area ourselves when they wouldn't take them from us. Traci stood outside to make sure they weren't taken off or rummaged through and didn't get on the bus until the storage doors were closed. I don't know why we were still surprised at this, but we were. Mumbai offered the same as the other cities in India (poverty, dirt, and the pervasive smell of urine) except it was more expensive. We were

accosted by beggars as soon as we arrived, beggars that ignored every single passing local. A little girl with two fully formed arms saw us walking down the street and quickly withdrew one of her arms to the inside of her dress and then

Child Wears Make-up To Ward Off Evil Spirits

pointed at the empty sleeve and put her upturned hand out to us. I was sure that she was poor and had a horrible life, but it was getting harder and harder for me to see that part of people's lives. All I saw now was the incessant begging and lying. I wish everybody in our country could see true poverty. Mumbai had beautiful architecture, and I was sure it offered much more than I was giving it credit for but really I just didn't want to see anymore. I wanted to go home to a place of my own with a clean bathroom and a bed that didn't leave me covered in bites when I woke up in the morning. I wanted to put on clean underwear and clothes every day and to look like I had just showered that morning. I wanted to drink the water out of the faucet and do something productive with my day. I wanted to stay in one place for more than 3 or 4 days. I wanted to see my family again. I was leaving for Hawaii in only a few days for my facial surgery; Traci is leaving tomorrow to catch a train to the south of India. Our impending separation had been in the background for several days now, making conversation strained. Although neither one of us brought it up, it was always lingering in the background. I couldn't wait to get back to the States, but dreaded that good-bye. Traci drove me insane some days and I was so looking

Sidewalk Shave

forward to not being attached at the hip 24/7 but we had been traveling together for a long time, and it would be hard to actually say good-bye and leave. I knew I would miss my best friend. I cried right now, thinking about it. She was so emotional that I hoped it would not be as bad as I thought it would be. I hoped she would be okay. She seemed to have the rest of India figured out and hopefully the time at the yoga retreat would give her time to get Africa figured out and from there she could get Europe figured out. It was time for me to go home where people smiled without a malicious reason for doing so, where they didn't barrage you with lies upon meeting, where I was not charged a higher price for food, for the internet, or for a bus ride because I was a Westerner, where I could drink the water and eat the food safely. Yes, I had seen the world and found my adventure,. I would return home with a whole new appreciation for my America. I hoped that Traci would find what she was looking for too.

The Impoverished Streets Of Mumbai
http://j.mp/kkhpW8

A Letter to Traci

Dear Traci-

I start this letter to you as we discuss our imminent parting in one, two, at best three weeks. I know you believe that this will be easy for me, but you are wrong. Although it may be harder for you, it will also be difficult for me. I will miss you, probably within the first several minutes of saying good-bye, but for sure the next time I see something amusing or strange, and you won't be there to share it with me. Or maybe it will be when I'm trying to find my seat on the train, and I will look back to see if you're behind me, and you won't be. Or maybe it will be when I wake up in the morning and I'm hungry, and you won't be there to make oatmeal for us, or when I forget something on the train, like my insulin kit, and I have no one to blame but myself. I will miss you many times during the day and night, don't doubt it for a minute.

It has been a GREAT 18 months, and there is no one else in the world that I could have done this with but you, and thank the Lord above for giving us this time and awesome experience. We are only a handful in the world who have taken this on and are still friends at the end. I would not trade this time for anything, so thank you for sharing this part of your life with me.

When or if you are ever feeling low, pull this out and re-read it. What I love about Traci: I love your optimism about being able to change the world and hopefully spending time in India hasn't dampened that forever. I love your ability to feel so deeply for others, your empathy for other's plights in life, and the loyalty you have and the love you feel for others, especially me. I appreciate how hard that can be at times. I love your ability to make others feel good about themselves by pointing out their strong points instead of their weak points and your creative thinking that never ceases. I love your excitement and enthusiasm about life, and your gentleness in spirit. But most of all I love that you can still love me throughout the trying times that we have put each other through throughout our decades of friendship.

As you continue on alone, I have no doubt that you will be absolutely fine. You do have the strength, smarts, and ability to get you through the next four or five months and then home to your family who adore you. Remember you can do anything you want to if you truly want to. This is not the end of anything but instead the start of something new. You will shine at your retreat as you will shine in Africa. I have no doubt of that. Remember, what you put out returns. Unfortunately that includes the good and the bad, so destroy that phony traveling journalist card.

There is no reason to be too sad. You are continuing on with your dream – not many people get to say that. I am continuing on to receive a new face, not many can say that either. Except you – you get to say both! Ha! Ha!

Go in peace and happiness, and rest your soul. Nothing will happen that you cannot handle. God has gotten you this far right?

I will see you in a few short months. I love you, Traci Renee.

Your Forever Friend –
Amy Oberstadt

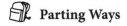 **Parting Ways**

Traci's Diary Entry
May 25th, Mumbai, India

I watch the clock turn for hours as long periods of night settle, and the alarm goes off for the very last time of our journey together. My brain is numb with fatigue, and my heart quivers with conflicting emotion. Silence fills the room. It is another day of departure, only this time we are departing from each other. She lays awake on her bed, and I lay awake on mine, separated by an old scuffed up nightstand, but there is so much more between us than that. Finally, we both sit up and stare at each other in silent sadness. She is the first to break the awkward noise by offering to cook me oatmeal while I shower so I will have a fully belly before catching my plane from Mumbai to Coimbatore for my spiritual retreat. It is time to say goodbye. We embrace and we cry.

I am off to a sluggish start to meet my world unknown, 40 days at an Ayurveda Retreat. The bickering banter hasn't been so bad, it was just us. I'd do it again, and there is no one else that I would or even could do it with than Amy. It's our differences that balance us out and make our friendship strong. I wouldn't have embarked on this trip without her, and it is hard to go on, but go on I will, for go on I must. I am much stronger and more capable than she knows and gives me credit for.

For Amy

True friend, you are
As the sparkle to the sea
Baring flamboyancy
Like the merging starkey ripples
Reflecting tomorrow's trusting rays
Of today's moons in the sky.
Warmed by the beautiful sun,
Your face, your heart
Inborn to enrich countless lives
With existence alone
One day, someday, we will grow up
Too soon, but not apart
Our hearts bonded with friendship and trust
Sticking together
In the times of life
Side by side
A true friend
A best friend
Though oceans away and sunsets too
Sisterly love will sail
Sail agelessly, through the silent trials of life
On and on, ahead toward the heavens and stars
To lengths still only imagined
On through dark nights, cold winters, and troubled times
In to the warm weathers of our hearts,
Yours and mine
True friends, like true love, sisterly love will

Live in our hearts...forever

Thank you for being the best friend I ever had
I will miss you more than any words can express
You are the first true liberator of my life
The first person to truly validate me
And teach me the great lessons of life
The keeper of my darkest secrets, greatest triumphs, & deepest
pains
My sister, my council, my co-explorer
The one I rely on to seek comfort & hard truth
I will miss you dearly, sorely, always...

From my heart to yours, with love,
Traci Renee Robbins Bogan

The Not So Spiritual Retreat

Traci's Diary Entry
May 26th, Coonor, India

The 8 AM ride to the airport is quiet and lonely. After a year and a half of adventuring the world together, I feel like half of me is missing. I don't even notice the chaos of India this morning or how long it takes the beat-up, old, yellow taxi to haul me to the airport because I am lost in the chaos of my own head. The weather is a perfect match to my mood this morning, grey and drizzly. I have a big lump in my throat and feel like crying. I have to force myself to put one foot in front of the other and move. I know the second half of this sojourn is going to be much different than the first half and probably a lot lonelier. I'm scared, but I am ready. Airborne two hours later, on a two hour flight, I look down to catch a final glimpse. Amy is lost in the sea of the lawless metropolis. Goodbye my friend.

And so it begins, I set off to find my peace and my place in India, in myself, and in the world, 6,000 feet above India in the beautiful, mystical, and tranquil Nilgiri Hills, more ancient than the Himalayas and more spiritual than the holiest cathedral. From Coimbatore I somehow, by the grace of God, survive the white-knuckle two-hour cab ride to Coonoor. Most of the driving is spent with my hands covering my eyes as the driver weaves and swerves through chaotic horn-blowing traffic, narrowly missing, cars, rickshaws, unattended children, and monkeys, thinking he possesses ownership of the road. The one-lane hairpin curves are usually taken on two wheels. My hands ache from clutching the door handle next to me and the headrest in front of me. It seems that only inches separate our cab from the sheer unguarded cliffs. We are fortunate to have had only two near miss head-on collisions, one with a car and another with a bus. Not only have I been terrified the entire ride, I am nauseous and throwing up in a bag. It is hard to believe that this enigmatic road leads to the doorstep of a tranquil "spiritual" retreat, where I am somehow expected to relax.

Finally, six hours later, with barf bag in tow, I arrive at the promising Ayurveda Retreat. I have looked it up online and it costs 47,000 rupees or $1,000 USD for 40 days. In a country where a Westerner can live like a maharajah on less than $20 a day, the price tag to attend this spiritual retreat seems exorbitant, but hopefully it will be worth it. The compound is encircled by a footpath, with benches, pavilions, and alcoves that invite me to stop and admire the blazing colors of wild flowers and take a second look at the odd looking insects that are grazing on them. It is sunny here and surprisingly warm, I'm guessing 80 degrees. I was thinking it would be much cooler and shadier, due to the elevation. Several cottages are strewn around the grounds sandwiched between floral beds and loamy soil gardens. I stroll past wild peacocks and monkeys and make my way to the reception villa. Such modesty seems appropriate for a place specifically set aside for tranquility and meditation.

Excitement and anticipation finally replace my grey and drizzly mood and the motion sickness nausea as I toss the double-knotted two pound barf bag into the trash bin, just in the nick of time before the receptionist rounds the curtain and welcomes me. I check-in with a smile, turn over my passport, and pay the required advance for my 40 day stay, and they hand over my room key. The room is basic, though much cleaner than some of the hostels and hotels that Amy and I have stayed at. It contains a small table, a dresser, and a bed with mismatched bedding, a rock hard mattress, and a paper-thin pillow. There is no architecture to applaud, no gadgetry to maneuver, no home interior to ogle, just simple wooden floors, dingy white walls, and a shower with no hot water. After I get settled in, I roam the beautiful green and floral grounds, breathe in the fresh mountain air, and admire the gorgeous backdrop of India, 6,000 feet below. I already feel tranquil. I stumble upon a wrought iron picnic area in the garden, grab a seat, and review the menu of services. The list is a little thinner than I am expecting and some of the services they have promised me in our email conversations are not listed on the menu, such as unlimited daily yoga, Indian cooking and gardening, and myofascial tissue release therapy. Oh well, maybe it's an added or an off menu service. There aren't very many people here, maybe seven or eight, and they all appear to be European or American. We all smile and say hello, but none of us go out of our way to make any real conversation with one another. But that's okay, I'm not here to socialize. I'm here to "find myself" and my purpose on this earth, and maybe they are too. We all seem to be in our own little worlds. The yoga bell is ringing across the way. I'm dizzy with excitement and off I go.

What most Americans think of as "yoga," is a style of basic body poses and movements called Hatha Yoga, one of many related but distinct spiritual disciplines of the Hindu and Buddhist origin, collectively called yoga. While the familiar Hatha Yoga emphasizes stress-reduction, flexibility, and health, the goal of Kriya Yoga is self-realization, a "direct personal experience of God" achieved through specific breath and meditative techniques and practices and lifestyle disciplines. Paramahansa Yogananda (1893-1952) is an Indian-born yogi, a master and teacher of Kriya Yoga. He adapted and expanded the discipline of Kriya Yoga into a "complete philosophy and way of life," and established the Self-Realization Fellowship to disseminate it, which is what this retreat claims to be. This is what I have come here for.

Okay, this isn't what I have come for. There is no Kriya Yoga here. It is just the same watered down version we do back home. The only difference is there are no designer props and accessories, fashionable over-priced and under-sized outfits, name brand supplemental and nutritional products, and Hollywood style yoga studios where pricey monthly memberships can run as much as a car payment. After the 90 minute class, I ask the yoga teacher when we are going to start Kriya

Yoga, and he looks at me with a puzzled look on his face. He enlightens me to the fact that they do not offer Kriya Yoga here because many of the visitors are Western. They teach Hatha Yoga, so visitors can easily adapt and pick up where they left off back home.

STRIKE ONE

"Okay, what time is the next yoga class?" I ask.

"It is always late afternoon, around 1500 hours or 3:00 PM"
he says.

"You mean there is only one 90 minute class per day? I was told you offer unlimited daily yoga," I snap.

"It is unlimited in the fact that you can take the same class everyday while you are here," he calmly replies.

"Well, what else is there to do here the rest of the time? There seems to be no structure or daily schedule to follow," I ask.

"That is correct. You choose to do whatever you want here. It is like a vacation," he smiles and says in the most peaceful and loving tone.

"I'm not here for a frigging vacation. I'm here to find myself and find my purpose in the world, and I thought you were going to help me," my voice escalates.

STRIKE TWO

I storm off to the front desk and file my grievance with the owners of the retreat and quickly discover that many of the services they have promised me on their glorified website and in our email exchanges don't even exist. They promise me an "all-inclusive" stay, including transportation to and from the retreat, unlimited daily yoga with mat, Kriya yoga, myofascial tissue release therapy in conjunction with Ayurveda oil massages, Indian cooking and organic gardening classes, and a full medical evaluation, diagnosis, and treatment plan for total body, mind, and spiritual transformation. At the end of the first day I receive from this "all-inclusive" retreat, a bill for 3,000 rupees or $45 USD for the two-hour white knuckle cab ride to their facility and another charge for 400 rupees or $6 USD for my internet usage, informing my parents of my arrival. I get one 90 minute yoga class per day on a burlap sheet. Authentic yoga mats are an extra charge and any additional yoga lessons will cost me 200 rupees or $3.00 USD per hour and appointments must be set a day in advance. I'm allotted a one hour Ayurveda oil massage per day and the masseuse has never heard of the myofascial tissue release therapy that I had specifically inquired about. The "full" medical evaluation consists of answering a plethora of in-depth questions about my personal history and past emotional traumas and then sitting in for a 5 minute consultation, with three different medical practitioners, who each give me three conflicting prognoses and three different treatment plans. The Indian cooking and organic gardening class is nothing more than an invitation to watch the non-English speaking cooks and gardeners perform their daily duties. This isn't the deal.

STRIKE THREE

After a sleepless night of soul-searching, I decide to move onto a more authentic ashram or spiritual retreat in the area, with a real "guru." When I go to checkout in the morning they refuse to refund my $1,000.00 USD payment, no paltry sum of money for this backpacker. We get into a hair-curling screaming match after I call them out on their blatant lies and drastically lacking services that in no way match the services agreed upon within our email contract and tell them I am going to report them to the police if they do not refund my money. They insist that the police are their friends and not only will they take their side, but I will have to pay them many bribes to get out of their country with no passport, as they threaten to conveniently "lose" mine. They besmirch me with slander and threaten to post my confidential medical history report, bearing the specifics about the childhood sexual abuse I endured from ages 5-14, all over the internet. Not even my phony travel journalist card will loosen their grip of harassment or change their mind. I am truly fearful of these people and their threats. I was scammed at a @#$%^&* spiritual retreat! I cannot think of anything more disgraceful! I am sick and tired of this. I have reached the boiling point of intolerance to their filth, pollution, lies, prejudice, and scams and am crawling to get out of this country and their pathetic way of living.

Security personnel are alerted and I am escorted off the premises and bundled with my backpacks into an awaiting rickshaw. They extract another 3,000 rupees from me for the ride and for the return of my passport. I ask the driver to take me to the nearest travel agency, so I can leave this shithole on the next flight out. He passes through two small dry and drab towns, driving 45 minutes to a dead end road in the middle of nowhere. I see the most beautiful sight in India, a lonesome travel agency cradled in the shadows of some old trees. I grab my bags and rush in, with a plea to leave on the next available flight despite the cost of the ticket change, but a woman explains that it is 2:00 PM and the agency had closed at noon. She is just there cleaning. She further informs me that the office will be closed for the holiday tomorrow and that if I want their services, I will have to come back in 2 days. Hanging my head low, I somberly walk outside and discover my rickshaw is gone. Nothing is working out for me here. Feeling abandoned, lost, and broken, in more ways than one, I stand in the middle of nowhere and cry. Finally, one foot moves forward, and then the other… now I walk and cry, lugging two heavy backpacks in an unknown direction to an unknown place, in the smoldering heat.

I walk and walk in the dry barren countryside until I notice a barely visible Taj Hotel and Yoga Center sign that is hidden by an overgrown brush. The sign says 5 miles ahead. I drag my tearful and spiritless body the whole way. "Where is everyone?" I wonder. Normally, people are loitering in every millimeter of the streets. Have I found the only section in India uninhabited by people? Exhausted, hungry, sweaty, and panting, I stumble in, collapsing in the nearest chair with my packs still on. Out from a red curtain steps a saintly, soft spoken man. He has a clean shaven look and is wearing a flowing white robe. There is a line of colored powder between his eyes. He grins, "Welcome my American friend. You are just in time for our four o'clock Kriya Yoga class, a deep dive into self-realization. Don't be late – you have a lot of work to do. We are beginning in nine minutes."

It is as if he has been expecting me. His presence touches me profoundly. His eyes reach me deeply. His energy fills my emptiness. "Who is this holiness?" I wonder, "This great seeing man." Just as quickly as he has arrived, he disappears behind the curtain. A moment later the front desk clerk emerges from behind me and says, "I can hold your bags if you would like to attend the yoga class that is starting in eight minutes." He helps me to my feet and peels my bag off of my sticky body. He takes in my discombobulated gaze and half cocked smile as a subtle yes. Still dazed, thinking about all that is happening and still feeling the presence of the white robed man, I just stare at the red curtain, still swaying from his departure, awaiting his return. "Miss, you shouldn't be late now, the head swami (spiritual teacher) is waiting for you." The hook-nosed Indian clerk motions his unoccupied hand in the direction of the little white yoga pavilion. Some magical force fills me with enough invisible strength to move me across the courtyard to the yoga center, a gem, secluded in the folds of a botanical garden. Something is just different about this place. I enter just in time to grab a yoga mat and find an open spot on the floor amidst twenty or so international students from Australia to the UK, ranging in age from eighteen to sixty. Some seem committed, others seem skeptical. The white robed swami gazes at me and begins speaking before I am fully situated... "Your biggest obstacle on your spiritual path is your preconceived notion of what yoga should be. Yoga is more than just the physical postures usually practiced in the West; it is about attaining unity of body, mind, and spirit through self-discipline. To master this, we must practice 'The Five Points' of yoga: Proper exercise (Postures), proper breathing (Pranayama), proper relaxation (Savasana), proper diet (Vegetarian) and positive thinking and meditation (Vedanta & Dhyana)" he contends.

"Let us begin with a guided meditation to soothe your mind," he whispers. "Close your eyes… inhaaaaale deeply, exhaaaaale completely…watch your thoughts as if you were an outside observer and then let them pass by." During the session, I feel a deep stillness and fall hard asleep. I experience intense, lucid dreams in short 60 second intervals between the rest periods of positions and breathing techniques. The trance-like experience unlocks something in my body that allows me the unconscious freedom to review an amazing recollection of memories. I recall odd images of places I have long forgotten about, have visions of old friends I haven't seen in years, and recall various memories of my life from youth to the present. It is a strangely beautiful experience. This place has a strange magic. I am where I need to be. This is what I came here for. It feels healing.

Two hours later, stomach growling and body trembling with exhaustion, I bow out in silence, grab some fresh fruit and make my way to another meager sleeping room with the same basic accommodations as the last place, paying a few extra rupees per night for my own room instead of a dorm. After an unanticipated cold shower, I fall onto my lumpy mattress blanketed in exhaustion, lingering depression, anticipation, and wonder. I write in my diary and then cry myself into an 11 hour sleep, in the safe guardrails of my new home for the next 40 days.

The Real Spiritual Retreat: Week One, Day One

Traci's Diary Entry
May 30th, Coonor, Tamil Nadu, India

This retreat is not a "vacation" like the last place, but a retreat into self and I'm here to fully immerse myself into it.

The white robed swami is a yogi named Vinod Kumar, a man who would come to change my mind and my perception of India. We have a deep and instant connection, and I savor our interchange of energy. I feel as sure as the sky is blue that I have found where I need to be through a strange twist of events and ills that have led me to here and to him.

5:00 AM: Wake up call. Clanging bells jar me awake. My blanket of exhaustion turns to rejuvenation. My depression turns to joy. My anticipation turns to excitement. My wonder turns to knowingness. I spring out of bed, eager to begin my spiritual "boot camp" and soul seeking. I splash cold water on my face, throw some shine on my teeth, and slip into the awkward and over-sized clothing; the white pants symbolize purity and the yellow shirt, learning. I curiously follow the flicker of candles, sound of bells, and groggy students across the dark courtyard to the little white yoga pavilion.

5:30 AM: Herbal drink. Devotional music echoes over the loudspeaker of a neighboring temple as we sip our early morning green tea or soy coffee. The room is silent except for the music.

5:45 AM: Mantra chanting. A mantra is a word or phrase sung or spoke as an incantation or prayer. We mimic different mantras 11 times each and then chant the vibratory word "OM," which means GOD, 108 times. The birds are chirping and the sun spreads its rays across the open-air room with an exquisite orange and gold undertone. On cue, I close my eyes and inhale.

"OOOOOOOOMMMMMMM."

After 108 intense repetitions, my body was trembling with delight. It is an intense and electrifying connection of mind, body, and spirit, a full-blown full-body orgasm. I'm on cloud nine.

6:15 – 8:00 AM: Asana practice. An asana is a yoga pose or series of poses that allow you to release the stress and stiffness in the body. Asana class is taught in a very traditional Hatha Yoga style (that Americans have adopted). It includes lots of twists, inversions, and holding postures for sometimes up to 5 minutes. We also incorporate breathing techniques, called pranayama.

8:00 AM: Karma yoga. Karma yoga means "discipline of action," paying it forward, or leaving something better than how you found it. Karma yoga sometimes involves cleaning, cooking, gardening, painting, taking out the trash, or planting trees around the facility as well as in local communities. My specific job is to piece together 100 lunch sacks for the needy outside of these walls. I guess I'd rather be doing this than cleaning the toilets. But when I really sit and think about this, we the students are their housekeepers!

9:00 AM: Breakfast. After being awake and active for a number of hours, everyone is anxious for breakfast. We each sit in front of a bowl containing chunks of papaya, banana, guava, carrots, and cucumber. I gobble mine down in seconds flat and patiently wait for the main course. I wait and wait and wait. After ten or twelve minutes, the server comes by and drops another ladle of fruit into our bowls. This can't possibly be the main course! It is. I know I'd give anything not to have to eat oatmeal anymore but this isn't exactly what I'd had in mind. Hopefully eating fruit every morning for breakfast will grow on me or at least make me feel healthy. I leave hungry, and lunch is another long three and a half hours away.

10:00 –11:00 AM: Lecture. There is an array of lectures on all aspects of yoga, including its practice, goals, philosophy, meditation, ayurveda, anatomy and physiology, and a range of other topics. Today's message is: Your Attitude + Your Choices = The Sum Total of Your Life. It is very thought provoking and powerful .

11:15 AM: Yoga Nidra. This is a powerful, ancient form of guided meditation that induces relaxation and healing of the body, mind, and spirit. Swami says that regular practice of Yoga Nidra is a healthy habit that rests, restores, and renews the body, mind and spirit, offering the opportunity to process and release the accumulated stress and tension that cause physical and mental illness. Regular practitioners report that they experience better sleep, less physical pain, and more emotional ease and well-being. For others, like me, it is also a chance to catch a quick nap and have some more lucid dreams.

12:30 PM: Lunch. A stone-faced volunteer leads us to the dining hall, where bowls and plates line the floor, and we are motioned to sit. There is a plethora of wall postings that say "Eat in Silence." But, of course, some wiseacre belts out, "Hare Krishna" at the top of his lungs a few times and a few others instantaneously follow suit until the server stops serving and deadpans them until they fall silent. Others stare at the group of distracters in pity. The only sound is an old heavy spoon clanking on our metal plates as the volunteer resumes his duty plopping a scoop of rice onto our plate. "Is this all we get?" I wonder. A moment later, a second equally unamused server carrying a big metal pail with a ladle hovers over our plate and dumps a ladle of vegetable stew over the rice and unskillfully drops two pieces of Indian flatbread chapatti (like a Mexican tortilla) in the general vicinity of our plates

and leaves the room. There isn't a utensil in sight. I observe other students scooping up the runny rice mix with their fingers before shoveling it into their mouths, with the brown watery broth  streaking down their arms and chins. These guys are amateurs I think to myself, as I scoop the rice-stew mixture onto a chapatti and roll it up as a make-shift burrito, just like Amy and I did at the Sikh Temple in New Dehli, where Babu brought us. All eyes move over to me with a blend of jealousy and disdain as I take a clean first bite into my new Indian burrito. I'm pretty sure I just started a new trend.

1:00 – 3:00 PM: Free time. These two precious hours are our chance to have a power nap, hand-wash our laundry, prepare for a yoga lesson, study, read, hit the local market down the street, or access the real world via a three minute phone call or ten minute internet session. I catch up on my laundry and send my parents a few photos in an email and let them know that I am in good hands and in a good place and space. I know they must worry about me, but I also know they are excited and proud of me for following my dream.

3:00 PM: Lecture. Sitting on the floor, cross-legged, the head swami instructs us to close our eyes, rest our hands palm-side up on our knees (palms apart), and surrender our thoughts. Five seconds later he instructs us to place our palms together in prayer position (palms together) and surrender our thoughts.

> *"Palms apart. Palms together. Palms apart. Palms together. Palms apart. Palms together. Palms apart. Palms together. Palms apart. Palms together," he whispers. This goes on in five second intervals for more than ten minutes.*

> *"Palms apart. Palms together. Palms apart. Palms together. Palms apart. Palms together. Palms apart. Palms together. Palms apart. Palms together," he whispers.*

> *"What does this have to do with the meaning of life?" I wonder.*

> *"Palms apart. Palms together. Palms apart. Palms together. Palms apart. Palms together. Palms apart. Palms together. Palms apart. Palms together," he whispers.*

"My arms are just killing me," I notice.

"Palms apart. Palms together. Palms apart. Palms together. Palms apart. Palms together. Palms apart. Palms together. Palms apart. Palms together," he whispers.

"All right, ENOUGH!" I scream inside.

"Palms apart. Palms together. Palms apart. Palms together. Palms apart. Palms together. Palms apart. Palms together. Palms apart. Palms together," he whispers.

"This is stupid," is going to be my new mantra.

"Palms apart. Palms together. Palms apart. Palms together. Palms apart. Palms together. Palms apart. Palms together. Palms apart. Palms together," he whispers.

Arms now burning; "SCREW YOU!" I sneer inside.

"Palms apart. Palms together. Palms apart. Palms together. Palms apart. Palms together. Palms apart. Palms together. Palms apart. Palms together," he whispers.

I feel this little ball of anger in the pit of my gut growing larger and larger with every sequence. I'm afraid if it bursts I'm going to get up and choke this guy.

"Stop," he whispers. "Notice your judgment and how quickly the need for control consumes you. This will prevent you from being receptive to any other possibilities that exist outside of the scope of what you know. We are going to learn how to control it – so it doesn't control you." He may have a point. I take a deep breath and feel myself accepting the possibility of change.

4:00 – 6:00 PM: Kriya Yoga. Diving into self-realization, a "direct personal experience of God" achieved through specific breathing, meditative techniques, and deep-dive mental processes. "You can be in a room twenty years, trying to get out through the walls, the ceiling, and the floor. It is when you finally discover the door that you find your way out. That's how it is with the soul. The average devotee may struggle his whole life trying to escape the bodily limitations by unscientific means and by the paths only of devotion or discrimination. By Kriya Yoga, however, if he is sincere, he can escape quickly. Kriya Yoga takes one to God by the universal highway: the spine." -Paramhansa Yogananda

6:00-7:00 PM: Havan. During havan we chant the OM or the Mahamrityunjay mantra 108 times. Havan is a sacred purifying ritual in Hindu culture and involves a fire ceremony. This is truly a delightful meditative experience.

7:30 PM: Dinner. All meals are vegan and are repeated each week. Today we have chapatti (Indian bread that resembles Mexican tortillas), toor dal (yellow lentils mixed with turmeric powder), beetroot (tastes like mushy red cabbage with white vinegar), and tomato salad (a tomato chunk with salad dressing on it) and buttermilk, a heavily diluted yoghurt with ginger and other spices that aids in digestion. It is surprisingly delicious and I devour it like I haven't eaten in days. When I look up, I notice that everyone is inhaling their food at lightning speeds, the aftermath of a skimpy breakfast and bland lunch.

8:30 – 9:30 PM: "Meaning of Life" discussion. Whoa! It's a heavy first day. Swami says "Starting a path of self-discipline is tough because it requires giving up the things that feel good right now in the quest for a far more elusive and intangible goal of self-realization or spiritual enlightenment. Lasting happiness isn't about instant gratification, but holding on to inner-peace when things don't go our way." Swami tries to get the point across by comparing the mind to a lake; thoughts are like ripples that keep us from seeing the bottom. Stress, worry, anger, sadness, discomfort, and jealously trigger waves in our minds. When the mind is still, like a calm lake, we can see past the shallowness of our shifting emotions to something deeper, making us more grounded. Swami contends "We are either living at effect (trapped in past, professional victim, judgment, blame, worry, fear) or cause (responsibility, mastery, peace, choice, allowing) and all of our behaviors are direct responses to unresolved issues within ourselves."

I can feel the swirl of discontent and restlessness in the air and can tell by the shameless heads bobbing, grimaced expressions and little mumbles that everyone is sitting in the seat of "judgment" and not "surrendering" to new information or other possibilities, as we are asked. There is no doubt that everyone in this room wants to be right about what they believe. I suspect stones will be flying, mud will be slinging, and tongues will be lashing by the end of this retreat. Here are the "Big Questions" we will be covering over the next 6 weeks:

- Meaning of Life – Why are we here? What is our purpose collectively and individually?

- Life After Death – What happens when we die? Should we fear it?

- Ethical Dilemmas – How do we decide between right and wrong? Who should be the judge?

- Social Justice – Is it right to steal from the rich to help the poor? Does accepting charity help or hinder a person's potential?

- Big Bang Theory – How and why did the universe begin?

- Time Travel – Is time travel physically or logically possible?

- Creation vs. Evolution – Are we descended from apes? Is there a God?

- Artificial Intelligence – Should intelligent computers replace duties and jobs of human beings?

- Extraterrestrial Life – Are we alone in the universe?

- Cultural Relativism – Are moral values relative or absolute?

- People Versus Church Versus Government – Who should decide what is best for our lives?

10:00 PM: Bed time. It seems as if I won't be making friends here. While I know I said that I wasn't here to make friends… it seems weird to be "silent" the entire time and be so close to a dozen other people who are going through the same intense soul-seeking as me. Seriously, how can we not talk about it? Bedtime is whenever the generator stops supplying power, which tonight is around 10 PM. I can cheat with my tiny battery operated headlamp and continue writing in my diary, as I'm one of the few who chose to pay extra for a private room and have no one to rat on me for breaking curfew.

Oh Rats

Traci's Diary Entry
June 5th

In the middle of the night some loud noise wakes me up from my sleep (with ear plugs in). I turn on the light, but see nothing. About 30 minutes later the noise becomes more prominent and transforms into a deep scratching. Upon closer examination, it appears to be coming from the desk drawer. Right before my eyes drops a long and thick swaying tail from the wooden backing of the desk. Something somehow got lodged in the drawer and is biting its way through to freedom. Suddenly it falls through. It is a large rat about the size of my shoe. I've never jumped on top of my bed so fast in my life. He scurries into the bathroom and is nowhere to be found, and I dart out across the courtyard to the office in my pajamas, and demand to change rooms at 2:27 AM. Aye, aye, aye!

I'm still feeling depressed. I can't seem to shake this collage of emotions, vacillating between mad, sad, angry, depressed, fearful, hopeless, exhausted… it's everything… it's Amy leaving, it's my sexual abuse, it's my broken engagement, it's not knowing what I want, it's not knowing where I'm going, it's not knowing what I will do when I get home, it's not knowing where "home" is. It's going home with empty pockets. It's not having a job. It's not having material possessions to fill an apartment. It's having to start over again. I feel lost and overwhelmed.

Today swami suggests that we start "Urine Therapy." He describes all the great benefits that drinking urine will have on our health.

I simply state that I will not be doing this. He shakes his head in dismay exclaiming, "I don't understand you Westerners. You have no problem going out and meeting someone in a night club and six drinks later you are at home licking each other's genitals and making a baby that you can't afford to take care of with someone you don't even know! But you're afraid to drink your own urine that is effective in treating a variety of diseases such as multiple sclerosis, colitis, lupus, rheumatoid arthritis, cancer, hepatitis, pancreatic insufficiency, psoriasis, eczema, diabetes, and yes, even herpes, caused by those very 'meet n greet' sexcapades you engage in! You people confuse me!" he sternly exclaimed. OMG! I had no rebuttal. It's true. We even reward such behavior with free government handouts. In fact, the more illegitimate children you have, the more state assistance you get. But that still doesn't change my mind about "Urine Therapy."

 Monkey Menace
Traci's Diary Entry
June 8th

There are signs everywhere that say "WARNING! Keep your doors and windows closed due to the monkey menace!" Monkeys roam freely and wildly everywhere. I'm still in complete awe to be  surrounded by these fascinating creatures and be so close and personal with them. They seem fearless of humans and often invade my personal space in search of goodies. I have braved a few hand-to-hand passes of fruit to them but still remain a bit frightened and intimidated by their immediate and bold presence.

Well, I am late for my yoga class this morning. I am in the bathroom in my hotel room getting ready when I hear a noise in the other room. I peek my head out the door and there is a large monkey vigorously rummaging through my backpack and devouring my instant oatmeal packs and granola bars. Despite the warning signs of monkey menace deposited around the hotel, I must have inadvertently left my door ajar when I hung my laundry out to dry on the balcony. I begin to recognize some of these varmints from their obvious ailments: a cut off limb, a missing tail, bleach looking spots. This particular monkey has a fat tumor on his cheek. I shout, "Get out of here," in an attempt to scare him away, but instead he lunges toward me, so I leap back into the bathroom and lock myself in. A few minutes later I crack the door ajar and see there are now three monkeys in my room ripping through my things in search of food. I whip my shampoo bottle at them, then the conditioner, hair brush, sandals, toothpaste tube, and each time I do, they rush the door, keeping me trapped inside the bathroom for forty minutes.

After making my way to the yoga class, I explain to swami that I have broken the "no late arrival" policy because the monkeys had me trapped in the bathroom, not because I have overslept or lost track of time. I am pardoned and allowed to join in on the class. So there we are in the middle of a quiet exercise, when we hear a loud noise in the rafters above. As we each peer up to see what it is, I blurt out "THAT'S the monkey who had me trapped in the bathroom this morning!

I recognize him from the big tumor he has on his cheek!" Swami started laughing himself silly and says "That is not a tumor on his cheek. That is where ALL the monkeys store their excess food!" The whole while I had thought this "tumored monkey" liked me because he is always hanging around my room. I see him every day on my route to my yoga class, and he even follows me to the marketplace a couple miles away to bother me for food. I have even named him "India."

Monkey's Invading Traci's Hotel Room
http://j.mp/kPTCgm

Seriously, two monkey dramas by lunch! Do I have "Harass Me" written on my forehead? There is a water leak in the dining hall so we are on our own for lunch today and get to roll our lunch period into our free time, extending our personal time from 12:30 to 3:00 PM. I'm having a lovely lunch in the hotel garden, bordered by "Trees of Peace" and blooming bougainvillea hedges, when all of the sudden, a monkey who has apparently been "casing" me drops down from a tree right before my eyes and grabs the sandwich from my plate. As I fall backward out of my chair in an attempt to get away from this aggressive little creature, I simultaneously hear a piercing POP! POP! POP! Things are blowing up on my table! The waiter is whipping firecrackers at the monkey to scare him away, not realizing that they are ultimately bouncing off me. I shout for him to stop, he comes up and offers to bring me a new lunch plate, and I kindly bow in gratitude. When he delivers it, he hands me a bill for 70 Rupees or $7.00. I ask what the bill is for and he says it is for the second lunch I had ordered. I must have had an apparent look of surprise on my face as he uttered, "Well, it's not our fault the monkey ate your sandwich. You've seen the signs about them. It's your fault for not paying attention!" There is no escape!

I began conversing with a staff member of the hotel. I ask him what it is like to work here and if he is happy doing his job. He informs me that he has worked for the TAJ Garden Resort for 13 years with no raise. When he asked for one 5 years ago, they suggest that if he is not happy with his wages, he should look for another job. They tell him that he can be replaced within an hour by someone who will appreciate the opportunity. Can you imagine this happening in America? The land of good and plenty... the land of pride and ego... the land of bigger, better, faster, more... the land of gimme, gimmee, gimmee... the land where we expect raises even if we don't do anything more to earn them. After even just a few years without a raise in America, someone would probably try to sue that employer for discrimination. And, of course, there would be some loathsome lawyer to take on the case.

I run out of Indian currency today and discover that there are no ATM's in the mountains. Advised by my hotel, I take a taxi into town on my afternoon break and visit the State Bank of India to exchange my American cash or Travelers Checks, but they direct me to the bank a block down. When I go inside, they too direct me to yet another bank down the way. Can you believe that this third bank redirected me to the very first bank that I started at? All of the banks say that they don't want American currency of any kind, and each bank points fingers at the other banks, insisting that it is "their" responsibility to make the exchange. After an hour of running in circles and getting the brush-off and in a moment of frustration, I loudly yell, "I am not leaving this bank until someone gives me some money!" A nun leaves her place from the line I am inadvertently holding up and hands me 47 rupees, the equivalent of $1 USD. They never do exchange my money for me until I return the next day with my new friend Pardeep, a big shot who manages the Taj and has some apparent clout in the town.

Discoveries, Fun Facts, and Useless Tidbits

- Cost of this 40 day yoga retreat: $240 USD.

- Cost of hotel room: $7 per night.

- Reiki treatments x 40 days: $21 or 950 rupees.

- Reiki Certification from a Reiki Master: $133 or 6000 rupees (not recognized in the good ole overly-regulated USA).

- Sleeper train across the country: 1,800 rupees or $20.00.

- Movie tickets to the latest show: 40 rupees or less than $1.00 each.

- McDonalds value meal: $2.00. Hot fudge sundae: 35 rupees or 70 cents.

- Air fare across the country: 6,000 rupees or $160.00.

- During the outdoor yoga session I got warm and unzip the legs off of my travel pants so they convert into shorts. Swami replies "Wow! Collapsible trousers! I've never seen those before! What an invention!"

Purging

Traci's Diary Entry
June 12th

I am having trouble sleeping lately and tossed and turned last night. I'm having some unsettled emotions over Amy bailing again. I receive an email from her this morning, but I'm just not ready to deal with it yet. I'm still too angry, but I know that behind all the anger lies hurt. When I break it down and break it down and break it down, I'm sad that she is not here to share the experience with me anymore. I miss her for comfort, fun, and safety. I'm feeling anxiety stricken and fearful of the unknown and feel too weak to carry on. I know my parents are worried sick about me being on this trip alone and are having their share of sleepless nights too.

Tough life! My days begin before sunrise and end at 10 PM. There are only about a dozen left in the program, as a few have dropped out. Our time is spent diligently.

The Daily Schedule:

5:00 AM:	Wake up call
5:30 AM:	Herbal drink
5:45 AM:	Mantra chanting
6:15 AM:	Asana practice
8:00 AM:	Karma Yoga
9:00 AM:	Breakfast
10:00 AM:	Lecture
11:15 AM:	Yoga Nidra
12:30 PM:	Lunch

1:30 – 3:00 PM:	Free time
3:00 PM:	Lecture
4:00 PM:	Kriya Yoga
7:00 PM:	Chanting
7:30 PM:	Dinner
8:30 PM:	"Meaning of Life" discussion
10:00 PM:	Lights out

After hearing the schedule, swami asks if there are any questions. I ask why we have to do this on Sundays. Swami replies "You breathe on Sundays don't you?!" It is an adventure of discipline like I have never imagined: no salt, no refined sugar, no caffeine, no alcohol, no sexual pleasure of any kind, no TV, no radio, no magazines, no gossip, no dead flesh, and we have to drink at least a gallon of water per day for 40 days. I am glad I am here, but a 90 minute break per day just isn't enough. A full day off would be nice to explore the adjacent towns and get to know the other students.

The 10 Commandments:
1. Be Silent
2. Be on Time
3. Be in the Moment
4. Attend all Classes
5. Listen
6. Give 100%
7. Surrender Pre-Conceived Notions
8. Love all things
9. Trust the Process
10. No Sex, Dead Flesh, Alcohol, Tobacco, or Caffeine

It hurts so good! I like who I am while I am here and where I am now at this point in my life. There is nothing that I would change if I could, and I wouldn't trade this experience for all the material wealth in the world. The more time I spend here with him, the more at peace and purposeful I feel. Swami is a simple man. I deeply admire and respect his unattached life. He loves everything and is attached to nothing or no-thing. He is one of the most intriguing and intelligent people that I have ever had the privilege to know. He knows something about everything. Maybe it is because he has no TV and devotes five hours a day to studying something new or because he has read all 6,000 books in his home library. I feel so lucky to be sharing this time with him. He has aged so gracefully, not looking a day over 45 though he is in his sixties. He has been studying yoga for more than 40 years; one decade alone was spent in the white caves of the Himalayas and Tibet with his great teachers or gurus. Then there is his 82 year-old mother, the woman who adopted him when he was in his twenties, and who is incredible. She is the wittiest and youngest 82 year old that I have ever met.

Yogi Vinod aka Swami (Spiritual Teacher)

She earned her M.D. in Toronto at age 40 and still regularly researches and submits papers on genetics. She has been recognized by Johns Hopkins, is sharp as a tack, and is the finest example of good, clean, and healthy yogic living that I've ever seen. Together they have a dream and are saving their money to open a communal living compound in their spiritual haven. An 82 year old with a bodacious dream moves me to dream even bigger.

Today we lay on the cool concrete covered with a sheet of fabric that they call carpet, resting our eyes and minds and focusing our breaths on a fast-paced routine that breathes in "GOD." I hyperventilate and think I am having a heart attack. It turns out to be a panic attack, which charges at me at lightning speeds about once a year. After disrupting the whole class, swami finally convinces me that I am not dying, and when I come around, he makes us do the process again. I am feeling ANGRY and RESENTFUL of him and the world, when all of a sudden I am released into a new dimension. It is like an out of body experience. It is the single most blissful orgasmic feeling I have ever experienced in my life. From head to toe, from mind to spirit, from body to breath, I am high on some ultimate drug of the spirit world. It is POWER! It is intense! It is indescribable! I don't want it to end! While we are in this euphoric state, he asks us to consider unconditional love, tolerance, and forgiveness and focus that energy upon anyone who has ever wronged us. Hell, in this state, I'll do anything. Swami says that one of the greatest challenges in life is to send love in the midst of hatred.

Next we have to purge all of the garbage that we've been hanging onto and hauling around with us all our lives. He guides us through a powerful exercise where we take a marker and write all of our regrets, bad thoughts, wrong doings, victimizations, negative sexual experiences, empty failures, and toxic behaviors in our lives on a balloon, and one by one we let each balloon go and watch it fly higher and higher into the sky and further and further away from our lives until we can't see it anymore. I am the last to finish; it seems that my years of mounting anger from child sexual abuse, heartbreak, being robbed, scammed, lied to, cheated, and abandoned will never end.

When I get back to my room I purge over my diary for hours, weeding out my garden of unhealthy things, behaviors, and people who no longer serve a greater good in my life. Amy makes the list. I know I am ready to make room for something new, so I begin to write new dreams. I realize that if I want to gain control of my life, I need to reinvent my dreams and reimagine my life and see myself in the picture, happy and healthy and living my dream. "What would I do if money were no object? What would I do if I could not fail? What would I do if I knew I only had 3 months to live?" It is a deep-seated release from all the heavy emotions that have unconsciously weighed on my mind all these years. My "Bucket List" graduates to a "Dreams Can," depicting 100 things I want to see, be, do, have, and share if money were no object, if I could not fail, and if I only had 3 months to live. I promise myself I will cut up the list and place them all in a can when I get home and randomly draw a "Dream" at least twice a year and find a way to make it happen.

"When we change our thoughts we change our world."
- Norman Vincent Peale

Traci's List Of 100 Things
http://bit.ly/nOkhcP

The Truth Revealed
Traci's Diary Entry
June 19th

Interesting day! During our afternoon break I am out exploring the property and gardens and I begin conversing with a few of the yoga students who were sitting around a table. In general conversation, I learn that two of them were scammed by the same ayurveda retreat that I was and that is how they ended up here. Sean and Dom from the U.K. reveal that the son, who also made my reservation, actually lives in Boston, not at the retreat with his family in India like he told us in his email. He targets and lures Westerners in with his fancy and misleading website, and his mother and father collect the cash upon arrival before their meager services and under-promises are revealed. Sean and Dom put up such a fight to get their money back that the people call the police on them, and now the police have been following them around and harassing them. They said the police even made them pay them money to retrieve their passports from the ayurveda retreat! SCARY! I actually feel relieved that it's not just me and it feels good to have others to talk with. We all wonder how many other people have been scammed out of their hard earned money and how they can continually get away with doing this to their visitors.

One issue that keeps relentlessly gnawing on my soul is my childhood of sexual abuse. Being molested by a loved and trusted family member is onerous to every area of my life and affects my every relationship. I'm not sure why this demon keeps rearing its ugly head, but it is all consuming. The weight is heavy and growing. This demon wants out! And I'm finally ready to let it; I'm tired of carrying the burden and shame of another man's ill. I wish Amy were here to console me like she did the first time I ever spilled my secret to her, when I was twenty years old. She helped break the news to my parents, who felt equally mortified and betrayed. They have each supported me every step of the way through the painful journey from victim to survivor.

This yoga retreat is intense. I'm emotionally exhausted and had another panic attack during an exercise about relationships. I again feel like I am having a heart attack and am going to die. Releasing all the crap from inside of me better be worth the up-front trauma I'm going through. The guided exercise forces me to look in the mirror and examine what it was about me that caused my engagement to end, why I stalled the eternal commitment for seven years, why I'm still chasing its variations, why I'm always aiming for someone or something just beyond my grasp, and why I haven't been able to commit and love freely, fully, and openly since. I then commit to making a few changes about myself that will better me for my next relationship. Autopsies are no fun and they stink. It is ironic that they used to be part of my job in the medical field, but who would have thought that I'd have to do one on myself and while I'm alive at that! I discover a number of truths during the exercise, and I feel like I am bleeding everywhere. I finally understand that the ultimate penalty for repressing my years of sexual abuse has been an early death of all my relationships. Hopefully now we can start plugging up these gaping wounds and breathe new life into my soul, before I bleed to death.

It feels good to be in one place for 40 days. I've been on the road for a year and a half already. I think I have mastered the art of living as a minimalist, fitting in, making friends, and feeling at "home" wherever I am. But I'm homesick today for the very first time. Sure there have been times that I have missed things or people from home, but never enough to run back home for, but I hadn't realized how wearing that living out of a backpack can be. I am with my whole life. There is nothing more to my existence right now. I'm all here. It takes a lot of energy to move to a new country or a new place and find a new bed to sleep in, figure out new ways to communicate, new places to eat, and new ways to get around, all while thinking about my safety and not getting taken advantage of again. Okay, so Amy was right, and I can see now how I had not carried my weight. Her way of planning, even just a little bit, made it easier than my way of just showing up in a foreign country, flipping open the Lonely Planet book at mealtime, activity time, and bedtime, and randomly choosing. I wonder if she would have stayed or stayed longer if I had done more. I'm sorry Amy. I'm sorry for being ignorant of your needs and what I now know you needed from me because I was too busy being right. Being constantly occupied helps keep my mind from missing my family and missing Amy or even dwelling on the fact that I am really alone and vulnerable two worlds away from home. As much as it still stings, I need this! I need to get a new life, just like Amy felt she needed to get a new face. I know that if she were here, neither of us would be able to achieve our objectives. I am off to bed, to recover from being emotionally bludgeoned today!

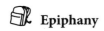 **Epiphany**

Traci's Diary Entry
June 22nd

Happy Birthday, Dad. I hope my card reaches him on time and
my e-mail lets him know that family is never far from my thoughts.
I've been missing home a little more lately. Of course I'd rather be
there right now than doing this soul-searching grunt work, but I know
this is what I need. My fevered search for life's meaning and my role in
it is unveiling itself right before my eyes. My final week of the retreat
and we have another emotional day in class. We sweat, bond, and cry
as we each face deep-seated shadows, truths, and fears about ourselves.
What I discover today is that I have never felt validated as a person or
deserving or worthy of my dreams. I finally understand that I must
OWN my life and take responsibility for it and all that happens within,
including transforming the pain and trauma of my child sexual abuse
into peace and purpose. I thought that by leading the charge in changing the Wisconsin Criminal Statute of Limitations for sex crimes on
children, that would be enough to heal me, erase the pain, and bring
closure. But I guess that was just a stepping stone, because I still feel
damaged. It isn't until today that I realize I have never released the guilt
and shame of being molested and holding in my secret. Today, that too
has changed! It isn't my fault! I am more than what has happened to
me and I am more than the life I had been living.

For More Information On
"The Bogan Bill" See:
http://bit.ly/oKUniY

🎒 Carry Prema

Traci's Diary Entry
June 25th

I'm sitting at a table in a quiet corner of the courtyard, catching up on my journal, during our afternoon break. Swami approaches.

"Carry Prema," he says as he sits beside me.

"I'm sorry, my name is Traci, Traci Bogan," I respectfully answer.

"Carry Prema in Sanskrit means 'wherever you go bring love.'" Carry means BRING and Prema means LOVE." He replies. "You are the name."

"Does everyone get a name?" Is all that I could think to mutter.

"Names are reserved for 'messengers.' I hand-pick the names myself, they are never re-distributed. I've assigned a few in 40 years," he informs me. "You are a messenger. You are Carry Prema!"

Swami touches the top of my hand with his and assures me that I am exactly where I need to be on my path. He explains that I have a message, a gift, to share and that I would not be able to do so and I would not be who I am today, without my life experiences. He enlightens me to the fact that my alleged "problem" is not my real problem... my real "problem" is that I have not found and embraced an empowering meaning. He contends that when I master my perception of what a "problem" is and shift my focus to that, I will master my life.

"How you react to your past and behave in your present, creates your future. When you embrace your history and take responsibility for your own happiness, a magic will happen that will transform you from a worldly student, to a teacher of the world. To lead is to teach. It is time for you to pick up the lantern, go forth on your path, and share your knowledge."

"How?" I whine.

"If you want new things in your life, you must do new things. Focus on living in CAUSE, you've been stuck living in EFFECT. If you master just this one thing, your whole life will change. Whatever you think and feel, decides your life."

"What am I a messenger for?" I worry.

"Carry Prema, you lend the world a sense of hope and possibility with your journey - which will inspire others to take journeys of their own. You will move some with your journey around the world, you will uplift others with your journey within, you will reach others by your journey through childhood sexual abuse, and you will lead others on the journey to living one's dreams. You have climbed Mt. Everest on many levels, in many ways. You are here to inspire others to climb theirs. Every day you are given a choice to be a beacon of light or a dimming shadow in someone's life. Be the light and show others how to take that first step. When you start living in CAUSE, not only will your world change, your role in the world

will change. It is all just outside of your radar screen.

"I don't know what to do next," I whimper.

*"Yes, yes, yes, you do," he demands. "When you shift your
thinking, it will all make sense. Practice THAT. Now go big
and honor your gifts. Be light, and bring love wherever you go,"
he ends.*

"BUT HOW?" I plead.

Swami stands up, moves behind me, and hovers his hands over
my crown, giving me a Reiki treatment. He whispers, "When you know
your chief aim and have a burning desire for its achievement and you
know WHY you must achieve it, the HOW will show up." He steps
away.

"SWAMI." "SWAMI," I beg.

As he walks away from me he speaks his lasts words, "Carry Prema,
your future is being born from this journey. These days are the pages
of your book and those pages are the foundation to which your stage is
built. We will meet there Carry Prema, we will meet again - there."

"Book? Stage? Meet again? Swami? Swami!" I gasp.

He walks forth in silence.

I sit in wonder.

At 1:07 AM, the cartoon character "Carry Prema, The Goal Scout" and the term "Dreampreneur" are born. I don't know what they mean yet, but I know they mean something.

Dreampreneur [dreem pruh-noor] noun, one who has the unrelenting will to achieve their boldest goals, most daring dreams, and live their authentic empowered life - despite all fear, obstacles, and opposition. –Traci Bogan

Carry Prema, "The Goal Scout"

 The Flame

Traci's Diary Entry
June 28th

We spend the first half of the class outdoors, and the second half of class indoors today. It is a nice change of scenery until a monkey sneaks up and unzips my backpack and steals Amy's camera and my passport documents during a quiet meditation, running up the tree before we can catch him. All heads turn on me once again for the massive interruption. Thankfully a hotel employee, with the help of a ladder, is able to retrieve the dangling camera

Swami & Traci

from the branch, and all of the passport documents that were ripped from their bag rain down all over the ground. Aye, Aye, Aye! I swear this stuff only happens to me!

We learn a powerful meditation at the end of class tonight using a candle flame. Hold a lighted candle stick at arm's length away so the flame is eye level. Relax your eyes and face and gently look into the centre of the flame without blinking, until your eyes get watery or until you see the green flame. Then close your eyes, but stay focused on the

Town Near My Hotel

image of the green flame as it appears on the inside of your closed eyes and continue watching it until it disappears inside of your mind. Do six rounds of this in one sitting. Your aim is to prolong the time of looking at the flame without blinking your eyes, which will aid in the clearing of your mind and strengthening your will power. Just surrender to all your thoughts and judgments and become one with the flame.

Two Curious Local Men

I use my afternoon break today lazing through the markets of a nearby town called Ooty. I buy a water color set for 67 rupees or $1. Though I haven't painted since I was a child and have no skill at it, it has been a fun way to relax before bed. I've already painted a dozen pictures, and they remarkably depict what I have imagined! This retreat is stirring up many emotions and events from my life that I don't even realize have been bothering me. It is an awkward peeling of the onion continued. And somewhere between my brush, the paint, and the murky water, I really understand today that no one can save me, fix me, validate me, or complete me – but me! I know. It is time!

Restaurant Kitchen

Restaurant Bathroom

 Leaving India

Traci's Diary Entry

June 29th

I bid farewell to the place that has helped weave perspective and meaning into my life and uncoil my tainted mind on my spiritual quest in search of a greater meaning. I am eager, anxious, and ready for whatever and whoever is coming next in my life. What began as a mediocre interest in learning yoga has developed into a deep yearning and hunger to know more, learn more, and BE

Leaving India

more in my life. These past 40 days have allowed me to take a good long hard look in the mirror and ask myself some tough questions and grow from their searing truth. I finally feel like I'm on my way.

India has brought out the best and the worst in me. She is both a traveler's dream and their worst nightmare, and the contradictions of rich and poor, war and peace, and democracy and corruption ensures that India never gets boring. I love her unordinary karmic rituals. I have climbed temple stairs, chanted mantras, gotten spit on by a camel for supposed luck, bent myself into yogic shapes, cleansed my sins in the Ganges River, walked in Gandhi's footsteps, bowed to a monk, got sprinkled with holy water, and was anointed with grey ash and colored powders. I have meditated, prayed, and cried my sorrows out, released balloons and anger, gotten Reiki energy tune-ups, and Ayurveda healing massages that turned my body brown. India's dark side is lingering and prominent; her beauty is short lived and graceful. Her mood has been bitter and sweet. She has left a sobering impression, but I will house the good with the bad and all that I have experienced and discovered in the Motherland. Amy may never again to return to India, this diverse country, but I am certain that I will.

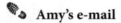 **Amy's e-mail**
June, 29th

Hi Traci-

I've sent you a few emails but haven't heard from you since we went our separate ways back in India. I am assuming that you are just too angry with me to e-mail and not that you are being held hostage some-

where. This e-mail will be the last that you hear from me as I will wait to hear from you when you are ready but I thought you'd want to hear how my surgery went. I wish I could say that it was one of the best decisions I had ever made but I'm withholding judgment at this point. My sister Vicki cried when I first got off the airplane because my face was still so swollen and bruised but it's only been 3 weeks since the surgery. Make-up helps a lot in covering the ugliness up but of course it is hot and humid so it doesn't last an entire day. I spend a lot of time indoors and avoid going to too many public places. I'm not going to look for work until I feel more comfortable with my appearance, but I don't have the luxury of an unlimited amount of time to wait. I wish it would just heal up and I hope that it eventually will look better but right now I just feel I look really different, not younger, than before the surgery. When I do go out I feel like people are staring at me so I spend a lot of time at home. I'm staying with my sister Wendy and she has made me feel very welcome and told me I could stay as long as I needed to. It still feels wonderful to be home and to see everyone at any time. My niece Tammy just had her 3rd little boy and Mom and I go for lunch pretty regularly. I am not ready to start dating so I hang out with my sisters a lot.

I think of you often and wonder what you are doing. I hope you are being careful and smart and if you're not you better start… there is a lot more world left for you to see after this trip. I will keep you in my prayers until I hear from you. I miss you Traci.

Adios my friend.
Amy

Stuck in Effect

Traci's Diary Entry
June 29th

Amy has sent me another e-mail checking in. I try not to care but
I can't help myself from reading them. I'm curious about what's going
on with her but I'm still too involved with trying to figure out what's
going on with me. Besides, I still feel betrayed and am still angry with
her for quitting another adventure we've embarked upon together.
I'm sure I'll get over it eventually, just not right now.

Making New Friends

School Bus In India

Family Pets

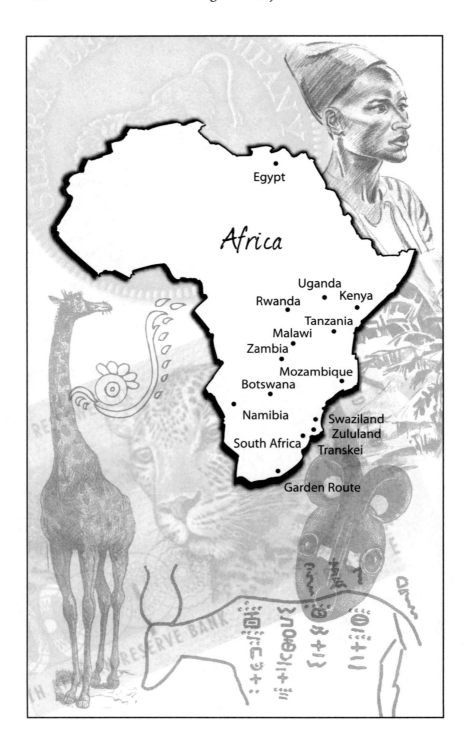

Africa

"If you surrender to the wind, you can ride it." - Toni Morrison

 **My African Dream - Come True**
Traci's Diary Entry
June 30th, Nairobi, Africa

I land in Nairobi. Literally! After eagerly boarding my flight,
I am filled with anticipation for my forthcoming African Overland
experience and with anxiety as I think about exploring a new country
alone. I sit quietly glancing between the blank pages of my sun-faded
notepad as the luggage handlers fill the plane's belly on the tarmac.
I'm in deep thought as to what to write about, my less than desirable
experiences in India or my excitement and fear about going to Africa.
A female flight attendant emerges before my seat and asks to see my
ticket and passport. As she walks away with them, my stomach sinks
deep into my seat cushion. I wonder if the evil man from the first
"spiritual" retreat in India has found a way to keep his promise and
detain me from leaving India for "defaming" his family name in my
complaints of their ill service and his taking me for a thousand U.S.
dollars.

Several minutes pass before a gentleman returns to my seat and hands me back my documents. He asks me to grab my belongings and follow him. I immediately become defensive and want to know why I have to leave and where he is taking me. He smiles and says nothing as he walks me to the front of the plane and motions with his left hand for me to sit in the aisle seat near the plane door. We both stare at each other as I cautiously reach my hand back and feel for the seat he is motioning to me, before taking it. I am stone-faced as he smiles and he makes sure I am seated before walking away. I am in the first class section. I sit there patiently, waiting for someone to come and escort me off the plane, but instead, someone comes and asks if I'd like coffee, tea, orange juice or a bloody mary. I choose the bloody mary, and as each sip coats my empty stomach and goes straight to my head, my defensive armor begins to dissipate, and I decide to surrender to the outcome and make the best of whatever is about to happen to me. As I stare out the window, awaiting my fate, the flight attendant taps my shoulder and orders me to fasten my seatbelt. Moments later, it occurs to me that our plane was rolling backward from the gate. Wow, they must have forgotten about me, I think. I am still stunned and dazed by the events that have unfolded, but after reaching cruising altitude, I realize that they probably will not be turning around to get me off the plane at this point. For the majority of the flight, I have no idea why they have taken my passport or why I have been escorted to first class, but I certainly am enjoying the unexpected perks, and it gives me great reason to mark a positive note in my diary. I shift my focus to a great start to my African arrival - alone. After a final, fattening Indian meal and short nap, the male attendant returns to my seat and tells me that the Captain wishes to see me in the cockpit, and he walks me there. The two young pilots, one of whom is very handsome, introduce themselves to me and motions for me sit in the third seat behind the main pilot and hands me a headset to put on. We make small talk and they share the names of a few of the gadgets and dials and let me press a few buttons. I finally draw the courage to ask them why I am sitting in the cockpit with them. They crack a smile as they briefly smirk at each other and confess that it has been a simple case of mistaken identity; one of them had been expecting a friend of a friend to be on the flight, traveling in backpacker clothes with a bulky backpack, and the flight attendant told them that I fit the bill. Turns out that friend of a friend never made the flight, but since I was already comfortably seated in first class, they decided to let me keep my premium accommodations and further extend the kind gesture with the cockpit tour. Lucky me! We laugh about the mishap, and I confess my disheartening story about being conned and threatened in India. Both of them chuckle and we are all equally glad that it has worked out so I can have a happy arrival and get a fresh new start in Africa. As we gear for landing, I get to help push levers and pull switches, and the handsome pilot pridefully boasts that we wouldn't be able to get away with any of this fun stuff in America because of the strict regulations in my country. I agree! It is the ultimate ending and new beginning. Indeed, I land in Nairobi... literally, or help land anyway.

I email my parents with my arrival, stubbornly refusing to respond to Amy's emails. I'm just not ready yet, but I know that our friendship will eventually survive my grudge.

Africa Encompassed: The Great Overland Encounter

Now let me set the scene for you. Ten years ago I came across an Adventure Center magazine that showcases different overland trips around the world, ranging from one week to one year. From that very moment and from that very magazine, I have dreamed of going around the world. The African Encompassed leg particularly has stirred my soul, becoming etched in my mind. I hung on to that magazine for years, and I knew that "someday" would eventually come, so when Amy and I decide that we are going around the world, we know that when we get to Africa, we will be joining the most comprehensive overland tour that the Adventure Center offers, which is "Africa Encompassed," a 91 day journey crossing half of the continent from Nairobi to Cape Town.

Trip Description: "On this trip we'll take you to far-flung places that would otherwise be impossible to get to. Give you all that Africa has to offer – the eden of Ngorongoro Crater, incredible wildlife on the Serengeti, stunning beaches of Zanzibar, gorillas in the rainforests of Rwanda, the majestic Victoria Falls, stunning views of the Great Valley Rift and Fish Canyon, and spectacular sunrises on the Skeleton Coast. You will canoe past herds of elephant in the Okavango Delta, ride horses on the shores of Lake Malawi, climb sand dunes or Kilimanjaro, and visit the Bushmen in Namibia. Whatever you imagine Africa to be, the reality will be even more amazing and poignant." This segment is written around and directly quoted from their itinerary (identified in quotes) with their permission. I highly recommend the Adventure Center. There is simply no other way to see Africa! **www.Adventure-Center.com**.

Accommodations: Small hotels, wild camping in national park and campsites (70% camping, 30% hotels).

The Tour Includes: an experienced driver, safari guide(s) and a camp cook while on safari; three meals daily, park fees; one pre-purchased gorilla permit; local specialist guides in Sossusvlei, the Okavango Delta, and Chobe National Park; all camping equipment; transportation in custom-built safari vehicles during safari, mokoros, and boat rides.

Cost: $3,985 + $500 kitty

Itinerary (my trip is reversed):

Day 1-2:	Cape Town, Township Tour, Cederberg
Day 3-4:	Orange River, Fish River Canyon
Day 5-6:	Sossusvlei, Namib, Naukluft National Park
Day 7-9:	Swakopmund, Cape Cross, Spitzkoppe
Day 10:	Twyfelfontein, Otjitotongwe, Cheetah Park
Day 11-12:	Himba Village, Etosha National Park
Day 13-16:	Bagani, Okavango Delta, Sepupa
Day 17-18:	Caprivi Strip, Chobe National Park
Day 19-22:	Livingstone (Victoria Falls), Lusaka
Day 23-25:	Chipata, South Luangwa National Park
Day 26-29:	Lilongwe, Lake Malawi
Day 30-31:	Iringa, Dar es Salaam
Day 32-34:	Zanzibar
Day 35-37:	Dar es Salaam, Arusha, School of St Jude, Mto Wa Mbu
Day 38-40:	Ngorongoro Crater, Serengeti National Park, Arusha
Day 41-44:	Nairobi, Masai Mara National Reserve

Day 45-47:	East Africa Mission Orphanage, Great Rift Valley Lakes
Day 48-50:	Kericho, Jinja (Nile River)
Day 51:	Ngamba Island Chimpanzee Sanctuary, Entebbe
Day 52-53:	Queen Elizabeth National Park
Day 54-56:	Gorilla Trekking, Parc National des Volcans, Kigali
Day 57:	Nairobi
Day 58-60:	Arusha & The Massai Village
Day 61-64:	Ngorongoro Crater
Day 65-68:	Serengeti National Park
Day 69-71:	Uganda
Day 72-73:	Kyabirwa
Day 74-76:	Kampala
Day 77-79:	Ngamba Island
Day 80-82:	Lake Bunyonyi
Day 83-85:	Rwanda
Day 86-88:	Ruhengeri & Volcano National Park
Day 89-91:	Golden Monkeys
Day 92:	Return to Kampala, Eastern Uganda

The Adventure Begins

Traci's Diary Entry
July 1st, en route from Kenya to Uganda

First stop: Nairobi. Throughout the course of the day the eager passengers trickle in from the airport. A small, shabby, shuttle-style bus carries a few of us at a time through the chaotic streets of Nairobi to a dingy little three star hotel called the Boulevard Hotel. By about four in the afternoon, we all have finally met. An appointed "cocktail

hour" before dinner helps break the ice and melt our guarded personalities. We share our first meal and some anticipation before settling
in to our rooms early for the big overland encounter, scheduled to
depart on June 11th, 2003. There is a nice mix of people ranging in age
from 20-60, from Canada to South America, from the U.K. to Europe,
and from Australia to New Zealand. I am the only American. I meet a
few nice folks at my dinner table. Avelyn and Charlie are both physi-
cians and are newlyweds. John is an attorney from the U.K. and his
wife Karen helps with his business. Sonja is a flight attendant. Vivian
is on holiday from the Netherlands and Katie is recovering from a
broken heart. Marika lives in Peru. Liz is from Namibia and wants to
see a baby gorilla. George is a lawyer from the U.K. who is moving to
Canada after this trip. Nicola is a full-time medical student from Nor-
wich who is between semesters, and Wilfred is an airline worker from
Germany.

The next morning at 8 AM we all pile in the overland vehicle, bags
and pillows strewn everywhere. Twenty strangers are embarking on a
journey of a lifetime
through the countries of
Kenya, Uganda, Rwanda,
Tanzania, Zanzibar,
Malawi, Mozambique,
Zambia, Zimbabwe,
Botswana, Namibia and
South-Africa. There are

The Bush Buster

three legs: East Africa and the Gorillas (30 days), The African Genesis
(30 days), and The Southern Cross of Africa (30 days). With each leg
people join and leave the tour based on their budget and length of
vacation time. I am one of the few in this group who get to stay for all

three legs and see Africa encompassed on a big green overland truck that I name "The Bush Buster."

Our contingent of 20 passengers, 2 drivers (James and Alloyce), 2 tour leaders (Mische and Gray), and 1 cook extraordinaire (Henry) leave Nairobi filled with excitement, uncertainty, and a roller coaster of countless other emotions. It doesn't take long for our defenses to drop and for our small talk to become filled with substance beyond talking about the weather and what we do for a living. Soon being on the big green truck for days on end turns into a proverbial campfire circle where we all share jokes, stories, laughter and pass around an occasional bottle or bag of "something" between our sightseeing and excursions. The couples are giddily in love, the single travelers are connecting, and everyone is forming a bond that will likely outlast this trip. I must admit there are times I am feeling a bit aloof and intro-verted and leisurely dip in and out of their conversations and my own thoughts, which are still dominated by the retreat and the words of swami.

Locals Carry Assault Weapons

It is a long way from Nairobi to South Africa, and I am a long way from home. Nonetheless, we're off to a great beginning, and I am immediately drawn to the vast cultural difference of Nairobi, having just arrived from spending four months in India. The country is full of rich red dirt and young adults roaming the streets with assault weapons holstered on their backs. We see things like giraffe and zebra as regular staple items on the menu.

Overlanding is not the most luxurious way nor is it the least expensive way to travel. It certainly is however, the best way to fully engage and appreciate all that nature has to offer, virtually hands-free. One advantage to joining an overland tour as opposed to backpacking on your own, as Amy and I had through China, Vietnam, Cambodia, Thailand, and India, is that you don't have to do much, worry about much, or plan much. It is all done for you, and they make it fun. The drawback is that it costs twice as much, and there is little room for solitude or to escape the personalities of twenty strangers who are sharing the journey with you. Just like with any shared group experience, you will have personality conflicts with some and make genuine and lasting friendships with others. It is much like the popular reality shows on TV. There is always going to be a know-it-all, a jokester, a passive one, a loud mouth, a quiet one, and a suck-up, but you just have to find your balance and make it work because nobody can be voted off this tour! If you're young at heart, have an open mind, a sense of adventure for the unexpected, and a positive outlook, you'll have a ball of a time.

Nairobi, dubbed "Nairobbery," is reputed to be a lawless city with high crime rates, muggings, and scams. It is not only the capitol of Kenya, but the principal economic, administrative and cultural center, as well as one of the largest and fastest growing cities in the whole of Africa. Nairobi comes from the Masai word, "Enkare Nyrobi" meaning the "place of cool waters" and has a cosmopolitan like atmosphere. There are ample good bars and restaurants, including one of the most famous in Africa: Carnivores. Our group (with the exception of me who has been on a strict vegetarian diet since China) experiences the delights of Africa's game in a very different way – by tasting them: zebra, giraffe, caribou, and crocodile. I hear words like "interesting," "not bad," "Hmmm," and "now I can say I tried that once." As for me, I prefer my experience with the most beautiful creatures in the world to be by observing them in their natural habitats, not on my taste buds.

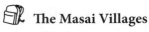

Pubic Bathroom In Nairobi
http://j.mp/ldQymq

The Masai Villages

Traci's Diary Entry
July 7th, Uganda, Africa

"We organize a visit to the local Masai villages to meet the people of the tribe and to learn about their pastoral way of life. While there we are treated to a traditional dance and music show. The Masai cling to their old tribal ways and still live the lives of their forefathers as pastoral cattle herders. A Masai's major concern in life is the welfare of his beloved cattle. According to their legends, Ngai (God) gave the Masai all the cattle in the world so the Morani (warrior) feels that it is his duty to collect all "stray" cattle, even those that actually belong to neighboring tribes. A Masai man can marry as many times as he desires as long as he can offer the woman's family a certain number of cattle as a dowry. Cattle are their form of currency. The more cattle one has, the richer he is."

We are met by a grey haired, tall, black man, wearing a red, plaid, sarong styled 'sheet' secured over his shoulder. He has beaded bracelets on his wrists and he is carrying a beaded stick. His

The Masai Village Welcomes Me

ear lobes are stretched nearly beyond recognition with many colorful beads dangling from them. This man is introduced as the chief of the tribe. For a fee of 100 Kenyan shillings each (78 Kenyan shillings to 1 USD), paid to the chief, we can each enter the village and visit the huts, pet the chickens, watch the locals dance and sing, and freely take photos.

The huts are dark, dry, small, and smell akin to a barnyard. Each is not more than ten feet in any direction and made of poles intertwined with twigs, branches, mud, and cow dung known as wattle. The roofs are low, flat, and covered with sticks and straw. The inside of the homes have dirt floors. They are lit by candles and have a thin wall made of wattle separating the sleeping and eating space from the corral where the livestock

Masai Hut

sleep. They are kept close to protect them from predatory animals. Rent is 390 rand/month or $48.00 USD. Once we sit down in their home, they offer me a drink of blood. I am not sure if it is from a cow, a goat, or a lion. Nonetheless I kindly decline, and Mesembi, the man of the house, doesn't seem at all surprised by my refusal to partake in their tradition. I wonder how many visitors actually do. I quietly watch them enjoy their glass of blood through my video lens. I visit with the family for about fifteen minutes and giggle as the wife battles with a

calf to get milk from a mother cow. One minute the calf nudges the woman aside and secures his mouth on his mother's teat, and then the woman shoves the calf away and starts milking the teat

until it squirts milk in her bucket. Back and forth they go for several minutes. The children play barefoot in the dirt amid the chickens and goats, kicking a lone ball around. Many of them are unaware of the flies

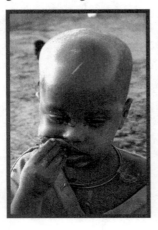

that are invading the corners of their eyes and sticking to their skin. I feel like I am being eaten alive and can't go for more than a minute or two without swatting them away. The children seem to wear a smile and have a curiosity about my colorlessness and straight hair, reaching out to touch me but only when safely clinging to the leg of a parent.

Though the semi-nomadic Masai Village tour is a bit "touristy," I can't blame them for collecting a few dollars for opening their homes to you and sharing their unique culture and heritage. This allows them to support their families through self-sustained income and they continue practicing their retained traditions

Masai Villagers Singing

despite the ever widening modernization and industrialization of Kenya. A few of their traditions and customs include piercing and stretching their earlobes, eating custard made from the blood and curdled milk of their cattle, and making decorative cuts on the women's faces for beauty. They worship their sun god, named Ruwa, who lives on Mount Kilimanjaro. The women and children keep their heads shaved while the Morani (warriors) wear their hair in long braids dyed with red clay.

I am surprised to learn that they outsource the making of some of their "traditional" clothing and goods to China. A few of us get a good laugh as we watch another overland group scrambling around to different vendors bargaining to purchase "authentic" Masai blankets and scarfing them up three and four at a time after we learn that they are manufactured, not handmade. The excursion is well worth the money spent, and they showcase the "happier" side of village living. No mention is ever made, nor will they answer my questions about their practice of female genital mutilation (clitorectomy), polygamy, or their killing practice which is contributing to the depletion of the last 2,000 lions left in all of Kenya. When a Masai boy turns Morani or warrior class, he is expected to be brave enough to enter the jungle and spear a lion. If he holds the tail of a lion as it dies, he is awarded the lion's mane and gains great honor in his tribe. Despite our vast cultural differences and spiritual practices, we were still able to connect and reach one another. I leave the Masai Village admiring their resistance to the temptations of the modern world and willingness to stay true to their cultural beliefs. As we board the overland and pull away from the little brown village of big hearted people, I ponder something that Masembi says to me as I am visiting his home. It captures the spirit of Africa beautifully: "I was born African. I don't have a lot of money, but as long as I have my two arms, my two legs, my eyesight, and someone who loves me, I am a rich man."

A Handmade Bow & Arrow Made From Animal Hide And Intestines
http://j.mp/m7Xqfq

Life Inside Of The Masai Village
http://j.mp/irDVXU

Discoveries, Fun Facts, and Useless Tidbits

- UGANDA: Capitol: Kampala. Population: 17.4 million. Literacy: 48%. Life expectancy: 51 years. Per capita income: USD $220.

- Uganda is known as the "Pearl of Africa." According to Winston Churchill, Uganda is one of the most beautiful and friendly countries in Africa.

- RWANDA: Currency: 4000 Rwandan franks per 1 USD. Life expectancy: 40 yrs. Literacy: 70 percent. Rwanda is one of the smallest nations on earth, and is the size of Vermont.

- TANZANIA: Currency: 950 Tanzania shillings per 1 USD. Life expectancy: 60 yrs. Literacy: 40%. Per capita income: $120 USD. Mount Kilimanjaro is located in Tanzania and is the largest mountain in Africa. Women can breast feed in public without covering themselves and they don't get any strange looks but they can never expose their knees and must wear skirts.

- MALAWI: Currency: 75 Malawi kwacha to 1 USD. Literacy: 50%. Life expectancy: 49 years old. Per capita income: $200.00 USD. Lake Malawi takes up 20% of the country's area and game parks reach altitudes of 3,000 meters.

- ZIMBABWE: Currency: 55 Zimbabwe dollar to 1 USD. Literacy: 73%. Life expectancy: 60 years. Per capita income: $640 USD. Zimbabwe is a landlocked country in Africa, situated between the Zambezi and Limpopo rivers. Once upon a time, the country was ruled over by Mutapa Empire, renowned for its gold trade routes with Arabs.

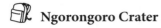 **Ngorongoro Crater**

Traci's Diary Entry
July 14th, Tanzania, Africa

I have dreamed about going on an African safari since I was about twelve years old, and the same image always emerges in my mind. I can see vast open lands, golden savannahs, dense brush, and plush wet jungles interspersed with an abundance of wildlife, kind of like a real life stage play of the Lion King. I conjure seeing a lion kill, or the Big Five (lion, leopard, elephant, buffalo, & rhino), and perhaps the elusive

leopard, all from the safeguard of an open roof, safari jeep. I see myself in my white, hard-top, safari hat, khaki pocketed shorts, and ankle trekker shoes with a pair of binoculars dangling from my neck and a camera in tow. Well, it didn't play out exactly like that, but it is just as surreal and exceeds my storybook expectations from my dreams of childhood. Time slips out of gear for me for the rest of the safari and I don't care if it ever goes back.

"The Ngorongoro Crater is a remnant of the world's largest unbroken caldera from an exploded and collapsed volcano. It measures about 20 kilometers or 12 miles across. The encircling rim is 600 meters or 2,000 feet above the crater floor, and it covers about 260km² or 100 square miles and has streams running down from the mountainous forested rim." It is its own self-contained ecosystem where plants and thousands of wildlife thrive in a fishbowl like existence in a setting of almost sublime beauty that they cannot migrate from. The crater road has a deep, steeping, pitch that is so treacherous, not even The Bush Buster can navigate its terrain, so we have to rent several specially modified 4 X 4 landrovers for this excursion. Our jeep whines with resistance as it makes the long and dusty, jagged descent to the flat, grassy bottom of the crater where we begin our search for game. In no time, we get a close encounter with the elephants, wildebeests, zebras, rhinos, gazelles, flamingos, rare birds, and buffalo that each had looked like specks of pepper sprinkled between the grasslands, from above just an hour earlier. By the thousands, they graze, laze, and migrate around a watering hole. But we have come here to see the big cats and maybe even a lion kill, and nearly a full day has passed without a single sighting. We wonder if we will ever see one when finally, someone spots two lionesses off in the distance through his binoculars. As they slowly prance their way toward our vehicle, everyone is delighted and clumsily sets off into a nonstop clicking frenzy of cameras as if we are each getting our first glimpse of our favorite celebrity. We are all so busy "shushing" one another that it sounds like a massive air blast rushing into a bicycle tire that is about to burst. I am relieved that these two beauty queens aren't distracted by our amateur implosion of excitement, and they strut right past our truck and up the pot holed dirt road, past the lines of other vehicles pulled aside, as if they know they were on the "catwalk" of an official runway show, getting their pictures taken for the cover of National Geographic. For that moment, there is nowhere else in the world that I want to be, and if I never see anything else for the rest of my three month safari, it is still complete.

Cars Brake To Let A Lioness
Cross The Road
http://bit.ly/j0wD80

As we make our way back to camp for the night, I fold my arms behind my head and look up at the near setting sun that kisses the foresty crater rim, and silently give thanks. I feel the presence of God or life or some other profound unfamiliar emotion that smells like creation and feels like love.

 Serengeti National Park
Traci's Diary Entry
July 21st, Tanzania, Africa looping back into Kenya

The Serengeti Plains lives up to everyone's expectations with their classic East African scenery of rolling grasslands dotted with acacia trees. Throughout the plains are water holes and rivers, which not only support water mammals such as hippos, but during the dry season attract many animals of the plains. These rivers are the prime areas for game viewing, and each morning we take a drive along them in search of big game. The main predators of the Serengeti have developed the unique practice of migrating north each year, along with their herds of prey. Though the lions still establish a territory during the wet season which they will defend against other prides or lone males, when the dry season encroaches, they are found along with hyenas and other predators accompanying the great herds of migrating wildebeest and zebra. This great migration usually happens in late April, May, June, and July. Our camp is in the middle of the plains, surrounded by animals and the nocturnal noises of the hunters and the hunted, right on the shore of Lake Victoria.

We spend 2 nights camping in one of the crown jewels of Africa. The Serengeti is one of the largest national parks in Africa, flat as a pancake and dry as a bone, spanning fourteen thousand square miles, and that does not include the portion of the park that extends across Tanzania's border into Kenya (where the park's name

The Serengeti Wildlife Expanse

changes to the Mara). Its ecosystem spreads out from the park into Ngorongoro and up into Kenya with the Masai Mara. The sheer scale of wildlife here is extraordinary, and a vast array of animals in the millions moves during the migration.

Our site is located in the middle of what the park rangers call the "Lion Zone," which is great when you're out during the day in search of the majestic cat, but a bit scary if you are sleeping outdoors with only a thin canvas tent as a barrier between you and a curious lion who happens to meander past your area in the night. Because the campsite is open grounds with no protective enclosure, we are given precise instructions on what precautions to take to ensure our safety. Shine your flashlight (torch) in search of the green glow of eyes before leaving your tent during the night. Always dispose of your food scraps in the safety bin. Keep your shoes inside the tent or the hyenas will steal them. Close the door to the toilets when you're done using them and if the door is open as you approach it, do not enter that stall. One of the neighboring tour leaders tells us a story about a previous overland trip where the cook goes to the bathroom in the middle of the

The Long Drop Toilet Hut

night and finds that it is already occupied by a lazy resting lion who had been attracted to the coolness of the floor in the long-drop hut. He had been able to pull the door shut to contain the lion and radio the park officials for help. No one had been hurt, but a later story confirms that two campers had not been so lucky. They had encountered a lion in their camp at some point in the night, and one of them was mauled to death. No one really knows what happened but those two stories, fact or fiction, are enough for me to instantly decide that I will not be making any trips to the long-drop hut at any time of the night. I opt to use a canister in my tent as a bathroom and empty it out in the morning, a ritual that I will follow and get harassed about from a few of my fellow travelers for the remainder of the three month camp-style trip.

I awake just before daybreak, to the magnificent yet chilling roar of lions. I toss and turn most of the night due to the unfamiliar cries and calls of wildlife hunting and being hunted, so close to my tent. As I squint, with one eye open, through my tent's window screen, a low hanging full moon still shines brightly, and I lay there wondering if anyone from back home is admiring the same brilliance in the sky in the same moment that I am. I miss them in that moment. I roll onto my stomach and groggily stare out to our campsite through my screen tent door. Faint sounds of nature intermittently permeate the silent morning African air. It is a ghost town compared to the roaring fire and laughter that had filled its space just a few hours earlier. The ground is damp and littered with empty Serengeti and Kilimanjaro beer bottles, unburned logs, and sitting stumps from our late night bonfire gathering. The fire has gone out but her embers still glow a deep fiery orange. It is around 5 AM, and we have made it through the night without having to fend off curious lions, scavenging hyenas, mischievous monkeys, or lumbering elephants. Another two hours pass with me lying there thinking about all I have seen and done on this round the world adventure. I think about my family and am missing Amy, before I exude enough energy to open the other eye and join the rest of the overlanders who are just coming to life themselves.

Each of us is assigned weekly rotating duties for each leg of the trip. These range from sweeping out the truck to doing dishes, from gathering fire wood to helping the cook prepare meals, from grocery shopping, to loading and unloading the equipment and every camp related job in between. It is a way to get to know different passengers in a different light and to ensure a check and balance system so that everyone carries his or her own weight throughout the course of the trip. I wasn't interested in getting to know the other passengers. It seems I have brought the quiet of solitude of my Indian retreat along with me to Africa. I chose to bunk alone and sit in the back of the truck alone on the long rides. I know I gave off some "leave me alone" vibes to any of my fellow travelers' overtures of friendship. If I had a partner for my chores we worked with a minimum of communication. It isn't me, but it's what I need. This week my job is to assist Henry, our cook, with preparing meals in our mobile makeshift kitchen. Wilfred, a quiet gray-haired airline worker from Germany, is always fidgeting with his glasses. He has often been my chore-partner and he again volunteers to help me. I don't mind as he is a bit of a loner and puts the same amount of effort in getting to know me, as I do him. I'd like to think that he is respecting my privacy and that he thinks I am respecting his privacy, rather than thinking I am an unfriendly jerk. I'm just still adjusting and processing all that transpired in India, mentally and emotionally. Breakfast is the easiest of meals to help with, especially during bush-camp because all we have to do is set out a bowl of fresh fruit and yogurt, a few boxes of cereal, some instant oatmeal packages, and a gallon of milk and juice and voila, breakfast is served. Wilfred and I knocked it out in minutes flat. By 8 AM we are back on the Bush Buster in search of Africa's Big 5.

The Lone Tree

We drive the washed-out, axel-breaking dirt roads around the game park and my stomach is upset from being tossed around so violently. It feels like my spine and insides have been jiggled to mush. Taking a drink of water or snapping a photo while on the five mile an hour crawl is nearly impossible on some parts of the road, but we pull over each time we see something that is camera or awe worthy, which seems like every five minutes from the last landscape or animal we have pulled over for. As we round a bend, we see groups of giraffes hovering into view high above the acacia trees. I snap a photo of a lone giraffe grazing on greens that turns out to be one of my favorite photos. They

do not seem threatened by our presence, peering over to get a good look at us. We see two giraffes fighting by clashing their necks together. It looks like two 12 foot construction cranes taking repeated swinging blows at each other, until one retreats. By late morning we have already encountered 3 of the Big 5 and even lost count as to how many of each we have seen, though it is literally dozens of some, hundreds of others,

My Favorite Photo

and even thousands of a few. The abundance of lions, elephants, and buffalo along with gazelles, warthogs, giraffe, wildebeests, monkeys, gnu, hyenas, and zebra become so common that they don't even

register anymore as being a big deal. It is like we have overdosed on them in just a few hours and are waiting for the next new drug of unseen animals to mesmerize us and keep us high for another ten

Monkeys

minutes. Someone finally asks our tour leader, Mische, where the rhino and leopards are, and she has to lovingly remind us that we are not in a zoo, but out in the wild lands of Africa and that there is a chance we might not see them at all. We trek on in verbal silence for a small stretch, with the Beatles playing in the foreground from someone's MP3 player and nature's cries, howls, and grunts raging in the background. It is with great excitement that our driver James receives word over the radio that a rhino has been spotted a few miles off on some washboard trail. Off he speeds going nearly airborne between potholes, until we land in front of a mass of the same safari vehicles with curious onlookers as ours. "Rhino!" someone declares triumphantly, breaking

the first quiet spell of The Bush Buster. His thunderous elongated body is just making its way to a nearby watering hole. We have now seen the holy grail of the Big 5. The black rhino has been pushed to the brink of extinction by illegal poaching for their horns and by loss of their habitat. The horn is still used in Chinese medicine and is said to be able to enhance male sexual stamina and fertility and cure different health ailments. The black rhino is more aggressive than the white rhino due to having poor eyesight, and it has been known to charge vehicles, but we mainly see his big butt walking away from us.

Last but not least, we see the master of camouflage and the star of the show, the elusive leopard. Leopards are nocturnal, secretive, well camouflaged, and stealthy. Leopard sightings are rare. As we drive, twenty pairs of eyes scan the tree lines and golden brush hoping to be the first to spot the leopard. In some areas the brush has been bitten down to its brittle and frail looking roots. Dust devils swirl about, and once in a while we pass kopjes, islands of rock scat-

The Elusive Leopard

tered amidst the endless plains that are often the abodes to resting prides of lions. The searing heat of the African afternoon has taken its toll and caused some of the park's animals to seek shelter for an afternoon nap, and our hopes of seeing the elusive leopard begin to fade. We bounce along from pothole to pothole, getting covered in red Serengeti dust, that blows out orange from my nose. I feel the onset of a nap sneaking up on me, and I just stretch out in my seat and get comfy when out of nowhere, someone pipes up and shouts, "There he is. There he is!" My head bounces up from its sleepy nod, and there he is, lazily plastered on a large acacia branch with his oversized paw dangling down from the tree. Within a nanosecond, we all are jockeying in the seats to get the best view. This spotted cat is beautiful and looks like a soft and cuddly domestic animal. The sleepy beast seems unfazed by the chorus of camera shutters emerging from the starstruck tourists, and at one point even lifts his head, half-cocked and looks at us as if to say, "Would you mind keeping it down a bit? Can't you see I'm trying to nap here?" Meanwhile, about 40 gazelle obliviously graze under the shade of the sprawling acacia tree, just below and all around the branch that holds the napping leopard. What a sight to see! Our Big 5 is complete.

We cross back into Uganda for a day trip and visit a school and hospital, just over the Ugandan boarder. It breaks my heart.

School Cafeteria

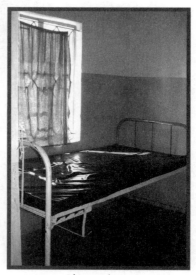

Hospital Bed

School With Dirt Floors
& No Desks

A Look Inside Of A
Ugandan Hospital
http://bit.ly/l83CXJ

Inside Of A Local
Home In Uganda
http://j.mp/IZMWsE

🎒 Welcome to the Jungle

Traci's Diary Entry
July 27th, Rwanda, Africa

Rwanda is called the "land of a thousand hills," and it is famous for its treks through the Virungas Jungle to see the last of the world's 650 mountain gorillas. Much of the country is covered in green, lush, mountainous jungle and is surrounded by the Volcano National Park. Rwanda, a landlocked republic, is situated on the eastern rim of the western arm of the Great Rift Valley, with a population of about 10

Virungas Jungle

million. It is part of the watershed of Africa's two largest river systems, the Nile and the Congo. The two main tribal groupings are the Hutu and the Tutsi and the heart-wrenching genocide that took place in 1994 is just the most recent chapter in a long and bitter relationship between the two groups when 1,000,000 people were slaughtered in just 100 days. Rwanda seems to be healing and is now considered to be one of the safest and cleanest places in Africa, even hosting a community "clean-up" day, where all the citizens gather on the last Saturday of every month and beautify their homeland together. The rich, red, dirt roads are a social gathering place for locals as they all walk long stretches to the markets or to the fields, carrying their bags of goods on their backs and waving hello to passerbys and chitchatting with their neighbors along the route. Around 90% of Rwandans are subsistence farmers, growing sweet potatoes, beans, bananas, corn, tea and coffee.

I have a funny realization tonight when Wilfred and I are given the job duty of assembling the "chef's tent." At each new location I look

Field Workers

for Wilfred to help me pitch the tent, and he never shows up to help with his share. I assume he is a slacker and shirking his duties. Two nice girls in their twenties, Nicola and Vivian, always seem to come around to help me. I think they feel sorry for me having been abandoned by my chore-partner. After nearly a week of this, I finally complain to the trip's tour guides, Mische and Gray, that I am tired of Wilfred hanging around the kitchen every time it is time to pitch the tent. It turns out, that the "chef's tent" is the KITCHEN tent, not his personal sleeping tent that I have been assembling, and Nicola and Vivian are actually the ones assigned to that job. Poor Wilfred has gotten stuck assembling the double-sized KITCHEN tent all by himself. He never once complained that I am never around to help him.No wonder those two helpful girls have been so nice and buy me a drink at the shebeen (bar). I apologize to Wilfred and we share a warm beer, a good laugh, and a little bit about our personal lives.

🎒 The Gorilla Trek

Traci's Diary Entry
August 3rd, Rwanda, Africa, Volcano National Park

Finishing the book Gorilla's in the Mist: The Story of Dian Fossey, brings an air of excitement to the leg of the trip I am most looking forward to, trekking to the mountain gorillas. Blurry-eyed but beaming with excitement, we start with a fast grab and go early morning breakfast and pile into the Bush Buster. I promptly fall asleep for the two-hour drive to Parc National des Volcans (Volcano National Park).

We pull in just before 7 AM and join the masses of other tourists who have each eagerly shelled out the equivalent of $500 USD to obtain their trekking permit. (The cost is just $30 for Rwandans –

Our Gorilla Bound Group

let's do that in America!) The Minister of Tourism limits the number of visitors per day and breaks us up into groups of eight. We each board the standing room only back beds of old rusty pickup trucks (called yutes) that deliver us to different entry points of the four habited groups of gorillas. The ride to the foot of the Virungas Jungle is worse than the Serengeti. For a solid 15-20 minutes we cling on to each other's jackets and elbows with white knuckles as we stand shoulder to shoulder in the early morning chill. Our limbs flail, our bones rattle, and our bowels roll about as we jump down the unmarked lane of dirt and jagged rocks, mistakenly called a road. It feels like we are the human-equivalent of a cattle truck on our way to slaughter. One of our African guides is riding in the back with us, bearing an assault rifle. He seems unphased by all the jolting and laughingly suggests that we are getting an "African organ massage" at no extra charge.

Slightly unkempt children, with sun-worn faces and dirty clothing held together by patches covering patches, chase and then swarm our yute demanding "pens, pens, pens" as we arrive. We disembark to the sight of local children around 7 or 8 years old, working in the adjoining fields, plucking rocks from the soil and dropping them into worn woven baskets that are later balanced on their heads and walked to a dumping point in the field near the foot of our entry point. I jokingly ask the young lads if they are earning their allowance, but none of them know what an allowance is, even after I explained it to one of their mothers, who doesn't seem amused. As I climb my first step into the plush, damp and pungent smelling jungle, the atmosphere instantly darkens and images of those hard working children along with my half-hearted comment and my lack of knowledge concerning their lifestyle, race through my mind. For a moment I reflect on how spoiled children are back in my American homeland of "good and plenty." For whatever reason, one specific incident springs to mind. Just prior to leaving for my trip, a friend and his eight year old son accompanied me to the store to pick up some last minute items. His eight year old threw a full-blown temper tantrum in the middle of the store after his dad said he could not have a $40.00 video game. Ten minutes later he rewarded him for his embarrassing behavior by caving in to him and letting him buy the game with no consequences or mention of the incident again. For just a few moments, anger and sadness rushes through me as I flash between that memory and those young African boys' reality and I can't help but wonder how many grueling weeks or months they would each have to work in the sweltering heat to earn $40.00 and how many starving mouths $40.00 could feed. My friend should have given me that money to allocate to a worthy cause during my trip, instead of rewarding his misbehaving son with a video game. I hike lost in slow motion thoughts about American ways and American parenting as I trudge through overhanging vines, past slippery moss covered rocks, and balancing over the bouncy thistle and branch mattress jungle floor. This daydream consumes me until I inadvertently brush past some stinging nettles that I mistake as a booby trap of kamikaze mosquitoes attacking me. It simultaneously startles me and whisks me back to the present moment as quickly as a pinprick instantaneously pops a balloon.

Rwanda is the hot spot and place of preference to see mountain gorillas. Trekking here is more comprehensive than in Uganda with a variety of different treks of varying levels from moderate to strenuous. There are four habituated groups. The Trebize and Sabinyo group both have 13 gorilla members and are considered low impact treks. The Amahoro Group, which resides on the slopes of Mount Visoke, also has 13 members, but is considered an intermediate endurance trek. And the largest is the Susa Group, which lives in the foliage of the Karasimba Volcano. It has 35 members, including three silverbacks, and it is the most strenuous trek and the original group studied by conservationist Dian Fossie. I am assigned to the Amahoro Group and hike about 1.5 hours through bamboo forest and thick vegetation. We follow two guides, one armed with a pagna bush knife, and the other with an assault rifle. We are steered to the gorillas' location by trackers whose job it is to follow the goril-

las and monitor their wellbeing, location, and safety from poachers. They radio their location to the guides, ensuring that each
visitor gets to see the gorillas on their once of a lifetime trek.

The forest canopy is dense and soupy and enclosed by a thick
drapery of mist, must, and dusk. The sky is nowhere to be seen, though
an occasional beam of sunlight somehow fights its way past the front-
line of foliage. Parts of our hike seem more like mountaineering; we
scale steep muddy hills, deep ravines, and swampy vegetation. I have
to grip the branches of the forest and the arms of our guide on occasion in order to climb my way up or over the slippery mossy bedrock.
We pass plants in every shade of green imaginable from fluorescent
lime to deep forest green, and some greens are so deep that they almost
appear black. We marvel at century old trees and plants, from towering, old, ancient haunted looking ones to fresh baby sprigs, just sprouting up from the bouncy carpet below. As we carry on, we catch paired
flashes of every denomination of rainforest animals and birds. At times
it seems like we are on Noah's Ark. We take in the sweet aromatics of
soothing eucalyptus, the faint smell of fresh rain, the subtle smell of
dense nature, and the pungent smell of musty swamp water, all in a
single breath and all in a single space. The heartbeat of the jungle is
mesmerizing with its chorus of pitches and squawks, its orchestra of
clicks and knocks, its symphony of flutters and peeping, and its sonnet
of rubbings and warbles. Her vocals of grandeur are so persuasive, that
my mind runs wild with exaggerated images of the faces, sizes, shapes,
and fangs attached to each electric noise that pierces the tranquil
enchanting Eden.

Finally, nearly an hour and a half into our trek and the moment
we have all been waiting for, our guides halt us and point out some

belching and grunting sounds belonging to the gorillas, who are just on the other side of an incline of some dense undergrowth. With piqued anticipation, we quietly take a few adrenaline rushed steps up

and round a patch of wild brush and vicious stinging nettles. There surrounding us are six mountain gorillas, our ancestors. They are so peaceful and beautiful, so humanlike, interact-ing with their babies. They play, feed, lounge, and tumble about, right before our eyes. We all just stare in amazement from our front row seats. The moment is surreal, and my whole body rushes with delight and dizziness as I stand dead center in the climax of realizing one of my biggest dreams. The beauty of the moment leaves me breathless and speechless, and I scan my surroundings and pinch myself to make sure it is real. I'm still filled with such emotion that I'm weeping as I write.

A curious baby gorilla draws playfully closer and mimics the facial expressions I make at him while his mother lays resting in the

background unfazed by our presence 3 feet away. I hear someone say "Move. Move! Move!!" but I am so fixated on the baby gorilla in front of me that it doesn't register that they are talking to me, nor do I hear or see papa gorilla approaching our group from behind. Suddenly he is just there. I stand frozen and in disbelief that he is just standing beside me, before he firmly trudges past, shaking the earth and crushing the bamboo stalks with his powerful strides. His coarse,

damp hair tickles the left side of my body as he rumbles past. He lumbers over and single-handedly scoops up the cute, black-haired, baby fur ball and moves a couple feet further away from us, before he sits gawking at us in the same fashion as we are at him.

There are only 650 mountain gorillas left in the entire world. They all live in Rwanda, Uganda, and the Democratic Republic of the Congo. It is heart wrenching to see these beauti-

Traci & Papa Gorilla

ful creatures and know they are in grave danger of extinction. I hope each of our $500 dollar park entrance fee aids directly in their survival from the ignorance, selfishness, and irresponsibility of man. By the end of my visit, I understand what kept conservationist Dian Fossey living in the forest for 18 years protecting these human-like primates and why she died for them. "The man who kills the animals today is the man who kills the people who get in his way tomorrow," said Dian Fossey. Sadly, she got in their way. R.I.P. Dian Fossey, you beautiful soul.

It is truly a magical and intense hour in their presence and one of the greatest wildlife experiences of my life. I feel rich in "oneness" with God and nature and feel disconnected from man and ego. It is a piercing moment of freedom. Being face to face with some of the last of the 650 gorillas left in the world is just as celestial as the first time that I knew I was in love. There are certain moments in our lives that we would like to freeze in time.

Feet Away From The Last Of The 650 Mountain Gorillas Left In The World http://j.mp/lLilFl

The Great American Rift Valley

Traci's Diary Entry

August 11th, On The Bush Buster

We drive a big loop `d loop and cross back into Kenya, finding ourselves in the heart of Kenya's western highlands, also known as "The Great African Rift Valley." The popular tourist destination is known for its stunning mountain scenery, lush tea plantations, and rich and diverse flora and fauna. We spend nearly all day in the Bush Buster rolling past the spectacular, hilly, country-side, in awe of the golden valleys, steep waterfalls and sparkling lakes, a mesmerizingly stark contrast to the Serengeti. We make numerous stops for elephant

Elephant Mud Bath

crossings and to stretch our legs and seize the once in a lifetime photo opportunities along the way. We make a special trip to the Kericho Tea Plantations, where the green waves of tea look and smell good enough to swim in. For much of the ride I am occupied in thought. What am I going to do with my life once I return home? The question weighs on me. I have no idea where "home" is any more. I miss my family in Wisconsin, but I miss my life in Hawaii too, where I have lived for the past decade. I don't want money to be the deciding factor on where I live, but I have a feeling it is going to be.

Scan Me!

A Herd Of Elephants Crossing In Front Of Traci's Jeep
http://j.mp/lNK4GX

The Bush Buster breaks down and delays our arrival to Lake Kisumu, the 3rd largest town in Kenya, by 90 minutes. I am most

looking forward to a hot shower, having gone two and a half days without one. I leap off The Bush Buster and make a selfish dash to the shower stall area to reserve my place in the already long hanging line of toiletry bags outside the hut. It's amazing how perception of luxury becomes a simple flushing toilet and a hot shower when living out of a backpack in the middle of the wilderness. It is cooler here and the sun is just beginning to set. I decide to fulfill my solo camp chore, which is sweeping out the truck, as I wait for my turn in the shower. After about 45 minutes, my turn finally comes. A hot water shower at last! The long travel day and the red Serengeti dust have been washed off of me, and I am ready for bed. Feeling unsociable as night falls upon us, I grab a hot chocolate and amarillo and my diary and go off into a quiet corner of the camp. Wearing my favorite over-worn black hospital scrubs, I reminisce of home and unload my heavy mind onto paper. Others set up camp, prepare dinner, get the campfire ready, and deepen their friendships. I envy that they all seem happy and I still feel so displaced.

Around 5 AM there is a grunting noise in the small confines of our campsite that sounds like a pig, and it seems really, really close to my tent. I am paralyzed with fear. "Can anyone else hear this?" I wonder. "Does anyone have a gun?" I pray. I can't even move, let alone look, so I don't. But there is something massive looming about, and I can feel its presence moving the ground beneath my makeshift bed. About ten minutes later, I hear Nicola and Vivian shuffling around outside so I peer my head out of my tent and whisper "What is going on?" Nicola quietly exclaims that a 2 ton mud-caked hippo was just grazing on a patch of grass right beside her tent, and his body kept swaggering and brushing into her tent wall. She has gotten a good look at him as she unobtrusively steals a peek out of her tent window. A hippopotamus sleeps in or alongside the water during the day and at night forages for grass close to the water. Our tents are in prime grass-picking quarters. Hippos will attack when wounded or agitated. Thank God we didn't startle him as they can bite a medium-sized crocodile in half, in one chomp. Hippos are responsible for most human fatalities and injuries, rendering them the most dangerous mammal in Africa. Nicola says her heart is thumping heavily as she realizes the only thing separating her from the hippopotamus had been

Pug Mark

the thin layer of canvas from her tent. With the grunting now off in the distance, I scurry out from my tent and join in on their investigation of the big wet pug-marks he leaves behind. We see movement in the water and follow the ripples; the mammoth semiaquatic beast has lugged his enormous body back to the swamp behind us, leaving a trail of muddy evidence from his visit. Whew! What a way to start the morning!

Discoveries, Fun Facts, and Useless Tidbits

- Doctor's offices are called 'Body Part Specialists.'

- Ketchup is called tomato sauce and is all artificial flavoring and coloring.

- Ice cream is also artificially flavored and colored. Boy they don't know what they are missing.

- A vodka and lemonade or orange juice would be a shot of vodka served with a can of Sprite or orange soda. They do not have lemonade or orange juice as we know it, nor could anyone comprehend my explanation. They just thought we were weird.

- A BBQ is a "Braai" which I am told meant burnt flesh.

- Instead of saying, "What's your name?" They say, "What are you called?" Instead of saying, "His name is Bob." They say, "He is called Bob."

🎒 Elsamere

Traci's Diary Entry
August 16th, Lake Naivasha, Kenya

I just finished reading the last page of the epic best-selling book Born Free as we roll into the campsite where we will be staying for the night. We are told that there have been a lot of burglaries in the area and that if we see any suspicious activity we should immediately report it to security. We get our tents set up just before dusk. Sure enough, just past dark, I notice a man wearing a long black trench coat peering into the vehicles parked at the site. I quickly rush to report it to the camp security, but it turns out the man in the dark long trench coat is the security. We both get a good chuckle out of that!

I haven't seen a shower in days but spot a tap and a bucket a few yards from our tents. I quickly rush over and cup my hands and splash the discolored water on my face and sneak in a sponge bath. That is my shower. I use distilled water from the canister in our truck and my faithful tin cup that had I picked up in China for $1 to brush my teeth, and I feel like a new person. I adore my tin cup. It serves as my cup to drink from and to brush my teeth with. It becomes the bowl that feeds me oatmeal and instant soup and transforms into the canister that stores my diced vegetables and boiled water to kill the parasites on just about everything that I eat. My tin cup and I have survived twenty-some countries together, and when I get home, I will place the shiny silver cup high upon my kitchen cupboard shelf and display it like a trophy.

After breakfast the next morning, a little boat ride delivers us to the picturesque banks of Elsamere Island, the former home of the conservationists George and Joy Adamson, who became world famous for their pioneering conservation work and relationship with an orphaned lioness named Elsa, for which they named their home. Born Free is based on the true story of how they rescued Elsa as a cub after her mother had been killed by poachers; they raised her, taught her how to hunt, and successfully rehabilitated her into the wild. The Adamson's were the first to prove that it is possible to rehabilitate lions, and they eventually raised and released another twenty. Sadly, Joy was murdered in 1980 at the age of 70 by suspected poachers, and George was shot to death nine years later by a Somali poaching gang at the age of 81. They had committed their lives to the lions and had died for them, just as Dian Fossey had died for her love and conservation of the gorillas. Elsamere is now a museum that showcases a collection of paintings, artwork, books, guns, and personal items belonging to the Adamsons. Even the jeep that George was killed in sits in front of their home. I am filled with emotion as I silently stroll through their home, taking in every touching remnant of their lives. I wonder what it is like to love and believe in a cause so much that you not only live for it, but are willing to die for it. I am filled with immense gratitude and respect for their lives, their work, and their cause, and it gets me thinking about my own mission and message in life and how I can best serve,

so my life is not in vain.

Afterward, we go to the lion park and on a jeep safari and I have my own encounter with a lion.

Traci's Encounter with a Lion –
Too Kool!
http://j.mp/iUwitR

African Reflections

Traci's Diary Entry
August 25th, Happy Birthday To My Sister, Jenni

There is just so much we have seen and done, and I'm not doing a good job keeping up with my diary. We've seen Livingstone and Victoria Falls, the Cradle of Humanity, Lake Malawi, the oldest desert in the world, limestone buildings, The Okavango Delta, Etosha National Park, overpopulated dirt cemeteries, Fish River Canyon, and Chobe National Park. We have enjoyed a clam bake on the Zanzibar, exchanged money in the black market, and volunteered at a soup kitchen… Here are my highlights…

Cemetery Of Sand
Graves In Botswana
http://j.mp/l6DijN

Highway Signage

Traci Walking The Streets With
2 Million Zimbabwean Dollars
http://j.mp/luUTtZ

Village Dinner

Himba Hut

America is Not the Only Place with Stupid Laws… Check Out This One from the Center of Disease Control
http://j.mp/m2lrXG

Boys Selling Pottery On The Roadside

White Picket Fence Dreams

Himba Woman

📖 The End of the Great Overland Encounter

Traci's Diary Entry

August 28th, Cape Town, South Africa

After 91 days of travelling through vineyards, canyons, deserts, salt pans, inland waterways, waterfalls, lakes, tropical coastal islands, savannahs, and mountain rainforests, we have made it! This myriad of terrains is only matched by the warmth and friendliness of the continent's people and the amazing density and diversity of its wildlife. The Bush Buster rolls in just before lunch. Within minutes of arriving at "civilization," it is over. What took hours to pack for our departure takes just minutes to unload upon arrival. We each hurriedly grab our packs, say our good-byes, and scatter like cockroaches into the unknown abyss of Cape Town, South Africa. Alone again. I check into a nearby hostel and lay on my bed for hours contemplating my trip around the world, my 91 day safari, what I am going to do in South Africa, and what am I going to do when I go home, wherever home is going to be. My crashing thoughts are so overwhelming that I crash - literally! Three hours later, after emerging from a restless slumber, I decide that if it is to be, it is up to me! I rush downstairs and pick up a map and circle everyplace I want to go to, everyplace I want to see, and everything I want to do in South Africa, just as I had done with Amy. I choose Table Mountain, Robben Island, shark diving, the Garden Route, the Wine Lands, the Trans Skye by horse, Swaziland, Zululand, and JoBerg. I purchase a one way multi-stop ticket on the Baz Bus from Cape Town to JoBerg and book a one way flight from JoBerg to Egypt, departing in 20 days. One decision and 40 minutes and my next destinations and my fate are planned. I can do this! Look, choose, move!

Walking the Streets of Cape Town

Traci's Diary Entry
August 29th, Cape Town, South Africa

South Africa is a country with 3 capitals: Pretoria (Administrative), Cape Town (Legislative), and Bloemfontein (Judicial). South Africa is the most developed and sophisticated economy on the continent. The currency is 8 rand to 1 USD. It has a literacy rate of 76% and an average life expectancy of 64 yrs.

Compared to coming from Botswana, Cape Town is a true first-world civilization. My gosh, I found a restaurant that had TVs in each stall of the bathroom, and I've never even seen that in America. Still, I don't feel safe walking the streets alone here. I have met too many travelers who had been carjacked, mugged, robbed, or cheated. There is a memorial plaque on the side of the road for Amy Biehl of New Port Beach, a 26 year old student, who was bludgeoned and stoned to death on the eve of her birthday by a mob of blacks chanting anti-white slogans.

As friendly as I am, I don't connect with anyone at my hostel to hang out with, so I steal a butcher knife from the kitchen, lock my bags in my room, and hit the streets with my new shiny weapon in tow, hidden up my sleeve. Curious children follow me and demand "pens, pens, pens" and touts shove safari and hostel brochures in my face at every turn.

One fella begins walking next to me. "Hey, where ya headed?" I have an unsettling feeling that he wants something from me. I cling tightly to the straps of my day pack. "You don't remember me, do you?" he asks. I have never seen him before, and don't like his aura. He was not going to be my new friend.

"It's John. John, from the hotel," he says. Ah, this is the "remember-me-from-the-hotel" scam that I had just read about in my "Lonely Planet" book, I thought.

"I'm not staying in a hotel," I deadpan.

"I mean the hostel. You don't recognize me out of my uniform, he said.

"I'm out of my uniform too," I lie. "I'm a reporter," and I hold up my phony journalist card, which also reveals the shiny knife hidden in my sleeve.

"Son of a bitch," he snarls and darts off.

Within minutes another fella steps in sync with me and walks beside me. "Welcome to my beautiful country. Where are you from?" he asks.

"Neverland," I sneer, tired of being conned and targeted as a rich Canadian or American.

"Neverland! You are kidding me! I am going to Neverland University next year. Can you tell me what it's like there over a cup of coffee?" he asks.

"If you want money – GET A JOB," I yell, intentionally rolling up my sleeves so he can catch a glimpse of my shiny butcher knife.

"Shit! Lady, you're crazy!" he whines and bolts across the street.

"Shit is right! I'm not taking any shit from you people! Do you hear me?! Now I'm going to have a scam-free vacation and try to enjoy your beautiful country!" I holler, loud enough for the entire coast to hear. Damn that feels good, I think, as I add a spring to my step.

The Lonely Planet guidebook, my bible of travel, does a good job shedding light on the scams of Africa, but where have they been for the rest of the countries I visited?

Discoveries, Fun Facts, and Useless Tidbits

- The bathroom is not the bathroom or the restroom; it is the toilet or the "dumpster."

- A liquor store is a "bottle shop" and booze is only sold at certain times on certain days (never Sunday) and only at this place. You can't walk into a 7-11 and buy a beer.

- Fetch is a huge word here. "I will come and fetch you in 10 minutes" or "Fetch me the salt please."

- Everyone must pay 12 cents per bag at any store, even expensive clothing shops where you just spent $100.

Reaching New Heights

Traci's Diary Entry

September 3rd, Cape Town, South Africa

I cannot help but be impressed by the setting of Cape Town. Behind the town, Table Mountain dominates the skyline. I am reading my map to see what trail I want to take from the 550 networks of walks to the summit of Table Mountain, when I hear a woman holler in my

On Top Of Table Mountain

direction, "Hey, I'm from Canada too – where do you live?" I have to come clean and tell her that I am an American, just posing as a Canadian to keep safe during the confines of my world tour. Her name is

Denise, and she is a physician from Canada on holiday. We become fast friends and decide to hike the Kasteelspoort Path together and take in the stunning views of the Atlantic and Indian Ocean and Cape Town sprawl. The climb is resplendent with rich flora and indigenous forested kloofs (ravines) that we crawl around. After our 90 minute workout, we reach the summit. There are beautiful vistas in all directions. It is magnificent. Drenched in heat, we cheat and take the cable car back down. She asks if I am interested in taking a ferry ride with her to Robben Island. I accept her invitation and proceed to get motion sickness and violently puke over the side of the boat the entire ride there and back. I'm so embarrassed, but the good doctor gets me a towel, rubs my back, and assures me that it's a short ride and I'm going to be okay.

Robben Island is a cultural heritage site about 7 miles or 11 kilometers offshore from Cape Town. Our guide is named Togula, a former political prisoner with Mandela Nelson. He has spent 10 years in the prison before general amnesty was granted to all political prisoners. Hearing him tell the story of the island from an intimate first-hand experience is a unique and powerful experience. He leads us over to Nelson Mandela's cell, where Mandela spent 18 of his 27 years in prison during South Africa's pre-democracy years. There is a hushed silence as each person takes his or her turn standing in front of this famous cell. The flashes

Nelson Mandela's Prison Cell

from cameras in the dim facility look like fireflies glowing. I go to the end of the line, so I can be last and spend more time peering into his cell and in his life. I can't imagine what life would be like in a 6 x 9 cell for nearly two decades without having done anything to deserve it. I stand there imagining the strength and fortitude it must take to extend the hand of forgiveness despite 27 lost years. Mandela is an example of a multi-dimensional being and super conscious living.

My visit here, like the one to the Killing Fields, the Oklahoma Memorial, the Vietnam Museum, the Hanoi Prison, Arlington Cemetery, Tiananmen Square, the Holocaust Museum, and the World Trade Center is another reminder of the cruelty of man. The 20th century had been the bloodiest in history, and I don't foresee the 21st century

being any better. We haven't learned or unlearned anything; we just
keep repeating history and getting nowhere. War. War. War. Bloodshed. Bloodshed. Bloodshed. Hatred. Hatred. Hatred. Ick! Ick! Ick!

> *"There is only one way to dispel darkness, and that is with light."*
> *- Unknown*

 **Leaving No Stone Unturned**
Traci's Diary Entry
September 7th, The Garden Route, South Africa

I board the Baz Bus at 8 AM. It is no match for the Bush Buster
but at least it has air conditioning. I can hop on and hop off, anytime,
anywhere at any of the attractions or hostels on the route between
Cape Town and JoBerg. What fun! How easy! The only thing missing is Amy. The Garden Route is one of South Africa's most stunning
scenic routes, aptly named for its lush, natural gardens, spanning 400
miles. It's sandwiched between the mountains and the Indian Ocean
and is best known for its picturesque coastline from Mossel Bay to
Port Elizabeth with its stretch of pristine beaches, charming seaside
villages, old wineries, majestic mountains, warm Indian Ocean waters,
plush forests, and a myriad of activities. I take in the charming towns
of Mossel Bay, George, Oustshoorn, Knysna, Plettenberg Bay, Natures
Valley, Storms River, Wild Coast, Transkei, Lesatho, Swaziland, Zululand, Durban, and Joberg all in the span of 20 jampacked days. There is
nothing that I haven't seen or done.

I have gone shark diving, sand boarding, abseiling, zip lining,
dune buggy racing, cave crawling, water fall jumping, tree climbing,

quad biking, river rafting, canoeing, ostrich riding, horseback riding, and fly fishing. I have made a drum, petted a whale, hiked the ship-

wreck coast, and trekked wild jungles. I have had a rendezvous with a European entrepreneur, kissed a girl, slept with a pet chicken, been French kissed by a giraffe, bottle fed baby lions,

Traci Sky Dives Above Cape Town

petted a leopard, been eaten alive by bed bugs, and chased by a wild zebra. I have tasted beetles, bugs, alligator, snake, scorpion, zebra, giraffe, llama, and caribou. Wheeeeew! What an adventure! There is just no stone I am going to leave unturned on this journey or in this life.

Traci Petting A Whale At 4:08. What An Awe Inspiring Moment http://j.mp/l9ALp1

Traci Get's To Play With One Of The Last 7,500 Cheetah's Left In The World http://j.mp/kjDWKx

---

Discoveries, Fun Facts, and Useless Tidbits

- Oregano is pronounced Oragaano .

- A bus is called a trolley.

- A flashlight is called a torch.

- A swimsuit is called a water costume.

- A boat is called a water bus.

- French fries are chips and chips are called crisps.

- A shirt is a jersey and a jacket is a jumper.

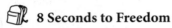 **8 Seconds to Freedom**

Traci's Diary Entry

September 18th

The Baz Bus drops me off at the buzzing and vibey Tube 'n Axe
Backpackers Lodge in Storms River. I immediately hit it off with
"Lucky Stephen," one of the transplanted owners, originally from
Europe. We sit around the blazing bonfire for the next four hours,
sipping cocoa, listening to the impromptu eclectic sounds of wannabe
musician backpackers, and chatting like old friends who haven't seen
each other in years. After being in an emotional funk since the yoga
retreat and through most of the African Overland Tour, I finally feel
ready to connect with other people again and it feels good to have
found someone I so quickly and easily cohere with. I love Lucky
Stephan's vibrant entrepreneurial spirit and I love how he is living his

dream of moving to Africa from Europe to open a destination back-packer's hostel. He has adopted the name Lucky Stephen because everyone back home says he is "lucky" to be able to go and live his dream. He invites me to watch him make his 125th bungee jump the next morning at "Face Adrenaline." I excitedly agree. There it stands - my biggest adrenaline fear. Towering 708 feet or 216 meters above South Africa the Bloukrans Bridge, is the highest bridge in Africa, and

the third highest in the world. It is in the Guinness book of world records as the highest commercial bungee jump. Lucky Stephen talks me into going to the top of the  bridge with him, rather than watching from the bottom. I have to sign a waiver to just walk across the catwalk of the bridge. I am terrified just doing that. I can't imagine what he is about to do! Crazy! When we get to the top, I can't believe the line of people waiting to do this. All of a sudden the worker grabs my catwalk ticket and tells me to harness up. A smirking Lucky Stephen informs me that he is one of the jump masters at Face Adrenaline and has been able to pull some "bungee cords" to get me a free jump. With eyes bigger than saucers, I sternly belt out "THERE IS NO WAY I AM JUMPING OFF THIS BRIDGE!" I think I have been clear that I am only here to see the pulse of this adventure, not to partake in it!

I don't really know how it happened, but the next thing I remember is being moved along, like a cow being led to slaughter. Here I am, standing on the ledge of the bridge, toes slightly hanging over, all trussed up and harnessed leg to leg with Lucky Stephen. It is a good thing my legs are bound together, otherwise they would have been trembling uncontrollably and might have prematurely vibrated me right off the ledge. I look down, with adrenaline coursing through my veins as the innate feeling of survival is thrown into question. My body is battling both nervousness and excitement in a rush of anticipation that can only be rivaled by the first time you know you are in love. I break down and bellow to the wind, in a voice loud enough for Lucky Stephen and the whole world to hear. I regurgitate every reason why I can't do it. Somehow, as I face my biggest "adrenaline demon," my biggest "inner demon" decides to unhinge itself. Unwillfully, I cry to the wind, releasing all of my angers and pains about how being sexually abused as a child had fucked up my life and my love life. I cry so hard that streams of tears and snot are falling off of my face and puddling onto the bridge. Lucky Stephen does everything to comfort me and assure me that I will live. He does everything he can to get me to let go of the baggage he now knew that I had. People scream profanities at us to jump or get off the bridge as I stand crying and unknowingly set a new record of contemplating the jump for a whopping 33 minutes. I suspect the only reason we have gotten away with it for that long is because Lucky Stephen works here .

Finally, he sternly grabs me by the lapels, stares at me square in the eyes and shout, "YOU NEED THIS!" He starts jumping up and down, with my shirt still wrapped around his clenched fists, shouting for me to jump up and down with him. The momentum starts to build, and the adrenaline starts to pump and then rush and he hollars at me to let it all out and start anew, jumping together, in unison,

I scream from the top of my lungs and from the bottom of my soul "I AM WORTHY OF HAPPINESS! IT WAS NOT MY FAULT! I AM ENOUGH! YOU DON'T OWN ME ANYMORE! YOU ARE NOT WORTH MY LIFE!". And without warning, Lucky Stephen swan-dives off the Bloukrans Bridge, jerking me off the ledge with him!

We drop 708 feet in 8 seconds falling 75 MPH. It is a silent abyss of free fall that is quiet like death and blissful like heaven. "Have I died?" I wonder. "Is this what heaven feels like… or death?" It is the most piercing sound of silence I have ever heard, and I don't want to return to earth from wherever I am! Suddenly, I am winched

back into the sky and again plummeting to earth, a few hundred feet up, a few hundred feet down, back and forth, back and forth, up and down, up and down, and then it is over. I have indeed died, and my new life has just begun. In 8 flipping seconds, life finally make sense to me. It is as if someone has pinpricked my life, and I pop open like a burst balloon and all of my demons instantaneously escape with the air. I finally understand how Nelson Mandela was able to forgive those who had imprisoned him and cheated him out of 27 years of his life. It is freedom. It is rebirthing. It is living. For I too had just forgiven and released the man who had imprisoned me and cheated me out of two decades of my life, whose murder I'd often fantasized. I finally "got" that I would not fully live, that I could not fully live, until I let go and accepted responsibility for my own happiness and destiny and transformed that murderous rage into fuel. My lessons from India become me. I feel the release from the chains begin.

When we get to the bottom of that bridge, I wrap Lucky Stephen in my arms and we kiss for a tender moment beneath the iron beams that released me from my past life. This moment feels good and he feels good. "Where did this guy come from?" I wonder. He is the perfect man to help me through this debilitating imperfection in my life. I will always remember him as one of the people who helped me get back on the road of life. And for the first time, in a long time, someone has sparked something inside of me that has warmed me up to the idea of being in a relationship again, down the line. I feel hopeful of my future and my love life.

We sit by a meadow and as he skips stones across the water in silence, I take out a piece of paper and draw a line down the center of it. On the left side I write down my every bad habit and everything I didn't like about myself, and on the right side I write who I am going to BE from this day forward and I commit to a new creed, a new ME. Today is the day I reclaim my power and take ownership of my life. That bungee jump is the single most terrifying and transforming moment of my life. It is a true re-birthing. Who knew that conquering my biggest adrenaline fear would release my biggest inner demon? It is the best therapy I have ever had and I am excited to design my new life! I am "Lucky Traci."

My Creed

Today is a great day and I have the opportunity to show up as the BEST ME EVER! I am a divine student of life and a servant to the world. I strive daily to nourish my body, mind, and spirit with truth, love, and light. I am living my dream life & I inspire others to live theirs. I am a beacon of light to all people and I empower others to achieve their goals, fulfill their dreams, and live a life of purpose and design.

From This Day Forward:

1. I am the creator of my reality. I create the exact amount of my financial success with my habits.
2. I am in love. I am in a passionate, happy, adventurous, & romantic relationship.
3. I am good. I am lucky. I am resourceful. Lucrative opportunities always come my way.
4. I am an excellent giver and receiver. I am constantly building new and genuine relationships.
5. Avalanches of health, love, happiness, wealth, & opportunity fill my life.
6. My words always flow, my message is always received, & my prayers are always answered.
7. I think big "outside of the box" thoughts, relish small pleasures, & handle setbacks gracefully.
8. I am committed to constant and never-ending personal improvement and I take massive actions to create my future as I want it.
9. I retire healthy, wealthy, and happy and share sunsets and swing sets with the love of my life.
10. I am a Dreampreneur with massive influence, impact, and income as a world-renowned author and speaker. Money & happiness flow to me easily & effortlessly.

 **The Kraal**

Traci's Diary Entry
September 19th

I have heard numerous backpackers and hostel owners talking about the Kraal. They say it is wild and remote and alternative, some sneering that the owner, Dylan, is more into animals and nature than human beings; you either love it or hate it they exclaimed. I feel like I turned a corner and I love animals and nature, I knew I'd fit right in. The Baz Bus drops me off at the Kraal Backpackers Retreat on the Wild Coast of South Africa at 11 AM. The lodge looks abandoned. Encumbered by two bulky backpacks I peevishly venture in, wondering if the owner has given up on guests and become a recluse. I clear my throat as a subtle way to announce my arrival, but no one is there. The Baz Bus is gone and I feel deserted. I can see how some of the younger

Tranquil Farm Animals

backpackers would choose a more social or lively place over this seemingly abandoned ghost-town, but there is nowhere else I would rather be. I walk around the lodge and premises for several minutes before discovering a pen of farm animals sleeping on their sides: horses, cows, sheep, and chickens. I hear a voice behind me say "Hi, I'm Dylan, would you like to check-in?" Without turning around or answering, I ask if the animals are sick. He says "No, they are tranquil." I have never seen farm animals sleeping on their sides on the ground before, like house pets. I know I am in a special place. What a steal at 300 rand for my own private room or 150 rand for the 8 bed dorm. I am Lucky Traci.

The view from my simple room is spectacular; I can lie in my bed and stare into the sea and watch whales and dolphins playing. The Kraal is off the grid, catching its own rain water for cooking and showers, and running on solar energy and candles. They grow their own food and biodegrade all of their own waste. It is 100% ecofriendly. It is the new, most beautiful place that I have ever seen. It is simply surreal and beyond any feeling of human consciousness I have ever felt. I am more aware of life, breath, touch, taste, sound, smell, and sight. I feel close to God or some kind of presence from the spirit world. I feel safe. I feel free.

Later that night, a couple of other backpackers show up. Even though I feel like being alone, I am glad I am not the only one here. We are invited to a Witch Doctor's home (a simple cow dung hut) where we partake in a ceremony to put a "spell" on a local villager to prevent her from gossiping. We walk a half hour in the pitch black, with just one candlestick shared between us, lighting our way. I trip over jagged rocks and

Witch Doctor's Gossip Removing Spell

potholes on this wannabe dirt road, and twist my ankle. We each sip from the pot of brown witch's brew, on the dirt floor to prevent any evil spirits from entering our bodies as we participate in the "spell" ceremony. We dance in circles around the room and chant foreign words to the woman who gossips too much. It is entertaining at the very least. There are chickens roaming everywhere inside of the hut and dead animal skins and carcasses decorate the walls.

Contrary to what I am led to believe, Dylan turns out to be quite sociable and kind. He is a chef and is studying to be a natural healer, a perfect addition to the eco retreat. He arranges for us to visit a school on a rolling hill in the middle of nowhere; the children surround us like we are celebrities, asking for "pens, pens, pens." The teacher is from Holland and it is her last month at the school after 12 months of volunteering. She tells me that there will not be a teacher to teach the children if another volunteer does not emerge as no locals in the area are qualified for the job. I feel so connected and alive in the Kraal, that I could have stayed longer, and I seriously contemplate taking the job. What else am I going to do with my life? I am going back home to nothing or no-thing! At least here I can make a difference in the lives of these children and this community in exchange for room and board. I would leave it better than how I found it, and I would leave better than how I arrived! I write down all of my fears in the dirt. I include all the reasons I should stay in the Kraal and all the reasons I should go home. The next day I return to the school and ask if I can do a 6 month teaching stint in exchange for room and board and they deny me. It is 12 months or nothing. I would have served 6 months. I would have served 6 months! I cry as I leave the Kraal but feel some solace that this will be another of our adopted schools. I don't want to leave, and if I had a way to cancel my reservation for a 3 day horse safari to the Transkei, I would have. Never have I cried over the beauty of a place or the beauty of an emotion that a place has drawn out of me. I don't think that life can get any better, or that my spirit can get any healthier, or that my mind can get any freer. If I get nothing more from this journey, I have gotten what I came here for and more.

Local Transport As Seen From My Packed Truck

Traci's Interesting Truck Ride To The Kraal
http://j.mp/ipfTVA

Inside The Local School At The Kraal
http://j.mp/l2QbNX

 **The Transkei**

Traci's Diary Entry
September 24th, The Transkei, South Africa

I feel like a modern day explorer on a three day horse safari through the Tanskei of South Africa. The rugged, untamed landscape

and seemingly endless coastline is mesmerizing. My-oh-my, how quickly the Kraal has been knocked from its place as being the most beautiful place my eyes have ever seen! And to think, if they would have had electricity for me to email or a phone for me to call to cancel my reservation, I would have, and darted right to Joberg to catch my flight for Egypt. Thank God for unanswered prayers. I would have missed all of this. I must admit, I'm not too keen on horses after getting thrown from one a few years back, but the beauty surpasses my fears. Besides, horseback riding allows one to truly experience the diverse region in its natural splendor.

Horse Safari Through The Beautiful
Trans Sky Of South Africa
http://j.mp/keptYU

The Transkei, birthplace of Nelson Mandela, is steeped in culture and dotted with traditional Xhosa villages that maintain the tribe's customs and rituals of years gone by. This part of South Africa is largely undeveloped, and inhabited by the Xhosa people. They are one of the 2 major ethnic groups in South Africa, the other being the Zulu people. Jobs are very scarce. The people in the Transkei basically live on subsistence farming.

We meander through the sleepy coastal hamlets and tribal villages, stopping for meals and rest. Each place is bursting with the warmth and friendly hospitality for which the Wild Coast is famous. At night the villages come alive with fire, traditional Xhosa dancers, some excellent drumming, and legends of the Xhosa people. I revel in the solitude and rawness of it all.

This is a dream right out of a magazine or movie; a fleet of wild horses takes us along deserted glittering beaches, through rich red clay mountains, over emerald rolling hills and savanna grasslands, crossing shimmering streams to arrive at a deep red sunset dreamscape. These colors have sound. Indeed these are the colors of heaven! I just can't get past them. They stop me in my tracks for hours, keeping me lost in wonder and in search of soul. No high-def camera can ever transfer this experience to paper. The Transkei is the new screensaver of my mind.

What a beautiful experience Africa has been for me, but truly, the Garden Route, Wild Coast, and Transkei in South Africa have been the highlights, excluding the Gorilla Trek and let's not forget my time with the man who had seven wives. I am Lucky Traci!

African Ambulance

Discoveries, Fun Facts, and Useless Tidbits

- More people are killed in Africa by crocodiles than by lions.

- Many children in Africa don't get the chance to go to school. If you grew up in Mali in West Africa, for example, you'd only have a one in three chance of being able to go to primary school.

- Africa is almost an island. Its only connection to other land is the tiny Sinai Peninsula in Egypt.

- The only street in the world to house two Nobel Peace prize winners is in Soweto, South Africa. Nelson Mandela and Archbishop Desmond Tutu both have houses in Vilakazi Street.

- Swaziland: ruled by a 35 year old King and his mother. The King has 11 wives and 2 fiancés. It is rumored that the King plans to "beat" his father's record of 80 wives and 100 children, with 100 wives and 200 children.

- Swaziland is in the Guinness Book of world records for having one of the worst roads in the world with the most daily and yearly traffic fatalities.

Meet The Man From Zululand
With 7 Wives
http://j.mp/kovnoe

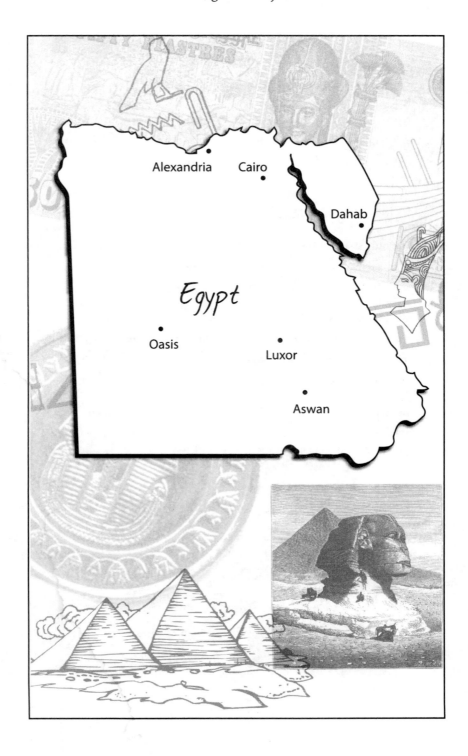

Egypt

"My favorite thing is to go where I have never been."
- Diane Arbus

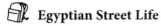 **Egyptian Street Life**

Traci's Diary Entry
September 30th, En route to Cairo, Egypt

On the 7th of October I say my farewells to South Africa and to my chains of sexual abuse. A new me boards the Egypt Air flight from Joburg to Cairo at 10:30 PM. I feel fifty pounds lighter. As overnight flight 33 slowly begins its descent through the early morning clouds, crossing over the orange tinted, sand carpet of the Sinai desert and approaching Cairo, I close my eyes and give thanks to another dream coming true. This after all is Egypt, a land famed amongst the world as an explorer's haven for five millennia. This primordial wonder has always been on my Bucket List, and armed with a fresh copy of Lonely Planet's Ancient Egypt, I am all set to explore this ancient land. I haven't been feeling so hot for a week or so. I hope I snap out of it here and reconnect with some good health to match my new attitude.

Immigration and customs are a snap. Despite everything in the airport being shut down at 6:30 AM, I manage to extract enough

Egyptian currency from an ATM to cover the cost a cab to my hotel, of course recommended by my new Lonely Planet guidebook. Pushing through the early morning swarm of taxi touts is the toughest part. Even they bicker and quibble and try stealing my business away from one another. Any traveler to Egypt will see a horde of taxis, both old and new. The new ones are black and white, metered, have working air conditioners, and working parts. The old ones are falling apart, some with no handles, definitely no air conditioner, and no chance of a working meter. Comfort is of course, based on price. Lonely Planet warns that a woman, especially a foreigner, should sit in the backseat opposite the driver. If you sit in the front seat, the driver might think you are available. I will heed the warning!

> *"Madame, Madame, where are you going? I give you best price," a few echo in unison.*

> *"The Oasis in Giza, Alexander Desert Road," I enthusiastically belt out.*

> *"No problem Madame, 300 Egyptian Pounds or $60," one driver shouts.*

> *"Madame, I have better price, only 200 Egyptian Pounds or $40," another haggles.*

I stridently make my way to an official looking taxi stand but not before a handful of independent taxi drivers follow me with protestations of constantly decreasing prices. I secure a ride at the taxi stand for 100 Egyptian pounds or $20 USD. After the driver deposits my backpacks into the trunk he looks to me with his palm out and demands "Baksheesh" (tip me now). I am flabbergasted by his brashness and flatly refuse. My "con" antenna is tingling. I sure hope this isn't a prelude to what the rest of the Egyptians are like.

As we weave through thick Cairo traffic in a fairly new black and white Mitsubishi Lancer, I gaze out the window, taking in the new sights one minute and daydreaming of home the next. The city is punctuated with both decrepit and modern buildings and dotted in between with clumps of brick houses of all shapes and sizes. The streets are overcrowded with people and cars, even at 8:30 in the morning. I wonder what my family is doing and I wonder how Amy is. The driver points out the window and turns around and says "Neel" which I caught on to be the legendary Nile River. We speed across the 6th of October Bridge, and I catch my first glimpse of the river which brings Egypt to life. I'm really excited to be here.

The Oasis Hotel is set amongst verdant greens and a carpet of wildflowers and is a good base to explore the Pyramids and Saqqara, 5 km away. What a thrill pulling into this driveway, but upon check-in I discover the prices have drastically climbed from Lonely Planet's listed price, so I dreadfully move to a nearby hostel and take a step backward into meager accommodations. But that's okay, there are so many other things to look forward to and besides, I'll only be in my room eight hours a day at best. After my first night in Egypt, I am startled out of a deep sleep and out of bed just before dawn by a chaotic noise. It draws closer and louder. It is some kind of war between blaring megaphones, music, and chanting that seems to be moving up and down the streets. I rush to the window to see if something or someone is under attack, but it is too dark to see, so I rush into the hallway to see if people are running from the building but the halls are quiet. I go back to the window and listen deeper. As I become present, I remember reading about the Islamic early morning prayer rituals of reading passages from the Quran. The racket of voices of a thousand men chanting is prayer and it echoes from mosques across the sleepy city. Feeling comforted that there isn't a war going on, I fall back asleep. Every day millions of Muslims bow down to Allah in prayer. They are required to pray 3-5 times a day, at daybreak, noon, mid-afternoon, sunset, and evening. It is interesting to see a man at his shop stop what he is doing, lay out a little personal rug and bow down in prayer. While I am not Muslim or even religious (I'm an investigator of every religion and a non-denominational believer in God. I'm Spiritual.) I admire the discipline of Muslims to what they believe in. "The essence of all religions is one. Only their approaches are different," said Gandhi.

What a strange dichotomy Egypt is. Arriving in Cairo after the tranquil Transkei is like being thrust from the third world back into the first world. Traffic spins about, cell phones and horns blare all around me, hurried people shove into me, and cars almost kill me. The western flavors of home dominate storefronts, like KFC, McDonalds, and Victoria's Secret. The market is buzzing in the early morning hours at Souk Mansour, a maze of narrow streets with sundry and merchandise that caters to tourists and locals alike; shoes, hookahs, western apparel, even giant iron safes lined the walkway. It is the typical disappointing hustle and bustle of big city living. Traffic is chaotic in Cairo. Crossing the street is an art, much like playing a human version of the video game Frogger. One has to find a space between cars and then weave lane by lane through the moving traffic that does not adhere to the painted lines of the street or the colors of traffic lights. When I first walk the city, I am surprised at the throngs of men holding hands, kissing on the lips, leaning on each other, sitting on each other's laps, and draping their arms around each other's shoulders, backs, and necks. I mean they were everywhere, and no one gives them a second look. If you see two men holding hands or kissing where I come from, it is reasonable to assume that they are gay. But here it is quite unremarkable to see two male chums sharing innocent affection with one another in the guise of friendship, not gayness. In fact, I have read that it is a crime to be homosexual in this country.

Loaded Bus

 **Will You Marry Me?**

Traci's Diary Entry
October 2nd, Cairo, Egypt

Egyptian men are some of the most handsome men I've seen on this whole trip, at least until they open their mouths and expose their yellow, rotting teeth and horrifying breath. One whiff can knock you unconscious but the turn off is not solely based on their bad breath and rotting teeth but it is the lewd and rude remarks that come out of their mouths. Sexual harassment here is overbearing despite the socially conservative nature of this traditional Muslim society. Egypt is 90% Muslim, 9% Christian, and 1% Catholic. I can't stroll through the city or bazaar for more than an hour without getting a hundred offers for dates, relentless catcalls, many of which are sexually explicit, and shameless groping, touching, and ogling. I see men with exposed genitals. One man grabs me by the arm and asks if I will kiss him on the mouth and flashes five Egyptian pounds at me (the equivalent of $1 USD), while another boldly squeezes my butt and yells "thank you" as he walks past. One man asks me if I like to be French-kissed on the bum while another stares at me and asks if I will marry him and bring him to America for 1,000 Egyptian pounds. Clearly, sexual harassment of tourists has no limits here. It is still hard to accept a culture that is more tolerant of sexual harassment than my own and offers more respect to their pets than its women.

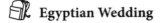 **Egyptian Wedding**
Traci's Diary Entry
October 4th

I went to a travel agency to book a flight to the Holy Land for next week or the week after. I am informed that it is not safe for me to go there because I am American. In fact, they outright refuse to sell me a ticket. I am pissed! I am right next door to the HOLY LAND and it is not safe for me to visit. Funny, we let everyone into our country and everyone feels safe and protected there. Hell, if they stay long enough, we even pay them! There is seriously a flaw in our world relations and a serious flaw in human beings. Nevertheless, it isn't a complete loss. Aladdin, the ticket agent, invites me to an Egyptian wedding, and I accepted his invitation.

Aladdin escorts me to the wedding. We meet in front of the travel agency, but he has to walk 10 feet ahead of me as if he doesn't know me for the whole 15 minute walk to the wedding grounds. He does not speak to me until we get into the confines of the outdoor wedding. This is a wedding unlike anything I've ever seen before. The wedding ceremony takes place in a big clearing of land, with more than 5,000 people in attendance. There is a huge Arabic tent called the Sewan and entertainment

Traditional Egyptian Wedding

includes belly dancers and singers with music blaring so loud that it is impossible to hear anything, let alone have any kind of conversation. Food, drinks, shisha pipes (water pipes used for smoking flavored tobacco or hash), and hash joints are passed to guests by the hundreds. Who am I to be rude and decline in partaking in Egyptian tradition? I consume everything that is passed to me, and it is all yummy. The customary food is "fattah," which is pieces of lamb meat embedded in rice and bread dipped in stew. The bride and groom leave their own wedding remarkably early, but the guests continue the festivities and celebration of their union. What a fun day and fun wedding! I feel very grateful to have been invited and exposed to such tradition. I am Lucky Traci!

Egyptian Wedding
http://j.mp/mo0lIQ

On the walk back, Aladdin still stays a few feet ahead. I assume that his invitation to join him for a beer at his favorite watering hole is an extension of this top-notch hospitality, and it is. Over bottles of Stella Artois, we talk about his life in Egypt and my life in the United States. He dreamily asks me about my America; he seems deluded by thoughts that everyone lives the life of a movie star and that every life has a storybook ending. I have to inform him that many people in America die with more debt than savings, and most citizens die with their dreams unmet. I realize that it's fashionable to talk about what's wrong with America rather than what's right with it, but I have to set the record straight and unveil the myth that real life is not like in the movies. I mean he seems totally aghast to learn that pretty little America is full of the same flaws and scars, ugly people, government control, and greed as his Egypt. Many Americans define who they are by their career. They live a life dictated by their children. They abandon their parents in nursing homes because they are too busy to care for them. They judge a man by the thickness of his wallet. They do just enough to get by and stay comfortable. The world is controlled by the same monopolies of basic commodities like fuel oil, energy, food, transportation, the media, taxes, and drugs. There is a misnomer called "health care" that keeps us addicted to prescription drugs, and America is no exception. In fact, it is the leader.

I explain that I am the same working slave to my government as he is to his, only I have a longer and looser noose around my neck, and I have access to more luxuries, opportunities, and personal choices than he does. But the moment I don't turn over a percentage of my hard-earned wages to an elite group of puppet masters who pocket my money and give it to causes that I don't believe in, I am thrown in jail.

I launch into another lyrical rant studded with superlatives. In the "Land of the Free" we are imposed to wear seatbelts, helmets, get vaccinations to enter school, eat genetically modified school lunches, and pay for insurance. When we act free and get caught, we are punished with heavy fines or jail time even if we aren't harming anyone else. In America it is illegal to go a few miles above the speed limit, smoke a natural herb, and walk down the street with a beer in hand. It's against the law be married to more than one person at a time but there is no punishment for fathering eleven children with nine different women, like the deadbeat who grew up in my neighborhood did, leaving seven of his children's mothers to rely on government assistance. We are forced to take a drug test to get a job but the people on welfare don't have to take a drug test to claim the free money that we are forced to give them. We can't offer a service that allows terminally ill patients to end their pain and their lives peacefully although we can do that for our beloved pets. When someone murders, rapes, or abuses another human being and they are sent to prison, they are often freed on early release for good behavior. Life in prison does not mean you will spend your life in prison. Our prisoners live nicer, eat better, and have more amenities than many poor people. America is no longer a rich land of manufacturing; it's become a complacent land of consumption. It is no longer the entrepreneurial melting-pot of the world, where people come to build a great life for themselves on sweat equity; it's become a melting pot of takers and lazy citizens. My barrage ends and it is my turn to ask him questions about his life and country. Poor Aladdin looks dismayed and I feel bad that I have deflated his American dream.

Discoveries, Fun Facts, and Useless Tidbits According to Aladdin

- A woman has an unmarriable reputation and name if she ever works in a bar.

- Every man must serve in the Army. The military monthly salary is up to 50 Egyptian pounds or $7.00 USD. Your length of service is based upon your education level.

- Prisons in Egypt are 10 x 10 cells with up to 100 people in them at a time. Sitting or lying down is not permitted. His friend who has just been released from prison said that it was so hot in there that prisoners were standing in their underwear. An 8 year prison sentence means that you will serve eight years in prison. You are not released early because you behaved well during your punishment. He assures me that the prisoners here do not live nicer than most poor people. "It is prison," he exclaimed, and just how it should be in my opinion.

- Thirty-five percent of Egyptian woman are hookers. The hourly rate for a hooker is 50 Egyptian pounds (big money) or $7.00 USD.

- Average rent for an average place is 700-1000 Egyptian pounds or $100-150.00 USD.

- Employees only get paid once a month.

- Education is compulsory in Egypt and free through high school. Notwithstanding this fact, the literacy rate for Egyptians is a low 57 percent.

- Egypt is in the process of becoming a major exporter of natural gas.

- Although the longest river in the world, the Nile is never more than 20 kilometers or 12.5 miles wide.

Ancient Relics, Artifacts, and Museums
Traci's Diary Entry
October 6th

I have always wanted to visit Egypt, but like most people, my imagination or notion of it consisted of the majestic pyramids, the famous Sphinx, the legendary Cairo Museum, decomposing mummies, medieval streets, hieroglyphic covered walls, women in black veils, men smoking water pipes, feluccas sailing on the Nile, yellowed papyrus paper and quill pens, falafels caked in cream sauce and nothing more. Beyond the pyramids there are temples, cultured highlights, impressive desert landscapes, the Red Sea coast, the Nile River, desolate sand, lime, and basalt deserts with bizarre rock formations. In reality, Cairo is a bursting at the seams with first world luxuries and contemporary distractions. Traditional third world life and first world modernization collide here and have created a perfect storm of progressive living. They have mastered the art of capitalizing on their infamous tourist attractions.

The first stop of my whirlwind tour as far as relics is concerned, is the Egyptian Museum in Cairo, the Holy Grail of museums. There are more than 120,000 treasures and artifacts from ancient Egypt. This outdated museum is absolutely stuffed to the brim with some of the most incredible ancient objects in the world. My guide Habine sheds some light on the enormity of the museum's collection. He said, "If you spent one minute looking at each piece, you will be here around-the-clock for nine months." Just like with most of my trip around the world and for each country I've been to and each city I have visited, I barely scratch the surface on what there is to see and do here.

Seeing a glimpse of a place is still better than not seeing it at all. I am exhausted after just five hours in the museum, until I hit the Mummy Room and get a second wind of fascination to the tune of another two hours. The "NO PHOTOS" sign becomes irrelevant after a museum worker suggests I snap a couple souvenir photos, for a small tip. Next stop is to the Pyramids and a restaurant serving Nile perch, a culinary treat that I've heard numerous tourists rave about.

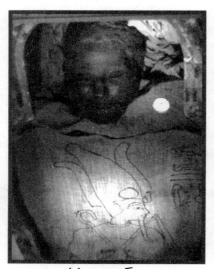

Mummy Face

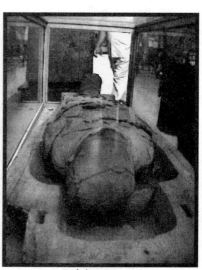

Mummy

The Real "Pyramid Scheme"

Traci's Diary Entry
October 9th, John Lennon's Birthday.

The Pyramids of Giza are uncanny and breathtakingly beautiful, an obvious choice of entertainment. I think everybody will agree. Millions of tourists like me flock to the Giza plateau to contemplate the pyramids of Khufu, Khafre, and Menkaure, but from the minute

I arrive at Giza to the minute I depart, I am subject to a constant barrage of "Hello my friend, where are you from?" "Want your picture taken?" "Want to buy my postcards?" "Want to come to my perfume shop?" "Want to go on my tour?" "Want to stay at my hotel?" They try shoving hats on my head, souvenirs in my hand, and food in my mouth. I am constantly hassled, like every two feet; there is no way to avoid it, touts were everywhere. I know these people are very poor and are simply trying to make a living but it isn't sales, it is sheer harassment. They mistake my politeness for weakness, and I have to get mean after the thousandth "NO!" All they want is my sterling, my Egyptian pounds and all I want is a moment of peace to take in the miracle that stands before me. I cave, and ask how much it is to take my photo in front of the Pyramids and the man says "3 Egyptian pounds," so I do. Bearing his rotting yellow teeth, he says, "Hey let me snap one more of you on my camel in front of the Pyramids," so I do, of course, knowing he will charge me another few additional Egyptian pounds for the minute long job. After he snaps my photo he says "You must pay me $50 USD before you can get off my camel." The dirty skinned, oily haired, middle-aged man refuses to let me down until I commit to an expensive ride or offer the equivalent in a bribe, known in Egypt as "baksheesh." I try to negotiate a price with him and muster some traveler excitement; I mean here I am, at the base of the Great Pyramid for gosh sakes. He won't budge and holds me prisoner on top of his camel for several minutes, repeatedly demanding $50 USD. Getting off a camel is just as difficult and awkward as getting on. There is just no way to easily jump off or slide down and I scrape myself in the process of a half slide, half jump maneuver and end up thumping the ground with my whole body. I leap up and chase him, as he sprints off with Amy's camera. I chase him on this sandy marathon until he finally drops the camera on the ground. I am going for blood this time and he knows it. Lucky thing I don't catch him because I am raging with

Just Before Getting Ripped Off

super-human adrenaline and anger from 23 months of being lied to, cheated, scammed, conned, ripped off, mugged, bitten, and robbed. I am about to take it all out on him. I am not consciously thinking and am reacting from hate.

If I had caught him, there is no doubt that I'd be sitting in an Egyptian jail cell right about now, unlikely to return home. The beauty of the Pyramids does supersede the near-prison experience and opens up my heart to the miraculous wonder before my eyes. The tourists, scammers, and commercialism still don't detract from the sight and experience of the Giza Pyramids. Despite what has happened, I am completely in awe in their presence, feeling the majesty of thousands of years of history. There is magic in those Pyramids and the experience has been worth it. They are beautiful; the people are ugly. I refuse to let them get the best of me and ruin my time.

A Guided Tour of the Road Less Travelled

Traci's Diary Entry
October 10th

The day starts out great. I stumble into an area of laborers that plays out like a scene from an old time movie. I watch this live black and white, third-world reality for nearly an hour. It is incredible to see people making cement blocks by hand in the twenty first century. Next,

I make my way to a temple and it is like Groundhog Day from yesterday, all over again. I think back to the lecture at the retreat, "Your Attitude + Your Choices = Your Life." I immediately return to my room. I'm opting out of this abuse. I need a chief aim, a plan, a strategy. I grab my map and make a list of what I all want to see and do here and calculate how long it will all take. I think Amy would be proud. I hightail it over to the travel agency to see Aladdin. He hires me a private female guide to drive me around to see attractions like the City of the Dead, Abu Simbel, The Egyptian Museum of Antiquities, Medieval Cairo, Temples of

Karnak, Hurghada, and the Temple of Luxor. A guide named Nefera will drive me around Cairo, Suez, and Memphis and then I will take a train to Alexandria and Luxor. Someone from Nefera's sister company will take over from there. I also book a 5 day cruise on the Nile River from Luxor to Aswan, and since I'm banned from going to Jerusalem, I decide that Greece is my next destination, leaving on October 31st. Aladdin books that for me as well. He is happy with his big commission and I am happy with my big plans, tout-free.

Tours, Tours, and more Tours

Traci's Diary Entry
October 12th

Via train or guided tour, a travel through Egypt is the most spellbinding history lesson I have ever had. I see everything and I go

Abu Simbel

everywhere. Tours, tours, and more tours, day after day after day, but one clearly stands out! Nothing prepares me for the lone masterpiece cradled in the middle of the Sahara Desert between blonde sand and brown water about 270 km south of Aswan near the Sudan border. I gasp when my driver rounds the mountain and I get my first glimpse of the massive rock temples of Abu Simbel, hewn out of rock cliffs during the reign of Ramses II dating from 1250 B.C. I have never seen such majesty. Giant statues guard the door and hieroglyphics cover the walls and ascend with the narrow passageways.

I stand in awe, gazing at the four colossal statues of Pharaoh Ramses II, wearing the double crown that symbolizes upper and lower Egypt. They form the temple's facade, two on each side of the temple's entrance. The carved sandstone monuments towers 65 feet in the air, hewn from the rock and cliff

Abu Simbel Hieroglyphics

face. Abu Simbel is the most impressive ancient Egyptian monument that I've visited so far, and it has left an indelible imprint in my heart and mind. The most remarkable thing about these temples is that they were originally built in a different location. After the Aswan High Dam was constructed across the Nile, the rising waters threatened to swallow the temples, so UNESCO funded the $42 million dollar project, and in the spring of 1965, workers injected the sandstone with synthetic resin and hand-sawed the entire complex into 1050 massive blocks. By the autumn of 1967, all the blocks were moved and impeccably reassembled at the current site just 210 meters from the old site. Admission into Abu Simbel is 35 Egyptian pounds or $7 USD. Adjacent to Abu Simbel is the Temple of Hathor which is free of charge with admission to Abu Simbel. What a delightful treat.

Each tour starts early in the morning and lasts past dinner or early evening. None of the tours provide lunch, and the tour guide never asks me once if I want to stop for lunch on any of the days we are together. Finally around 3:00 PM I ask how much longer it will be before we stop for lunch and she snaps her head around and sneers in a demeaning tone "You want

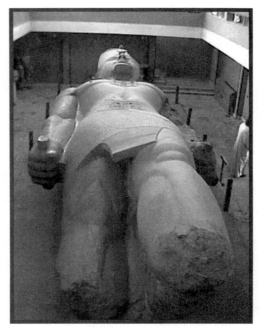

A Broken Artifact

to eat! You know that if we have to make a special stop for you we will get back an hour later don't you?" Of course, I want to eat. She knows that I haven't had breakfast because she picked me up from my hotel at 4:30 AM and everything had been closed! I was amazed how she could go so long without food or drink, and then it dawned on me that she must be Muslim and on her Ramadan fasting cycle, a month of fasting where participating Muslims refrain from eating and drinking and is intended to teach them about patience, humility, and spirituality. Nefera and the driver both sit in the car and wait for me to eat at a little café-style restaurant. It isn't until I order my food and go to sit down that I notice there isn't a single table or chair to eat at in the entire restaurant; everyone is eating and standing. I join them. Egyptian food is excellent. It is a marriage of Mediterranean and Arab cuisines. I opt for the yogurt and turmeric marinated vegetable kebabs, a delight on my palate and empty stomach.

 Feluccas on the Nile in Aswan
Traci's Diary Entry
October 15th

I've been very ill, having to return to my hotel to lie down several times in a day. I've had a fever, diarrhea, no appetite, and an upset stomach for some time now and when I really think about it, it's getting worse. On top of that I'm menstruating, and finding woman's sanitary products on this trip has been a chore. After the fourth store I do find some, but oddly, they are sold individually rather than in packages or boxes. I'm wishing now that Amy would have left me some of her antibiotics. I'm also wishing that she were here about now to take care of me. Of course, she has missed out on the best and most beautiful part of the entire trip, but actually, I just miss my best friend sharing this experience with me. My heart is still resolute. I miss her but I'm not ready to accept her back into my life. I know that I'll be all the way back home when I can let go of that last pain and see her departure as what Amy needed to do for Amy rather than another betrayal of Traci. It has turned out to be somewhat of a blessing as I have learned new lessons in self-reliance and have released the chains of my past.

I meet a nice woman named Maki from Japan on the train from Luxor to Aswan. We become fast friends and I persuade her to stay at the same hotel as me, recommended by Lonely Planet. We meet in the lobby at 9 AM and decide to go to the parade and wander the markets together today and then take a felucca ride. She is so nice, and I'm glad I have someone to do things with. I have truly enjoyed her company and feel safer travelling as a pair. It's impossible to escape the touts selling felucca rides. A stroll down the street attracts solicitations from all directions. Finding a reliable captain, however, is another story, as everyone here seems to overpromise and under deliver. Rather than interviewing captains, inspecting boats, and skimming guest-book reviews, we decide to follow the best advice I know, Lonely Planet. We head straight to Shukri Saad at the Aswan tourist information office for a list of names of reliable captains. We hire Mohammad, a toothless local who looks like he just got out of bed, and has the breath to prove it. Feluccas are traditional Egyptian slow sailing boats that can be crewed by just one man, and they have remained, over the centuries, the primary form of transportation on the Nile just as during the time of the Pharaohs. All the historical and cultural destinations are located along the banks of the Nile River and sight-seeing these places by felucca are an inexpensive experience worth cherishing and a great escape from the hustle and bustle of the city and the harassment of the touts. Mohammad uses a long pole to push us from the clunky dock out into the famous water way. The Nile is a gorgeous river to behold with every shade of blue imaginable. The sight of the waters flowing through the majestic desert is truly mesmerizing. Despite there being no wind today, he unfurls the sail. Within minutes, the sun has risen and it is starting to get hot on the boat. Mohammad pulls a separate canvas sheet over the iron ribs of a nearby pole above us, giving us a little shade. Eventually a small breeze kicks up and we use the sails for maybe ten minutes. We lazily drift past beautiful bedrock art soaked in exquisite colors of summer, quaint hamlets buzzing with locals attending to their daily chores, crumbling ancient tombs strewn with snap-happy tourists, colorful indigenous birds resting on fan-leafed palms called palmyra, grazing cattle cloaked on emerald green mounds, and aged leathery-faced fishermen loading their rickety boats in hopes for a day's catch. It is a wonderful experience for 60 Egyptian pounds an hour, especially since Mohammad doesn't shove his lips against ours as we climb off the boat, like the one next to us does to his pretty teenaged Asian passenger.

Maki and I speak of getting something to eat, and Mohammad mentions his brother's restaurant is across the way. We agree to check it out. Expecting an American version, I order a falafel and I receive a plate with one single falafel ball and one cucumber slice on the side. Turns out, I had to order the humus spread, lettuce, tomato, and bread each individually. Besides that and the fact that there are some hidden charges on our bill, the food is actually good and very inexpensive. While we wait for our meal to be served, we are not only given a couple of small dishes of chips, we are HAND-FED them! The service is stellar, though awkward, and each time our glass of soda or beer is even an inch low, our server comes over to fill our glasses from the remainder of our bottle and places a chip in each of our mouths whether we want one or not. When we get our check we noticed we have been charged for two bowls of chips that are ordinarily complimentary in America and we have been charged a service fee for EACH time the server has refilled our glass from our already purchased bottle of beer or soda.

Discoveries, Fun Facts, and Useless Tidbits

- Anytime I order sauce with a meal, I receive a single packet of ketchup. At least it is Heinz.

- No matter where I go in Egypt, when I order a glass of orange juice, I receive a glass of good ole fashion TANG! And when I order fresh mango juice from the restaurant of my fancy hotel, I am given an empty glass with a child-sized mango juice box that contains 35% mango juice.

- I bare witness on a number of occasions to straws being recycled at a restaurant. They simply rinse them off and stick them in the next customer's beverage. I always refuse the straw, knowing that a hundred mouths may have sipped from it before me.

- There are extra charges for napkins, salt, pepper, mayo, pickles, olives, lettuce, and tomato, at everyplace I have eaten so far.

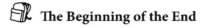 ## The Beginning of the End

Traci's Diary Entry
October 17th, Nile River Cruise Ship
Day 1

So far on my world tour I've been transported by elephants, camels, planes, trains, automobiles, scooters, bicycles, hollowed out trees, rafts, bungee cord, moto-cars, dune buggies, boats, rickshaws, tuk-tuks and donkeys, and I am expecting this 5 star cruise to be my favorite and most comfortable transportation. However, you're not going to believe this. Aladdin my travel agent makes a mistake and books me on a non-English speaking cruise ship. We've already set off to sea before the mistake is noticed. I'm on a Dutch and Egyptian speaking ship going on a five day cruise from Cairo to Alexandria. There isn't one single person aboard who speaks English, and I'm trapped on here for 5 days. This is an expensive lesson on this back-packer's pocketbook. I might as well be on vacation by myself. The only words anyone knows is "Hello!", "What's your name?", and "What country are you from?" When I board the cruise everyone says "Hello" and my guide drives me to the port herself, gets me checked-in, and helps with my bags. I settle into my cabin right away and kick my feet up and read a book for a couple of hours. It isn't until lunch, when I go to my assigned table that I realize the mistake. I comment to my table-mates that I have never been on a 5 star luxury liner that uses paper plates, plastic utensils, paper napkins, and serves wine and juice from a box, but the entire table just looks at me blankly. One lady shakes her head at me and speaks in a foreign language. I realize they are all speaking Dutch, so I call over the server and nonchalantly ask to be moved to a different group, but he doesn't understand what I am saying either. Panic stricken, I jump from my seat and ask another server, and another, until I run out of servers to approach. None of them can understand me, nor can I understand them. Someone has alerted a Egyptian supervisor or captain looking guy to come to my table, and he too begins talking to me in gibberish. Now I haven't been feeling well for weeks, but is my mind playing tricks on me? Is this some kind of practical joke? Am I on Candid Camera? Seriously, I glance at the ceiling in search of a camera, but there are none. This is no longer a dream, this is a nightmare!

I lose my appetite and go up to the sun deck where I sit on the edge of the pool swishing my feet in the water. It is a warm and sunny day, home to a beautiful coastline, and I am on a dream vacation, cruising the longest river in the world. The only thing missing is someone to share it with who speaks English. Moments later the Egyptian supervisor or captain looking guy taps me on the shoulder and motions for me to follow him. He takes me into a little control room and there on the CB radio is Aladdin!

"Traci, it looks like there has been a mistake, and you are on the wrong boat."

No shit Sherlock! I think, but don't say. "Aladdin! What are we going to do?" I ask.

"Well, if you just stay on the ship, I can refund you $100 of your $210 USD ticket price. Otherwise, you can switch boats when we arrive at the next port tomorrow afternoon. What do you want to do?" he asks.

"Well what do you think I want to do? Idiot!" crosses my mind.
"I'd like to disembark this luxury liner at the next port," I utter.

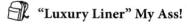 "Luxury Liner" My Ass!

Traci's Diary Entry
October 18th
Day 2

Deciding to leave the cruise is a no brainer. It has an American rating of about 2.5 at best. Everything is plastic, in plastic, or served on plastic. I can't read anything on this ship, and I have not a soul to converse with. The best part of this cruise so far has been the Egyptian massage at the end of the hall for $15/hr. I've had massages all over the world, and this by far is the best I have ever received. There are times I think he is close to crossing the line with his touches, but I let him get away with it. He must have enjoyed groping me as much as I enjoyed letting him because he ends up giving me an extra 30 minutes at no extra charge. That's right, a 90 minute massage for $15 and no tip, a far cry from the $65 an hour American prices. If massage prices were more reasonable in America, I would get them weekly. I never could understand how someone who rubs my feet makes more than I do when I was riding the rescue squad, working in the ER, or assisting in surgery. Another sad and unscrupulous American idiocy, but that's okay, I'm done with all that. I think swami is onto something, there is something bigger out there for me to do and it's on its way to find me.

I'm actually looking forward to going to Europe next and being in a world a little closer to my own. At least I'll have peace of mind in walking the streets, paying the same prices as the locals, eating inspected food, drinking cleaner water, and using normal transportation. Greece is my first stop, then onto Turkey, Italy, and France. Where I go thereafter depends on if I have any money left. I know Europe will eat up my funds very quickly; I will have to budget strategically. Amy's method of planning is really coming in handy these days.

I'm feeling terrible today, feverish. I go to the ballroom and see there is some kind of Egyptian costume party going on. They dress me up, but after ten minutes I have to come back to my room. I get sick in the bathroom for awhile and stand in the shower for a good fifteen minutes before lying down. Something is wrong, really wrong. Yes, I'm a little homesick. Yes, I'm a little beat up. Yes, I'm a little worn down. Yes, it sucks not having anyone to talk with here. Yes, I wish Amy were here. Maybe these things are tiny little contributing factors, and maybe after 700 days on the road, living out of a backpack, this trip is finally catching up with me. Still I think it is something deeper than all of that. I feel strange inside, and I cannot describe it. Something is just wrong, and I have no one to tell. I miss my mom and dad.

That is the last diary entry and photo taken of me on my world tour. Here's what happened…

 No Story Book Ending

Traci's Diary Entry
Racine, Wisconsin

On the second day of that luxury cruise, my planned departure day, I don't show up for breakfast or lunch. Somebody notices my absence. I'm assuming it is the crew who breaks into my cabin and finds me lying in a feverish sweat. I have vague recollections of it all. I have occasional flashbacks of several people standing over me, talking above me in a foreign language and shoving some sort of pills or medication into my mouth. The next thing I remember is being carried off the ship and then being adjusted into the seat of a train, where my head rests against the window. I remember the ride is long and I sleep much of the way. I have video footage aimed through the window from my seat, capturing the lovely scenery outside, so I know at one point I am coherent enough to record part of the ride back, I just don't remember it. I turn the video camera on myself and record my last will and testimony for my family. I tell each family member what they mean to me and that I love them. I tell them I want to be cremated and my ashes scattered in the wind as I feel that I am in process of dying.

A train attendant checks on me periodically, giving me sips of water and at one point offers me some broth. I remember asking her where I am, where my bags are, and where I am going. She tells me that I am going from Alexandria to Cairo and that I have been on the train for fifteen hours. She tells me I am sick and have a temperature of 104 degrees, and that the ship had made an emergency port stop. I am being taken to a medical facility in Cairo.

When the train stops after the seventeen and a half hours, two men are waiting to retrieve me from the train and transfer me to a medical facility. After a day and an intravenous round of antibiotics, I don't feel like I am dying anymore, but I am still quite ill and the decision is made for me to go home. We call my family to tell them that they have a sick kid on the way; I am on the next flight to America. It is time. I am wounded. I am done. I am severely ill for nine weeks, but not well for more than six months. It turns out that I have contracted three types of intestinal parasites and unknowingly been bitten between the webbing of my toes by a venomous Egyptian spider. I'll never know how, where, or when the spider got me, but the infection is big enough to slide a Q-Tip half way into the bite site. The first question my American infectious disease specialist asks is if I have ingested any water from the Nile River, one of the dirtiest waterways in the world. I tell him I have brushed my teeth several times in the shower on the cruise ship and may have inadvertently swallowed a little of the water in the rinsing process. As it had been a non-English speaking boat, warning signs about not drinking the water, posted in each cabin bathroom, are useless for me.

To this day, it all remains a blur. I do not know who any of those people are who helped me or how they coordinated the train to hospital transfer 17 hours away. I've never been able to thank anyone for their help and kindness, and I never saw or heard from Aladdin again.

Returning Home

Traci's Diary Entry
October 19th, Racine, Wisconsin, My old room of my parent's house

I don't even remember how I got to the airport, but with a little help from someone, I slung my now 82 pound backpack over my shoulders for the final time and board my plane back to my America. There are no weight restrictions leaving Africa, unless there has been some exception made for a sick person onboard. My pack is plum full of handcrafted souvenirs from Africa. I am surrounded by English speaking people the whole flight home, and I never utter a single word. I wasn't just ill. I was broken. I was broken in every sense of the word: physically, mentally, emotionally, spiritually, and financially. And it all came crashing down just as I was on the cusp of getting it all together, so I could return home with a concrete plan.

I spot my mom and dad immediately. They are standing in the reception area of the arrivals terminal. My dad has grown a few wrinkles and my mom has grown a few gray hairs. I have just grown, but I am not sure into who or what yet. Their appearance makes me vividly aware of how much time has passed, two long years. My journey has been challenging for them too and they have supported me and our sister schools every step of the way. I feel awkwardly oversized in their presence, and then we embrace and I know I am home; it is as if no time has passed at all and nothing and no one has really changed, but me. My dad nearly gets a hernia carrying my backpack to the car and asks how I have managed to lug it around the world. It is a quiet ride home. I am too tired and ill to engage in stories. I stink like spoiled oil and earth. My parents have to drive back to Wisconsin from Chicago with the windows open, on a chilly fall day.

When we arrive at their home, I strip in the garage, and my mom takes my smelly clothing and the contents from my backpack directly to the washing machine. I take a 45 minute hot water shower and burn through 3 razors. My dad takes my two backpacks outside and delouses them, where they lay for days. I straggle to the couch where I lay for weeks! Couch, doctor, bed, couch, doctor, bed, couch…

After 717 days of waking up in hotels, hostels, tents, huts, trains, planes, overland vehicles, and other people's houses, I am now in my old room of my parents' home, where I haven't lived for more than a decade. It is 3 AM; I stare at the ceiling for hours and reflect on my situation and replay swami's words over and over again. I am abruptly thrust back inside of a place and a life that I am not ready to be in. I haven't gotten closure from my journey. I haven't completed my plan for my future. I haven't made it to my European leg of the journey. I haven't returned back to Hawaii to live. I am not mentally prepared to be here. I still have two months of travel left in which to figure out my life's plan. It is a painful re-entry. It isn't supposed to happen this way.

Epilogue

Coming Full Circle

🎒 **Traci**

I spend six months recovering at my parent's house from my illness. Not to mention, I suffer severe reverse culture shock. Returning home after 717 days of backpacking around the world is as much of a culture shock to me as the day I planted my feet onto Chinese soil, two years ago this moment. I stand in front of the 4,000 boxes of cereal at the Piggly Wiggly and a prickling rush of anxiety crushes me like a ten pound weight. There is a mill of choices. Noise, fat people, clutter, ringing cell phones, gossip, chaos, processed food, and Western prices meet my every step. It takes weeks for me to transition from what used to be my normal life and to adjust back into the ways of America and the overconsumption of American living.

My journey has been laden with lessons and epiphanies that far supersede all that imperiled it. There has been more laughter than sadness, more tears of joy than of sorrow, more love than anger, more hellos than good-byes, more ahas than oh-nos. In the strangest corners of uncivilized places, I have discovered the wonders of the world and recognized the wonders of my own world. I have discovered the kindness of strangers and learned empathy and compassion. I have discovered the meaning of life, and I have found my purpose in life. I have discovered the devotion that other people offer to their God, and I have grown closer to my own God. I have discovered truth, and I uncovered my own inner beauty. I have discovered love and I have released my demons of hate. I have discovered how to forgive transgressions against me, and I have asked to be forgiven of my own. Best of all, I have discovered how to dream and how to live fully. It has taken a trip around the world for me to discover all that.

Happiness lives inside of me and home is wherever I am in the world. I have been shown the value of life in so many ways, and the meaning of living, through so many people. I may not be able to save the world, but certainly I can be the saving grace in one person's life and if attitudes are contagious, then I can choose to live one that is worth catching.

Six months after the fact, backpacking around the world has not only changed my life, it has changed the course of my life and my quest for enlightenment and self-mastery has deepened. The journey hasn't made me more worldly in terms of history or knowledge, but it has grossly eased the clamps of my ignorance and singular world views. It has never been about seeing destinations around the world for me; it has always been about the journey and the growth born from it. Life has become a much happier place since I decided I wanted a happier life and took ownership of it and responsibility for how I responded to the adversities, roadblocks, dream killers, and naysayers that I encounter along the way. I know now that there is nothing I am not capable of achieving.

And now when the weight of the first world rushes over me and tramples my thoughts and spirit at 3 AM, I think back to my retreat in India, lie down on the floor with real carpet, rest my eyes and my mind, and breathe in God. No panic attack! I guess I'll live through this transition after all.

I am the wealthiest, penniless person I have ever known.

Amy

Five months have flown by already, and I am still happy to be home, but often I find my mind drifting back over the last year and a half and remembering what I was doing a year ago at this time. It seems like it was only last week instead of a year ago that we were repacking our bags and making sure we had everything we needed. I read my diary entries before going to sleep at night, and I laugh at how we were dumped in the middle of the freeway with our backpacks and forced to find our own way to the bus station, or how the Chinese kitchen staff would laugh and point at us as we mixed all our vegetables together, or how we had to play charades in order to communicate what we wanted. We had some great times. I wonder how little Muong and Sun are doing in Vietnam or if Babu in India has found other lady tourists to watch out for. I look around at other people in this city and even in this state and then compare them to the people I saw on the other side of the world and the differences seem to melt away. There are good people and bad people in every country. There are honest people and deceitful people in every country. There are people who want to work hard and people who are lazy in every country. Most people all over the world want a better life for their children and are willing to do almost anything to make that happen. Most people that we met while traveling would give almost anything to have the chance to come to this country, but their perception of life in this country may be based on a television show rather than reality. There are times now that I wish we were just starting our trip so I could do it all over again, especially now that I am back to a full-time job, furnishing and keeping up an apartment, and trying to become reacquainted with the city I left 20 years ago. It seems somewhat foreign to me to not be planning which country I will visit next or how I will get there or what I will do once I get there. I already am thinking about when I will be able to take another 3 months off and go to Africa, and I will admit that there are days that I wish I would have just gone forward to Africa with Traci. Now that I have been home for awhile I feel like I am ready to travel again, but now I have a pet and a job. I am somewhat limited on how long I can be away, not to mention the fact that my current financial situation won't allow me to take 3 months off anytime soon, and my travel partner is still not talking to me. I am glad to be home but it sure hasn't taken long for me to get bogged down in the daily routine of life. But that's okay; I like where I am. I hope Traci has found the peace and purpose she was looking for.

Traci

A couple years pass before Amy and I speak again though I think about her regularly. Then on the anniversary of the day that she left me in India I extend the olive branch. We snap back together and into each other's lives with the elasticity and intensity of a new rubber band. She immediately drives down for a visit. We embrace and we cry. We stay up all night in true slumber party fashion, thumbing through thousands of pictures, watching hours of video footage, and reminiscing about our journey. We recollect all the silly things that happened on our trip, like when Amy ate the pot pizza and fell out of bed, or when

I knock the lady with my backpack on the subway and try to say "excuse me" but say something obscene enough for her to tell the entire subway car leaving everyone laughing and pointing fingers at me, or when the chef at our luxury hotel is seen picking a booger out of his nose and then resumes his bread kneading duties, or when we mistakenly show up to catch our train an entire day early. We laugh for hours and by the end of the night, we are talking about climbing the ancient ruins of Machu Picchu together. Oh my, how I have missed my best friend.

Amy

Finally after a couple years of silence Traci contacted me. It took her longer to come around than I had expected. I guess she was angrier or more hurt than I had ever thought. Her African expedition certainly sounded like it was incredible and it made me wish I had continued on with her so that I could have seen and experienced it too, but I chose a different path. We're already throwing around the idea of traveling to South America for a couple months. I'm glad I have her to travel with as there aren't many people our age who are willing to strap on a backpack and stay in hostels in order to explore the world. She seems much more mature and capable then when we went our own ways in India. She's the truest friend I've ever had and I've missed her much more than I ever thought I would. Since returning to Wisconsin I have landed a great job as a Physician Assistant that allows me a lot of vacation time, so I'll get to Africa yet. I'm taking online classes to earn a graduate degree and have bought a house and a lakeside cabin. After dating a lot of duds from online dating sites I was one date away from calling it quits when I met Dave. We've been together ever since. I've come to terms with my new post-surgery appearance, like I have a choice in the matter at this point. I like some of the changes, but not all of them. I still think it is very apparent that I've had plastic surgery done, and I still have a tendency to avoid mirrors as I do not see the reflection in the mirror that I am expecting to see.

📖 Traci

During the six months I'm laid up at my parent's house, I manage to write two books from the comfort of my parents couch: Romance-411: Your Little Black Book of Romantic Ideas, and Romance-911: Your Emergency Guide to Romance. They are bursting at the seams with all the fun ideas that I have collected from around the world. I even muster enough energy to attend a speech class at Gateway Technical College. Completing the course gives me the idea and the confidence to enroll in their marketing program and earn a marketing degree. That experience has led me to get involved in Delta Epsilon Xai, the co-ed marketing fraternity, where I meet a ton of exciting people and some of the nation's most decorated speakers. A chance 5 hour meeting with motivational icon, Victor Antonio and Kelly Perdue, winner of Donald Trump's famed TV show The Apprentice, helps shape my destiny and sets the stage for a new career. An ironic 3 AM phone call from swami helps set it into motion. I am Lucky Traci.

I've officially traded in my stethoscope for a microphone and have redesigned myself as a Certified Professional Speaker, Dreampreneur, and network marketer (see www.sendoutcards.com/planb). After stepping away from my loud life, I was able to quiet myself enough to hear my calling and meet my role in the world head on: to empower millions of people to achieve their goals, fulfill their dreams, and live a life of purpose and design so they can have, do, and be more than what they believe is possible. I am a Dreampreneur, inspiring others to become Dreampreneurs. I've retained the habit of living as a minimalist and have mastered the art of building my career around my life instead of the reverse. I pride myself on exploring new wonders of the world 100 days each year and am patiently awaiting that special entrepreneur to storm my life and share in my journey.

Amy

Since our reconciliation, Traci and I have met annually for 1 or 2 month adventures. We each take turns picking the destination and planning the details; she's become more of a planner, and I've become less anal. We've sunned in Mexico and started writing this book there with margaritas in tow. We've eaten sushi and slept pool side on lounge chairs with our backpacks after arriving at 1 AM at an overbooked resort in Bali. We've been flabbergasted by the breathtaking majesty of the ancient ruins of Machu Picchu and played with monkeys in the Amazon Jungle. We've hiked the golden trails of Copacabana and written our names in the famous salt flats of Bolivia. We took a tango lesson in Buenos Aires and had nightmares after visiting the famous La Recoleta cemetery. We've tasted fried scorpion and returned to China for a summer, teaching English by day and exploring new pockets of the fascinating country by night and on long weekends. This year, well who knows what this year will bring? Traci proposes that we drop our dream adventures into a "DREAMS CAN" and randomly draw one out: float in the Dead Sea in Israel, explore the Eisriesenwelt Caves in Austria, touch a cloud in Dubai, eat osso buco in Brissago, Switzerland, kiss the Blarney stone in Ireland, sleep in a castle in Scotland. The world is our oyster.

Here are a few highlights from trips we've taken since our reconciliation:

200 Year Old Coffins At La Recoleta Cemetery In Buenos Aires
http://j.mp/m5YA0D

A Glimpse Of The Ancient Ruins Of Machu Picchu
http://j.mp/kR6zzJ

Inside Of Our Tuk Tuk Drivers Home
http://j.mp/lKyiAW

An Inside Look In The Main Hospital
In Iquitos, Peru
http://j.mp/lgjAQt

A Wild Monkey Pulls Traci
Through The Jungle
http://j.mp/mOQ87P

A Very Unique Peruvian Garbage Day
http://j.mp/keEvVA

A School In Bali
http://bit.ly/mTTLgp

Traci

When we look back on our trip, one of the greatest benefits is that it has forced us to overcome a legion of fears, live out of our comfort zone, expand our worldly views, slow down, and appreciate what we have. Our homecoming is not an ending. It has become a new beginning. We've adventured through 30,000 land miles, 13 countries, and 3 continents together. We've both emerged stronger and more empathetic people, and our perception of what we can and can't do has been completely redefined. It has taken years to digest and absorb all of the lessons and epiphanies that slowly unveiled themselves to us on our journey and in its afterlife. It has been an intense education, a metaphoric master's degree in life, humanities, social studies, and personal development, and writing this book has been our thesis. Amy wanted to see the world, and I wanted to discover my role in it. We both got what we went for... and so much more. We are two friends, who veered off on two paths, from that one remarkable life changing journey.

Bali

Traci & Wild
Monkey In
The Amazon

Amy Holding A Sloth
In Peru

Traci & Amy Answer FAQs

Traci Bogan

Biggest Lesson

http://bit.ly/qetWIx

Just Do It

http://bit.ly/q65NpT

Favorite Memory

http://bit.ly/oGXn2R

My Favorite Country

http://bit.ly/qL55yZ

How Did We Afford It?

http://bit.ly/qsXwOQ

Would I Do It Again?

http://bit.ly/rskA4x

Traci & Amy Answer FAQs

Amy Oberstadt

How Did We Afford It?
http://bit.ly/rcRuiJ

My Favorite Country
http://bit.ly/qlFgI5

Lessons Learned
http://bit.ly/r8RstQ

Thoughts On Discrimination
http://bit.ly/p56fuj

Most Memorable Moment
http://bit.ly/pBvBmB

Trip Highlight
http://bit.ly/qZNl5l